HITLER'S TANKS

OSPREY
PUBLISHING

HITLER'S TANKS

GERMAN PANZERS OF WORLD WAR II

EDITED BY
CHRIS McNAB

OSPREY PUBLISHING
Bloomsbury Publishing Plc
PO Box 883, Oxford, OX1 9PL, UK
1385 Broadway, 5th Floor, New York, NY 10018, USA
E-mail: info@ospreypublishing.com
www.ospreypublishing.com

OSPREY is a trademark of Osprey Publishing Ltd

First published in Great Britain in 2020
© Osprey Publishing Ltd, 2020

This book is compiled from previously published Osprey books in the New Vanguard and Duel series. For a complete list, see Further Reading.
Artwork by Mike Badrocke, Richard Chasemore, Terry Hadler, Jim Laurier, Ian Palmer, Peter Sarson and David E. Smith © Osprey Publishing.

A catalogue record for this book is available from the British Library.

ISBNs: HB 9781472839763; eBook 9781472839770; ePDF 9781472839787; XML 9781472839794

19 20 21 22 23   10 9 8 7 6 5 4 3 2 1

Index by Sandra Shotter

Originated by PDQ Digital Media Solutions, Bungay, UK
Printed and bound in India by Replika Press Private Ltd.

Front cover: A Tiger I and infantry enter a village in the Soviet Union, January 1944.
(Photo by ullstein bild/ullstein bild via Getty Images)
Title page: A Panzer III in winter 1941/42.
(Photo by ullstein bild/ullstein bild via Getty Images)

Osprey Publishing supports the Woodland Trust, the UK's leading woodland conservation charity.

To find out more about our authors and books visit **www.ospreypublishing.com**. Here you will find extracts, author interviews, details of forthcoming events and the option to sign up for our newsletter.

FSC
www.fsc.org
MIX
Paper from
responsible sources
FSC® C016779

CONTENTS

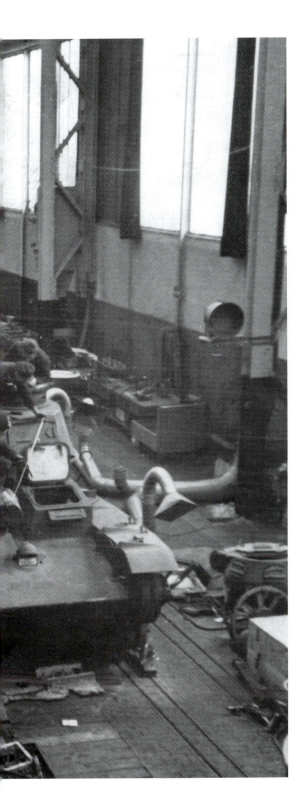

INTRODUCTION

Light Panzers are manufactured in the assembly hangar of a German armaments factory, 1940. (Photo by Heinrich Hoffmann/ullstein bild via Getty Images)

Although armoured warfare was, from 1916, a component of World War I, it was only in World War II that armour became truly central to the land battle model. And of all the combatants at the beginning of that conflict in 1939, it was Germany who, arguably, had most successfully integrated the tank into its tactical thinking, prominently in the tactical phenomenon that we now call *Blitzkrieg* (although that term wasn't significant in contemporary use). From 1939 to 1945, therefore, it was Hitler's Panzer battalions and divisions that would generally occupy the forefront of any land campaign.

The principal component of the Panzer division was, of course, its tank element. The establishment envisaged for the original Panzer divisions contained two two-battalion regiments, each battalion consisting of four 32-tank companies. Together with armoured command vehicles, this gave the Panzer division a total tank strength of 561 – a dream which never approached realization. Despite the rearmament programme, German tank production in the immediate pre-war years was sluggish and in September 1939 the majority of battalions possessed only five Panzerkampfwagen (PzKpfw) IIIs, sufficient to equip one platoon, a total of 20 per division. The balance of the divisional tank strength consisted of 24 PzKpfw IVs and light PzKpfw Is and IIs, supplemented in some cases by the recently acquired Czech 35(t)s and 38(t)s. Even so, the average number of tanks in the division was 320, so that battalions were forced to leave their fourth companies, i.e. 25 per cent of their paper strength, behind in their depots.

A German PzKpfw I armoured column during the Spanish Civil War. The tank immediately behind the motorcyclists is a Kleiner Panzerbefehlswagen, a single-gun command car variant. (AirSeaLand/Cody)

The early days of German armour. A captured German A7V heavy tank, only 20 of which were produced in 1917–18, is here manned by its British crew. (AirSeaLand/Cody)

PzKpfw IV tanks of the I. SS-Panzer-Korps on manoeuvres near Kharkov in early 1943. Many crew commanders are standing up in the open turret hatches for improved observation. (AirSeaLand/Cody)

By May 1940 the situation had improved sufficiently for each of the divisions of Heinz Guderian's XIX. Panzer-Korps to be equipped with 90 PzKpfw IIIs and 36 PzKpfw IVs, the divisional strength being fleshed out with PzKpfw Is and IIs. Other divisions had an establishment of 50 PzKpfw IIIs and 24 PzKpfw IVs, plus the lighter German models. Those divisions (6th, 7th and 8th) whose primary armament consisted of 3.7cm-armed Czech vehicles do not seem to have received an official allocation of PzKpfw IIIs, but Rommel's 7. Panzer-Division certainly acquired several, since he records the loss of six during the fighting at Arras on 21 May. Overall divisional strengths varied between 218 and 276 tanks, about half the theoretical establishment.

Following the startling success achieved in France, Hitler decided to double the number of Panzer divisions. This was achieved by halving the tank element, which was reduced to a single regiment of two battalions, although six regiments had a three-battalion establishment. By now the PzKpfw I and the 35(t) were considered obsolete, but the PzKpfw II was still employed for reconnaissance and there were sufficient PzKpfw IIIs to equip two 22-tank companies in each battalion.

At the time of the invasion of Russia, divisional strength varied between 150 and 200 tanks. In 1942 there was a further rise in the number of Panzer divisions in spite of the losses of the previous year and the slow growth in tank production. On the Eastern Front, the northern and central sectors remained relatively quiescent, and regiments possessed equipment for a single battalion only. On the active southern sector, the number of tank battalions was increased to three, but in practical terms this meant a mere 170 tanks. At this stage it was decided to increase the number of battalion companies to four, the old pre-war figure, but in the majority of cases the equipment was simply not available to implement the directive. Indeed, following the Stalingrad campaign and the withdrawal from the Caucasus, the average Panzer division possessed only about 27 tanks.

During 1943 the PzKpfw III declined rapidly in importance as a battle tank, its place being taken by the improved PzKpfw IV and the PzKpfw V Panther. The PzKpfw IV was originally intended as a fire-support tank to complement the main battle tank of the Panzer divisions. This mission changed after Germany confronted the Red Army during Operation *Barbarossa* in the summer of 1941. The appearance of large numbers of Soviet T-34 and KV tanks was a technological shock to the Panzer force. These tanks were significantly better than the PzKpfw III in terms of armour, firepower and mobility. As a result, the PzKpfw IV shifted from being a supplementary tank in the Panzer divisions to being the principal battle tank. Use of the PzKpfw III gradually faded, production of the chassis shifted from the tank version to the StuG III assault gun, and the PzKpfw IV began to outnumber the PzKpfw III in service by July 1943.

The Panther tank was also developed in response to the tank crisis that befell the Wehrmacht during the invasion of Russia in June 1941. It represented a significant shift in tank design philosophy, fostered in large measure by Germany's changing military fortunes. In the haste to put the design into production, however, insufficient attention was paid to the impact of the weight increases on the power train, and the Panther would be plagued by durability problems because its engine and final drives were better suited to the original, lighter proposals. By any other Army's definition, the Panther was a heavy tank. Although originally intended to replace the existing PzKpfw III and PzKpfw IV medium tanks, its cost and complexity limited the scale of its production. By 1944, the Wehrmacht was saddled with a mixed fleet of Panthers and PzKpfw IV tanks instead of an integrated fleet, burdening the Army with both logistics and training difficulties.

A German Leichter Kampfwagen II, a light tank of World War I. It was armed with a 3.7cm Krupp or 5.7cm Maxim-Nordenfelt gun, and had armour up to 14mm thick. (AirSeaLand/Cody)

The new, heavyweight Tiger I was also making an increasing appearance, first in North Africa in 1942, then spreading throughout the Eastern and Western Fronts. The Tiger I is the most famous tank of World War II. It earned its legend in the savage tank fighting on the Eastern Front in 1943, notably in the battle of Kursk, and became the boogeyman of all Allied tankers: Soviet, British and American. By the summer of 1944, however, it was no longer invincible once the Allies began deploying more powerful tank guns such as the British 17-pdr, the Soviet 85mm and the American 90mm. The increasing spectrum of threats partly led to the development of the Tiger II, a thunderous piece of technology. Although officially designated as PzKpfw Tiger Ausf B, the Tiger II was more often known by its unofficial name, initially coined by the Reich Ministry for Armament and Ammunition, 'Königstiger' (Bengal Tiger), which was incorrectly translated by Allied intelligence as 'King Tiger' or 'Royal Tiger'. By expanding on the thick armour and large main armament of the Tiger I, and the more modern design of the Panther, the 70-tonne Tiger II presented a formidable battlefield solution.

OFFENSIVE FORMATION

ABOVE In a relaxed moment, the crew of a PzKpfw IV stop to chat with some passing German infantry. Note how the mudflap is hinged up at the rear, to enable track inspection. (AirSeaLand/Cody)

All these vehicles took their place tactically within the Panzer division, a balanced formation designed specifically for offensive use. Much of its success depended upon its ability to generate extreme violence during the breakthrough phase of an offensive operation. With its tank brigade spearheading the assault, and close tactical support from the Luftwaffe, it would attack a sector of the enemy front not more than 5,000m wide. During its approach march, the tanks might be concentrated in a *Keil* (wedge), but for the assault itself it would deploy either into two consecutive waves known as *Treffen* (clubs) or two parallel groups known as *Flügel* (wings), for both of which the quadruple organization of tank units had been designed; each club or wing would be responsible for dealing with a specific aspect of the defence.

The sheer weight and speed of the attack would generally take it through the defended zone, and then the Panzer brigade would accelerate towards its designated objectives. Through the gap created by the tanks would pour the rest of the division: the armoured reconnaissance battalion, which would go into the lead and operate several kilometres ahead of the main body; the motorized rifle regiments, later called Panzergrenadiers, who would mop up any by-passed centres of resistance and hold selected areas of captured ground; the anti-tank units, which would form PaK-fronts against counter-attacks; the mechanized artillery batteries, ready to support the tanks with fire against specific strongpoints which were delaying their advance; the divisional service units, with their maintenance, supply and replenishment facilities; while within easy reach of their ground controller the Stukageschwader circled, ready to pounce down on pin-point targets in their role as flying artillery.

Concentration and continual movement were the twin pillars of Panzer division tactics. Concentration, because the intention was to have more barrels in the gun line at the point of contact than the enemy; continual movement, because once a breakthrough had been achieved, the enemy commander would be unable to react quickly with effective counter-measures against a mobile force whose location remained uncertain. If a heavily defended zone was reached it was by-passed, encircled and left for the follow-up troops, i.e. the infantry divisions, while the advance continued.

Parked up in France in September 1944, a German formation presents a variety of armoured vehicles, including three PzKpfw V Panthers and, second from the foreground, a 7.5cm PzKpfw 37L Marder I, a conversion of the French Lorraine 37L. The vehicle in the foreground itself is a turretless French R35. (AirSeaLand/Cody)

A vision of German armoured strength, as columns of Panzers drive forward over the steppe of the Eastern Front. The distances of travel in this theatre had an adverse effect on the long-term mechanical reliability of all German tanks. (AirSeaLand/Cody)

In the event of an armoured counter-attack, the Panzers would fight together, the burden of the engagement falling on the PzKpfw IIIs and, during the early years, the smaller PzKpfw 35(t)s and 38(t)s. If the engagement began to go against them, they would adopt defensive/offensive tactics, retiring behind their own anti-tank gun screen, returning to the attack once the enemy armour had blunted its potential against this. Should it be necessary to carry out a tactical withdrawal, this was undertaken by alternate bounds, the tanks working in conjunction with their anti-tank gunners.

It was, of course, the universal provision of radios that permitted this degree of flexibility, but the German Army also set much store on the personal initiative of the commanders on the spot. Command was exercised from among the division's leading elements, and more reliance was placed upon spoken as opposed to written orders.

THE TANK CREWS

Prior to and early in the war, every German soldier undertook 16 weeks of infantry training. They could volunteer for the Panzerwaffe (Armour Force) and would be assigned if possessing a mechanical aptitude. In the new German Heer (Army), the Panzertruppen (Armoured Troops) were considered an elite arm and were provided with some of the most qualified and motivated young soldiers. The Panzersoldaten (Panzer soldiers) considered themselves bearers of the traditions of the Hussar, the old heavy cavalry.

Training at the Panzertruppenschule at Wünsdorf, south of Berlin, was comprehensive and thorough. In January 1941 it was redesignated the Panzertruppenschule (Schule für Schnelle Truppen 'Wünsdorf'). With the expansion of the Panzer-Divisionen, a second school was established in June 1941 from the old Cavalry School at Potsdam-Krampnitz south-west of Berlin as Schule für Schnelle Truppen 'Krampnitz'. In four months of instruction, all students were taught driver and maintenance skills as well as the basics of all crew functions. Many future Panzermänner (tank men) had undertaken training in the Nationalsozialistisches Kraftfahrerkorps (NSKK, National Socialist Motorized Corps), where young men learned vehicle driving and maintenance skills. Many also served in the Reichsarbeitsdienst (RAD, National Labour Service), receiving pre-military training. Private ownership of automobiles was not widespread, and the NSKK served to familiarize members with motorized vehicles for employment in industry and the military. Gunnery was an important skill, and small-unit tactics were incorporated into field exercises.

Crude German Panzer training in 1931, the 'tanks' mocked-up by affixing wooden hulls atop standard civilian commercial vehicles. (AirSeaLand/Cody)

Prospective Panzertruppen officers and junior NCOs undertook special courses of instruction in which they also learned leadership, tactical and administrative skills, and political indoctrination.

The highest qualities sought among Panzermänner were speed of action, resourcefulness and cunning. The Panzerwaffe had been established in July 1938 from the Kraftfahrkampftruppen (Motorized Battle Troops) and inherited that branch's pink arm of service colour. They were better known by their black uniforms and the Totenkopf (death's head) collar insignia. The black wool uniform was replaced by reed-green tropical twill, but the Hussar death's head insignia was retained.

In September 1939 all armour, anti-tank, armour reconnaissance, motorized rifle and motorcycle rifle units assigned to Panzer-Divisionen were consolidated with cavalry units to become the Schnelle Truppen (Mobile Troops). They would not be redesignated the Panzertruppen until March 1943.

Tank crewmen were selected for training in specific duty positions according to their demonstrated abilities early in training. Cross-training was not neglected. A German pamphlet captured in Libya outlines the duties of a Panzerbesatzung (five-man tank crew):

The tank commander is an officer (platoon leader) or an NCO and is responsible for the vehicle and its crew. He indicates targets to the gunner, gives fire orders, and observes the effects. He keeps a constant watch for the enemy, observes the

A Waffen-SS tank commander on the Eastern Front in 1943 in his PzKpfw IV, his commander's position featuring the split hatch design rather than the single hatch. (AirSeaLand/Cody)

zone for which he is responsible, and watches for any orders from the commander's tank. In action he gives his orders by intercom to the driver and the radio operator and by speaking tube and touch signals to the gunner and loader. He receives orders by radio or flag, and reports to his commander by radio, signal pistol or flags.

The gunner, a junior NCO, is the assistant tank commander. He fires the main gun, co-axial machine gun or the sub-machine gun [for close-in defence] as ordered by the tank commander. He assists the tank commander with observation.

The loader loads and maintains the turret armament under the orders of the gunner. He is also responsible for the care of ammunition, and when the cupola is closed, gives any necessary flag signals. He replaces the radio operator if he becomes a casualty.

The driver operates the vehicle under the orders of the tank commander or in accordance with orders received by radio from the commander's vehicle. He assists with observation, reporting the presence of the enemy or obstacles. He watches fuel consumption, reporting as it drops to specified levels, and is responsible to the tank commander for the care and maintenance of the vehicle.

The radio operator is under the orders of the tank commander. In action and when not actually transmitting, he always keeps his radio set to 'receive'. He operates the intercom system and records any important messages he may receive. He fires the bow machine gun. If the loader becomes a casualty he takes over his duties. [Tank radio operators were taught not to just operate the radio, but to make minor repairs and send and receive Morse code, though this was seldom used. The radio operator also carried a backup battery in case the tank lost its electrical power.]

All crewmen shared in maintenance and repair duties as well as servicing equipment and cleaning the tank's weapons. Communications between tanks, subunits, higher units and supporting arms was considered most critical by the Panzertruppen. While most armies installed two-way radios only in platoon commanders' and higher echelon tanks, the Germans equipped all tanks in this fashion. Other armies held to the concept that tanks in the platoons were only to follow orders. It was thought that by eliminating two-way communications, response time would be speeded up. However, in reality this concept prevented subordinate tanks from achieving numerous tasks that included confirming the receipt of orders (or that their radio was even operational), requesting a retransmission of orders drowned out by static or garbled transmissions, reporting they had successfully completed an action or were unable to, reporting detected threats to other tanks, adjusting supporting fires, reporting their fuel and ammunition status or reporting they had mechanical problems. By allowing all tanks to transmit, the Germans were more responsive and able to pass information up the chain of command, which surely enhanced German combined-arms tactics.

As with all arms of service in the Wehrmacht, the downturn in German military fortunes from late 1942 began to have a profound effect on the recruitment and training of tank crews. The Panzertruppen were beginning to run thin on tank crew replacements in winter 1944, being in poor shape due to the horrible losses of the past summer on both Eastern and Western fronts. While there were formal Panzer crew training centres for both the Heer and Waffen-SS, the extreme shortages of personnel in autumn 1944 meant that most replacements were given minimal basic training and then sent to their Panzer units for specialist training.

There were three main sources of Panzer crew trainees in autumn 1944: wounded veterans returning to service, new draftees and displaced Luftwaffe and Kriegsmarine

TANK COMMUNICATIONS

The Germans divided communications into two types: external (radio, flags, hand signals, flare pistol, flashlight and hand smoke signals) and internal (intercommunication telephone, speaking tube and touch signals). Voice radio range between two moving tanks was about 6km in the desert and 10km using continuous wave (Morse code). Flags were used for very short-range signalling and were sometimes not usable owing to dust, smoke or fog. Signal flags were carried in holder tubes on the left of the driver's seat. When the cupola was open, flag signals were given by the commander; when it was closed, the loader raised the circular flap in the left of the turret roof and signalled through the port. Flag signals were given in accordance with a code, the meaning of any signal depending on the colour of the flag (yellow, green or red; US forces used the same colours) and whether the flag was held still or moved in a particular manner. Flags were soon discarded as being too conspicuous and were replaced by hand signals. The 2.6cm flare pistol was used mainly to signal to accompanying infantry and artillery using coloured smoke (during the day) and flares (at night). The radio set, in conjunction with the intercom, provided the commander, radio operator and driver with a means for external and internal voice communications. Verbal orders were transmitted from the commander to the gunner by means of speaking tube and touch signals. The latter was also used for messages from the commander to the loader and between the gunner and loader.

German infantry on the Don front in July 1942 cluster thickly on the outside of a PzKpfw IV, the soldier at the front bracing himself on space track links. (AirSeaLand/Cody)

personnel. The latter category represented the best potential, since in most cases the men were already accustomed to service life and had some form of military technical training. The Wehrmacht had a fundamentally different replacement policy from the US Army in 1944. Divisions were kept in the line, receiving few replacements, with the combat elements shrinking into smaller and smaller Kampfgruppen (battle groups). At some convenient point or when the division was decimated to point of uselessness, the entire unit would be pulled back for complete refitting. In the case of most of the Panzer divisions deployed in the Ardennes, for example, they were scoured out by the Normandy campaign and pulled out of the line in September 1944 for refitting.

It should be kept in mind that in a typical wartime Panzer division, about only one-third of the troops were engaged in direct combat, including the Panzer crews, Panzergrenadiers and some other units such as the reconnaissance battalion. Of the 14,700 men in a Type 44 Panzer division, about 2,000 were in the Panzer regiment, of which about 750 were crewmen. Another 5,400 were in the two Panzergrenadier regiments and reconnaissance battalion. Other elements such as the divisional engineers and artillery might occasionally be exposed to combat, but casualties tended to be heaviest in a narrow slice of the division. The administrative and support elements of the division tended to remain intact even in disasters such as the Falaise gap encirclement in France in August 1944, and so divisions were rebuilt around an experienced core.

When it is said that a division 'suffered 50 per cent casualties', these casualties were not evenly shared in the division; losses fell hardest on the combat elements. The Panzergrenadier regiments tended to suffer worst of all due to the usual hazards of infantry combat combined with the mobility of these units, which led to their frequent commitment. Most of the Panzer regiments lost one-third or more of their crewmen in Normandy and most if not all of their tanks, an appalling cost for any arm of service.

• • •

This book is a detailed study of the chief tanks that formed the cutting edge of Germany's armoured formations between 1939 and 1945. Specifically, it concentrates on the light Panzers – the Panzers I and II and the 35(t) and 38(t) – the PzKpfw III and IV medium tanks, the Panther (actually classed as a medium tank, but heavy in reality) and the two Tigers (I and II), each chapter also making a nod towards some of these vehicles' many spin-off variants. As with any study of wartime German production, we see in Wehrmacht tank development some of the most innovative engineering; when they worked properly, tanks such as the Panther and Tiger I had few equals on the battlefield. In balance, however, there is the persistent theme of German technical overreach, the armament industry producing relatively few advanced models when it might have been better served by manufacturing a higher output of less capable machines.

The crew of a PzKpfw IV make a powerplant change, having parked in front of an agricultural building to provide cover during this vulnerable time. (AirSeaLand/Cody)

CHAPTER 1

THE LIGHT
PANZERS

These PzKpfw I Ausf As are serving
with the Großdeutschland Division
on the Eastern Front in Poland in
January 1941. The Ausf A is
distinguished from the subsequent
Ausf B by the fact that the latter
had its rear idler wheel elevated off
the ground. (AirSeaLand/Cody)

Hindsight has been described as a mirror that enables ordinary men to be wise after the event. This may well be true, but it is also true that hindsight frequently offers a distorted perspective, so that the contemporary view of events and equipment held two generations ago is rather different from that held today. Thus, because of the spectacular nature of its victories from 1939 to 1941, it is tempting to regard Hitler's Panzerwaffe as a superbly equipped cutting edge for the rest of the Army. In reality, the Panzerwaffe excelled only in technique, and was very badly equipped. As we shall see, the PzKpfw III and PzKpfw IV medium tanks were in critically short supply, therefore it was upon a mass of light tanks that the Panzerwaffe relied to fill out the ranks of its under-strength divisions during its high years. This amply justifies a study of the latter, if only on the grounds that their apparent lack of potential makes their achievement all the more remarkable; nor, indeed, are they entirely without points of technical interest.

In terms of general tank design, the outbreak of war in 1939 found Germany behind the Soviet Union and France, almost level-pegging with Great Britain, slightly ahead of Japan and with a decisive lead over Italy. The United States was not yet a contender in the race, but was well advanced in the designs that led to the Lee and the Stuart. For this the restrictive clauses of the Treaty of Versailles, under which Germany was forbidden tracked armoured fighting vehicles (AFVs), are sometimes blamed, but the fact is that German tank designers were at work long before Hitler repudiated those clauses in 1935. During the 1920s, a secret experimental station was jointly

From 1935 to 1937 the Czechoslovakian Army acquired 298 LT vz. 35 tanks based on the Skoda S-II-a design. This tank is better known by its later German designation of PzKpfw 35(t), an example of which is here parked by a sunny harbourside in the early years of the war. (AirSeaLand/Cody)

A PzKpfw II Ausf F stops for a crew consultation behind a destroyed Soviet aircraft. Development of the PzKpfw III and PzKpfw IV only began in 1936; the PzKpfw III Ausf E would be the first true production variant of the former, but between December 1938 and October 1939 only 96 would be made, while only 134 PzKpfw IV Ausf C fire-support tanks would be produced between September 1938 and August 1939. To make up for this shortfall, and flesh out armoured formations with sufficient vehicles, the light PzKpfw II was thrust from its training role into front-line combat operations. (AirSeaLand/Cody)

established with the Red Army deep inside Soviet Russia, and much technical data had also been gained from work carried out discreetly in Sweden. Again, German military attachés throughout the world were fully conversant with the latest developments in tank design, details of which were contained in their reports; nor should the national reputation for expertise in heavy engineering be forgotten.

The reasons, therefore, must be sought elsewhere. First, and most important, was the fact that the newly formed armoured corps certainly did not envisage becoming involved in a major war as early as 1939, and did not believe that it would be prepared for such an undertaking until approximately 1943. Second, it was entirely reasonable that it should order for itself a simple, inexpensive machine, the PzKpfw I, with which to carry out preliminary crew training en masse. Third, while the basic concepts of its two main battle tanks, subsequently known as the PzKpfw III and IV, were essentially sound, it seems that the Army's procurement department, the Heereswaffenamt, seriously underestimated the time required for these to reach full-scale standardized production: this being the case, the Panzerwaffe felt compelled to order a stop-gap vehicle, the PzKpfw II, which was also capable of reconnaissance but which was simply an extension of the light tank theme.

It was certainly not compatible with the National Socialist ethos to make good the shortfall with vehicles purchased abroad, even if a trading partner could have been found. On the other hand, the conquest of Czechoslovakia was accompanied by the acquisition of the Czechs' own tank fleet and domestic manufacturing resources; in such circumstances it would have been extremely foolish to do other than return pride to one's pocket, since the Czech vehicles, known in German service as the PzKpfw 35(t) and 38(t) (the 't' standing for *Tschechisch*, i.e. 'Czech'), were similarly armed to the PzKpfw III and could be substituted for it.

PANZERKAMPFWAGEN I (SDKFZ 101)

German volunteers advance at a crouch behind the shelter of a PzKpfw I during the Spanish Civil War. German personnel were to train Nationalist crews for using the PzKpfw I, but once instruction was completed the instructors eventually transitioned to combat duties. This provided valuable combat lessons, such as the benefit of incorporating tactical aircraft and artillery to support armoured and motorized operations. (AirSeaLand/Cody)

The traditional policy of the Heereswaffenamt was to issue basic specifications for a project to a number of civilian manufacturers and then choose the best design submitted, and in 1932 it despatched competitive contracts for a light-tracked fighting vehicle that, for the moment, was known simply as the Landwirtschaftlicher Schlepper (LaS), or 'Industrial Tractor'. The Krupp entry, incorporating experience gained jointly with the Swedish Landsverk company during examination of a British Carden Loyd chassis, was selected, and the initial manufacturing contract was given to the Henschel organization under the interim designation of 'I A LaS Krupp'. The first prototypes were delivered in December 1933 and quantity production began in July 1934, the vehicle's official service title being PzKpfw (MG) I Ausführung (Ausf) A once the need for subterfuge had disappeared.

As might be expected in what was intended essentially to be a training machine, the design was very simple. The suspension consisted of four bogie wheels and a trailing idler, braced by an external beam and secured to the hull by bolts and quarter-elliptical leaf springs; track adjustment was obtained by altering the position of the idler. The

power unit was a four-cylinder horizontally opposed air-cooled Krupp petrol engine which produced 57hp at 2,500rpm, fitted with one Solex downdraft carburettor for each bank, and an acceleration pump. (A few models were fitted experimentally with an air-cooled diesel engine, but this produced only 45hp at 2,200rpm, insufficient for the vehicle's requirements.) Fuel capacity was 90 litres, housed in two tanks mounted in the rear corners of the driving compartment.

From the engine, the drive passed through a two-plate dry clutch to the gearbox, which provided one reverse and five forward gears, and thence across the front of the vehicle to the drive sprockets. Steering was effected by clutch and brake, cooling being supplied by a small fan. The driver controlled direction by means of steering levers, each of which had two hand-grips, one for normal steering and the other with a thumb-plunger to act as a parking brake; no handbrake was fitted. The instrument panel contained an oil temperature gauge, a revolution counter marked 0–3,000rpm with a danger zone above 2,500rpm and a speedometer marked 0–50km/h. Maximum recommended speed in gears was: first – 5km/h; second – 11km/h; third – 20km/h; fourth – 32km/h; fifth – 42km/h.

The second crew member, the commander/gunner, was housed in a small turret mounted to the right of the vehicle's centreline. All-round traverse was available for the turret's two 7.92mm MG 13 machine guns, which were mounted in tandem but capable of independent fire: the gun on the left was fired from a trigger on the elevating handwheel to the commander's left, the one on the right from a trigger on the traverse handwheel to his right. Maximum elevation obtainable was +18° and maximum depression -12°. A clutch was incorporated in the elevation handwheel which gave 'Operate' and 'Free' positions, and the mantlet itself could be locked in the horizontal. Ammunition was contained in 25-round clips, stowed as follows:

- one bin in turret containing eight clips
- one bin in hull containing eight clips
- one bin in hull containing twenty clips
- one bin in hull containing six clips
- one bin in hull containing nineteen clips

The commander's seat was suspended from the turret and rotated with it, although the floor of the fighting compartment remained static. His communication with the driver was by means of voice tube. Armour thickness was 13mm all round, proof against small-arms ammunition but little else. Trials with a captured example revealed that even sustained machine-gun fire was capable of jamming the turret ring and mantlet, while the air intake was considered to be highly vulnerable to grenade attack.

German mountain troops advance alongside a PzKpfw I on the Eastern Front in May 1942. Such light vehicles were extremely vulnerable to the Soviet 57mm and 76mm anti-tank guns. (AirSeaLand/Cody)

Those vehicles fitted with radio mounted a collapsible aerial on the offside of the hull, operated by a handle inside the fighting compartment. When the turret was traversed, a cam acting on the turret ring automatically lowered the aerial to prevent it fouling the guns.

No sooner had the Ausf A entered service than it was found to be badly underpowered for cross-country work. Some redesign was clearly necessary, and this resulted in the Ausf B, driven by a six-cylinder water-cooled Maybach NL 38 TR engine and fitted with an improved transmission. Being larger, the Maybach unit occupied more space than was available, this deficiency being remedied by extending the engine compartment to the rear. This, in turn, meant a longer suspension incorporating five bogie wheels, and because of this the idler wheel was raised above ground level to facilitate steering. In all other respects the Ausf B was almost identical to its predecessor. Some 300 Ausf A versions were built, and approximately 1,500 Ausf Bs.

In September 1939 it was decided to develop the design into a light fighting vehicle which could undertake the reconnaissance role and also provide support for air-landing operations. The work was jointly carried out by Krauss-Maffei and Daimler Benz, and resulted in the Ausf C. This vehicle, armed with a 2cm cannon and a co-axial machine gun, had a five-wheel interleaved suspension and was powered by a Maybach 150hp engine. While it reached the prototype stage, it does not seem to have passed beyond this.

A further development was the PzKpfw I nA verst (neue Ausführung, verstarkt – 'new model, up-armoured'), which is sometimes referred to as the Ausf D or F. Requested in December 1939, this vehicle lay outside the basic philosophy of the Panzerwaffe in that it was intended for infantry support. The project was again awarded to the team of Krauss-Maffei and Daimler Benz, which employed the same chassis and engine as the Ausf C. Armament consisted of two MG 34 machine guns mounted in tandem, and armour thickness was 80mm, giving a total weight of 18 tonnes. Maximum speed was 24km/h, quite acceptable for the role envisaged and comparable to that of British infantry tanks. The vehicle began entering service in June 1940, and 30 are known to have been delivered before the order was cancelled, although details of their eventual use remain obscure.

PzKpfw I derivatives

Probably the best known derivative of the PzKpfw I was the Kleiner Panzerbefehlswagen (small armoured command vehicle), which employed both the Ausf A and B chassis. This vehicle was fitted with a fixed superstructure in place of a turret, and was armed with a ball-mounted machine gun for local defence. Two radios were carried, the Fu2 and the Fu6, and the vehicle was manned by a crew of three. About 200 of these conversions were produced by Daimler Benz between 1936 and 1938, emphasizing the fact that from the outset tactical control from well forward was an essential element in the Panzerwaffe's operational technique.

A crewman inspects a bullet strike on his Kleiner Panzerbefehlswagen (SdKfz 265), a variant of the PzKpfw I Ausf A. (AirSeaLand/Cody)

Ausf B *Fahrgestell* (chassis) were extensively used as mountings for self-propelled guns, the conversions being undertaken by the Alkett organization of Berlin-Spandau in 1939. These included the Wehrmacht's first tracked tank destroyer, the PaK 4.7cm (t) Sfl auf PzKpfw I Ausf B, which, as its title implies, was fitted with a Czech anti-tank gun. The mounting for this 43.4-calibre-length weapon was protected on three sides by armour plate and provided a limited traverse of 15°. A total of 86 rounds of ammunition could be stowed, and a crew of three was carried. These vehicles remained in service on the Eastern Front until the winter of 1941/42, and were also encountered in North Africa.

The Type 33 15cm Heavy Infantry Gun, complete with carriage and wheels, was also mounted on the Ausf B chassis, the 38 conversions made being designated 15cm sIG 33 auf PzKpfw T Ausf B. The mounting was protected on three sides by 10mm armoured shields that gave the vehicle an ungainly appearance, increasing its height to over 3m: the shields and weapon combined to bring the overall weight to 8.5 tonnes, which grossly overloaded the chassis and curtailed mobility. These conversions were manned by crews of four, and saw active service during the Polish and French campaigns.

Turretless, open-topped chassis were used for driver training and as supply carriers, and some Ausf B chassis were issued to tank recovery and repair units as tractor units.

The Ladungsleger I (Explosive Charge Layer I) was an interesting venture into the field of assault engineering. The equipment consisted of a pair of telescopic arms

PzKpfw I Ausf A tanks are readied for operations by German engineers. About 300 Ausf As were produced, as opposed to c. 1,500 of the Ausf B variant. (AirSeaLand/Cody)

mounted on a framework above the engine deck on an Ausf B. These could be extended to deposit a 75kg charge on to the roof of a pillbox or similar fortification, the charge being detonated by remote control once the vehicle had moved out of the danger radius. A prototype was completed towards the end of 1940, but the idea was not widely developed.

PANZERKAMPFWAGEN II (SDKFZ 121)

As already mentioned, the PzKpfw II was intended to be a stop-gap machine pending the arrival of the PzKpfw III and IV, and its main armament specification of one 2cm cannon could still be regarded as adequate – but only just – in July 1934, when the Heereswaffenamt put the project out to competitive tender under the cover name of 'LaS 100'.

After the various prototypes had been evaluated, that submitted by Maschinen-Fabrik Augsburg-Nürnburg (MAN) was selected for further development. Layout was almost identical to that of the PzKpfw I, and indeed the first four production models, Ausf a1, a2, a3 and b, possessed very similar characteristics, employing leaf springs and an external beam for the suspension of six small bogies, arranged in three pairs of two.

The commander and driver of a PzKpfw II Ausf F pose for a photograph in their hatches. As the PzKpfw II was intended to be an improvement over the PzKpfw I, and was not built for direct action against enemy tanks, all of its armour was essentially ineffective against anything greater than small arms and shrapnel, with the area under the turret front particularly vulnerable. (AirSeaLand/Cody)

The Ausf a1, a2 and a3 were all driven by a Maybach six-cylinder HL 57 engine, which produced 130hp at 2,600rpm. These three models, of which 25, 25 and 50 respectively were manufactured, reflected minor but progressive improvements, notably to the cooling system, but lacked final drive reduction gears and were soon shown to be under-powered. These difficulties were resolved by fitting the Ausf B with a Maybach six-cylinder HL 62 engine, which had an output of 140hp, and modifying the final drive to incorporate a reduction train. One hundred vehicles of this type were built.

The fourth production model, Ausf C, appeared in 1937 and incorporated an increase in frontal armour thickness from 14.5mm to 30mm. It also saw the introduction of the five-wheel quarter-elliptical leaf spring suspension for which the PzKpfw II is generally remembered. At this point it was decided to accelerate production and MAN were joined by the Henschel, Famo, MIAG and Wegmann organizations in building the numbers required. Until now the bow of the vehicle consisted of a one-piece rounded casting, but this was replaced on the Ausf A and all subsequent models by a square joint-welded combination of flat bow and glacis plates. The turret of the Ausf B was fitted with a shallow cupola, as was that of the Ausf C, these two models being identical in appearance although the latter incorporated several interior improvements.

In 1938 Daimler Benz were contracted to produce a Schnellkampfwagen (fast fighting vehicle) version of the PzKpfw II with which to equip the light divisions. This was achieved by replacing the standard suspension with a torsion bar system mounting four large Christie-type road wheels, the return rollers being dispensed with. In this form the vehicle was capable of a maximum speed of 55km/h. Two almost

OPPOSITE A rare colour image of a column of PzKpfw IIs moving in formation through a village, location unknown. During the 1939 and 1940 campaigns, the number of Panzer IIs, and support from mechanized, motorized and aerial assets, promoted a rapid German advance against an increasingly fragmented enemy defence. (AirSeaLand/Cody)

indistinguishable models, Ausf D and E, were built, the total production run being 250 vehicles. However, due to internal Army politics, very few actually reached the light divisions and the majority served in Panzer-Regiment 8 of Panzer-Brigade 4.

By 1939 the Panzerwaffe possessed a stock of 1,266 PzKpfw IIs and production was allowed to tail off, only 15 being completed in that year and nine in 1940. Hitler's decision to double the number of Panzer divisions immediately led to a resumption in order to flesh out the establishment of the new formations, the vehicle's by now deficient firepower and protection having been masked to some extent by the easy victories in Poland and France. The Ausf F began entering service at the beginning of 1941, protected by 35mm frontal and 20mm side armour: the effect of this modest attempt at up-armouring was an increase in vehicle weight to 9.35 tonnes, purchased at the cost of a reduction in speed by 10km/h to 40km/h. The series continued with the Ausf G and J, which were distinguished from the Ausf F by the addition of a stowage bin to the turret rear. Production did not finally cease until the beginning of 1944.

The PzKpfw II's turret was offset to the left of the tank's centreline, and the vehicle was manned by a crew of three: commander/gunner, loader/operator and driver. The line of drive passed from the engine through a plate clutch to a crash gearbox that provided one reverse and six forward gears, and thence across the vehicle's front to the drive sprockets. Maximum recommended speed in gears was: first – 5km/h; second – l0km/h; third – 12km/h; fourth – 21km/h; fifth – 30km/h; sixth – 40km/h. Steering was performed by levers operating a clutch and brake mechanism. Driver's instruments included a speedometer, a revolution counter calibrated from 1,000 to 3,200rpm, marked in red above 2,600rpm, a water temperature gauge and an oil pressure gauge. An electric starter was provided, but for low temperatures an inertia starter, operated through the vehicle's stern plate, was also fitted.

In addition to a 2cm cannon, the PzKpfw II was armed with a co-axial 7.92mm MG 34 machine gun. The 2cm was fired from a trigger on the elevating handwheel to the commander's left, and the MG 34 from a trigger on the traverse handwheel to his right, the latter giving 4° of traverse per full turn. The traverse mechanism operated through a dog clutch controlled by three levers marked as follows:

> **EIN ('geared'):** traverse gear engaged, traverse lock disengaged;
> **AUS ('free'):** traverse gear disengaged, traverse lock disengaged;
> **EST ('locked'):** traverse gear disengaged, traverse lock engaged.

In the 'free' position it was possible to turn the turret by hand quite quickly, using two handles on the turret ring. Zero marks on the hull and turret coincided when the latter was in the 12 o'clock (i.e. fully forward) position.

The 2cm ammunition was stored in 18 10-round magazines, for a total of 180 rounds, while the 7.92mm ammunition was held in 17 150-round protective leather bags, totalling 2,550 rounds.

A Panzer II conducts a fording operation. Following the Polish campaign, Ausf D and later versions would incorporate a low turret cupola and additional frontal armour. (AirSeaLand/Cody)

A PzKpfw II Ausf L Luchs (Lynx). As the PzKpfw II's final purpose-built reconnaissance iteration, the Ausf L Luchs had interleaved wheels and proved effective in its intended role. (AirSeaLand/Cody)

In dusty climates, the mouth of the belt bag was usually stuffed with a wad of grease-proof paper, keeping the rounds free from grit, which could cause jamming in the weapon's feed mechanism. Examination of belts stowed aboard PzKpfw IIs captured in North Africa revealed a mix of half-and-half alternate armour-piercing (AP)/AP tracer, or sometimes 100 per cent AP tracer, but often belts had obviously been filled hastily with whatever was to hand, no thought being given to sequence. Two types of gun sight were employed: an open sight graduated from 200–800m with 200m markings; and a telescopic TZF 4/38 sight with a magnification of 2.5× and a field of 25°, graduated from 0 to 1,200m with 200m markings. Attached to the tank's stern plate was a rack of five smoke grenades that could be released by pull-wires from inside the fighting compartment, enabling the vehicle to reverse into its own smokescreen.

The PzKpfw II remained under-armoured throughout its active service career and, as in the case of the PzKpfw I, its turret ring was vulnerable to sustained machine-gun fire. A small point of interest on later models was an aluminium dummy visor fitted beside the driver's real visor, clearly in the hope that it would attract a portion of the enemy's fire.

Normally, three radio sets – two receivers and one transmitter – were carried, the aerial being mounted at the nearside rear of the fighting compartment. Internal communication between the commander and driver was by means of voice tube.

In parallel with the standard PzKpfw II gun tank, a reconnaissance version had also been under development since 1938. Using experience gained from various experimental projects, MAN produced a prototype in April 1942, and the vehicle began entering service the following year under the designation PzKpfw II (SdKfz 123) Ausf L, later amended to Panzerspahwagen II (2cm KwK 38) Luchs ('Lynx').

PZKPFW II AUSF C SPECIFICATIONS

General

Production run: June 1938–April 1940 (22 months)
Vehicles produced: 364
Combat weight: 8,900kg
Suspension: five quarter-elliptic leaf-spring
Crew: three (commander/gunner, driver,
    loader/radio operator)

Dimensions

Length: 4.81m
Width: 2.22m
Height: 1.99m

Armour (degrees from vertical)

Glacis (upper/middle/lower): 14.5mm @ 73° /
    14.5mm round / 14.5mm @ 64°
Hull face: 14.5mm @ 9°
Hull side: 14.5mm @ 0°
Hull rear (upper/lower): 14.5mm @ 7° /
    10mm @ 62°
Hull roof (deck/engine): 14.5mm @ 90° /
    10mm @ 82°
Hull bottom: 5mm @ 90
Turret face (front/base): 14.5mm round /
    14.5mm @ 16°
Turret side: 14.5mm @ 22°
Turret rear: 14.5mm @ 23°
Turret roof (upper/front): 10mm @ 90° /
    10mm @ 76°
Mantlet: 16mm round

Armament

Main gun: 2cm KwK 30 L/55 (180 Pzgr 39 and
    Sprgr 39 in 18 ten-round magazines)
Sight: TZF 4/38 (2.5×)
Elevation: +20°/-9.5°
Secondary: 1 × 7.92mm MG 34 (co-axial) (1,425
    rounds in 19 × 75-round magazines)
Main gun rate of fire (cyclic/effective): 280rds/min /
    120rds/min

Communications

Internal: voice tube
External: FuG 5

Motive power

Engine: Maybach HL 62 TR 6-cylinder (water
    cooled) 6,191cc (petrol)
Power to weight: 103kW (sustained) @ 2,600rpm
    (11.57kW/tonne)
Transmission: Zahnradfabrik Aphon SSG 46
    gearbox; six forward gears, one reverse gear
Fuel capacity: 170 litres

Performance

Ground pressure: 0.62kg/cm²
Speed (maximum/road/cross-country):
    40km/h / 25km/h / 15km/h
Operational range (road/cross-country):
    190km / 130km
Fuel consumption (road/cross-country):
    0.89 litres/km / 1.35 litres/km
Fording: 850mm
Step climbing: 420mm
Climbing angle: 30°
Trench crossing: 1.7m
Ground clearance: 340mm

PzKpfw II Ausf C, Panzer-Regiment 35

The RAL (Reichsausschuss für Lieferbedingungen, or 'Reich Committee for Delivery Terms and Quality Assurance') paint was provided as paste, which was diluted prior to application. To ensure consistency, specifications were sent to paint suppliers, with details on preparation, after which test specimens had to pass examination and approval, and once at the assembly facilities inspectors used swatches to determine whether the post-application colour matched initial specifications. The PzKpfw II's interior was ivory, Elfenbein (RAL 1001), over a red primer, while the exterior sported a two-tone scheme of dark grey, Dunkelgrau (RAL 46, later renumbered RAL 7021), as a base coat, over which irregular patches of dark brown, Dunkelbraun (RAL 45, later renumbered RAL 7017), were spray-painted onto roughly one-third of the surface.

Vehicle identification generally comprised three digits applied to each turret side, indicating the company and platoon to which the tank belonged, and its individual number. Panzer-Abteilung command vehicles used prefixed Roman numerals (e.g. 'II01' for II. Abteilung), while regimental varieties used an 'R' (e.g. 'R01'). Initially, a white Balkenkreuz was used for nationality identification, but as these were found to be overly visible, crews often subdued them.

(Richard Chasemore © Osprey Publishing)

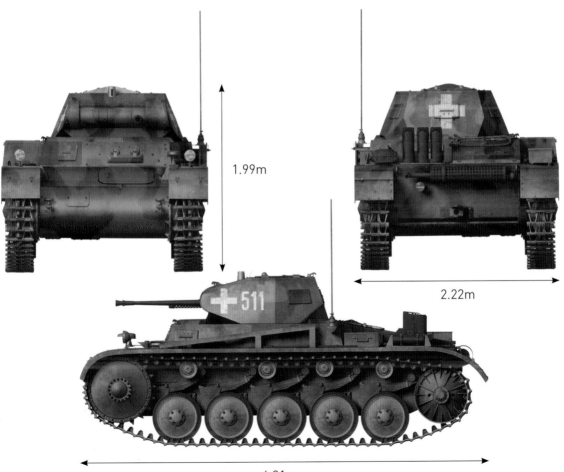

1.99m

2.22m

511

4.81m

The Lynx weighed 11.8 tonnes, was powered by a Maybach HL 66P 180hp engine and could achieve a maximum speed of 60km/h. The suspension consisted of five large interleaved bogie units carried on torsion bars. Frontal armour was 30mm thick, and the first 100 production models were armed similarly to the PzKpfw Ausf A–J; the remaining 31 vehicles, built before manufacture ceased in May 1943, were armed with the same 50mm L/60 weapon mounted by the PzKpfw III Ausf J–M, producing an almost unworkable

The photograph shows the rather impractical-looking Schwimmpanzer II, the flotation tanks prominently extending out from the sides. These vehicles were mainly utilized for river crossings on the Eastern Front. (AirSeaLand/Cody)

combination of too much gun for too little turret. Much emphasis in the design stage had been placed on medium- and short-wave radio equipment and this, together with an additional operator, resulted in an impossibly cramped interior.

Technically the Lynx was an Aufklärungspanzer, or armoured reconnaissance vehicle, and it was used exclusively by armoured reconnaissance battalions. Plans for a more heavily armoured version mounting a 5cm gun and co-axial MG 42 machine gun were completed in 1942, but the project was cancelled, although the turret was later fitted to the eight-wheeled Puma armoured car. Had this vehicle been built, it would have been known as the 'Leopard'.

PzKpfw II derivatives

During the preparations for Unternehmen Seelöwe (Operation *Sealion*), Hitler's planned invasion of the south coast of England, it was decided to form an amphibious tank battalion equipped with PzKpfw IIs. Unlike the amphibious versions of the PzKpfw III and IV, however, the Schwimmpanzer II would not have to drive along the sea bed to reach the shore; instead, as its name implies, it would swim ashore from its parent vessel, using a kit of flotation tanks attached to the return rollers, and powered by a propeller driven by an extension shaft from the engine. The turret ring was sealed by an inflatable rubber ring. Again, unlike the 'diving' versions of the medium tanks, the Schwimmpanzer II could use its guns during the landing, and was expected to.

The unit which would have manned these vehicles had the operation taken place was known as 'Panzer-Abteilung A', recruited from volunteers drawn from Panzer-Regiment 2. In due course this and other volunteer battalions were formed into Panzer-Regiment 18, which carried out an amphibious crossing of the River Bug during Operation *Barbarossa*. It is just possible that a number of Schwimmpanzer IIs may have participated in this, although the bulky flotation equipment made the vehicle more suitable for landing on a beach than for a river crossing in which it would have to negotiate difficult banks.

Another imaginative project was the conversion of 95 Ausf D and E chassis to the flamethrower role. The conversion was generally known as the Flammpanzer II but was also referred to as the 'Flamingo'; its official designation was PzKpfw II (F) (SdKfz 122). Two flame guns, each with a traverse of 180°, were mounted well forward, and sufficient fuel was carried for 80 two- to three-second flamings. The range of the flame guns was limited to 35m, and the vehicle was clearly vulnerable at such close quarters, particularly as the original turret had been replaced by a smaller one mounting a single machine gun. Photographic evidence suggests that in order to remedy this deficiency some vehicles were fitted with a battery of grenade projectors above their engine decks. Because of the space occupied by the flame equipment and fuel, the crew was reduced to commander and driver. The Flammpanzer II served in specialist battalions which were employed at the discretion of senior commanders.

By 1942 it was painfully obvious that the PzKpfw II's usefulness as a gun tank was at an end, and large numbers of chassis were turned over for conversion to other uses. It was, in fact, very fortunate for the Wehrmacht that they were available, since they served as suitable mountings for its first generation of tank destroyers, the 7.5cm L/46 PaK 40/ 2 anti-tank gun being fitted to Ausf A, B, C and F chassis and the captured Russian Model 36 7.62cm anti-tank gun to Ausf D and E chassis. Both these conversions were known as Marder II.

The 15cm sIG 33 was also mounted on Ausf A, B, C and F chassis, the conversion being lower and generally more business-like than that based on the PzKpfw I. Weight and space considerations led to later models being based on an extended chassis. The vehicle weighed approximately 12 tonnes and was manned by a crew of five.

Best known of the self-propelled mountings based on the PzKpfw II was the 10.5cm howitzer Wespe (Wasp), the official title of which was le FH 18/ 2 auf Fahrgestell PzKpfw II Sf: for reasons best understood by himself, Hitler decided that the name 'Wespe' should be dropped in February 1944. This vehicle began entering service in 1942 and equipped the light batteries of Panzer artillery regiments. It was built in substantial numbers, using most PzKpfw II chassis with the exception of Ausf D and E.

PzKpfw IIs (Ausf D and E) are rolled onto trucks for transportation. The PzKpfw II progressed through several wartime variants and conversions until production ceased in January 1944. (AirSeaLand/Cody)

PZKPFW II AUSF F

Key

1. Muzzle flash cowl
2. 2cm KwK 30 L/55 automatic cannon
3. 7.92mm MG 34 co-axial machine gun
4. Direct sight vision port
5. Gun mantlet 30mm internal
6. TZF 4 telescopic gun sight
7. Roof armour 10mm
8. Weapon mount and elevation mechanism
9. Fuel fillers ports in roof to right of turret
10. Commander's cupola/hatch with eight periscopes
11. Armoured fuel tank, 170 litres
12. Turret stowage bin
13. Commander/gunner's seat suspended from turret
14. Turret ring ball bearing race
15. Mounting for radio transformer
16. Wooden block for use with jack
17. Radio operator's position
18. Maybach HL 62 TR 6 cylinder 140 PS water cooled motor
19. Motor inspection cover
20. Right-hand side rear cooling air outlet grille
21. Exhaust silencer
22. Air intake grille
23. Fold-down 2m rod antenna for FuG 5 radio system
24. Armoured dispenser for six smoke candles
25. Side armour hull, 15mm
26. Mudguard storage bin
27. Adjustable idler wheel
28. Radiator
29. Antenna tray
30. 300mm cast dry pin track links
31. Side armour superstructure, 15mm
32. Quarter elliptical springs
33. Road wheels 550 x 100-55 tyres
34. Return rollers 220 x 105
35. Drive shaft
36. Ten-round 2cm ammunition magazines (total load 180 rounds)
37. Clutch
38. Driver's seat
39. Gear shift
40. Drive sprocket
41. ZF gearbox, six forward, one reverse
42. Steering levers
43. Tow cable hooks
44. Steering unit and final drive

45. Sloped front armour, 35 mm
46. Bar for stowing spare track links
47. Instrument panel
48. Glacis plate 20mm
49. Spare wheel
50. Dummy aluminium visor
51. Driver's front armour plate 30mm
52. Bullet splash protector for turret ring

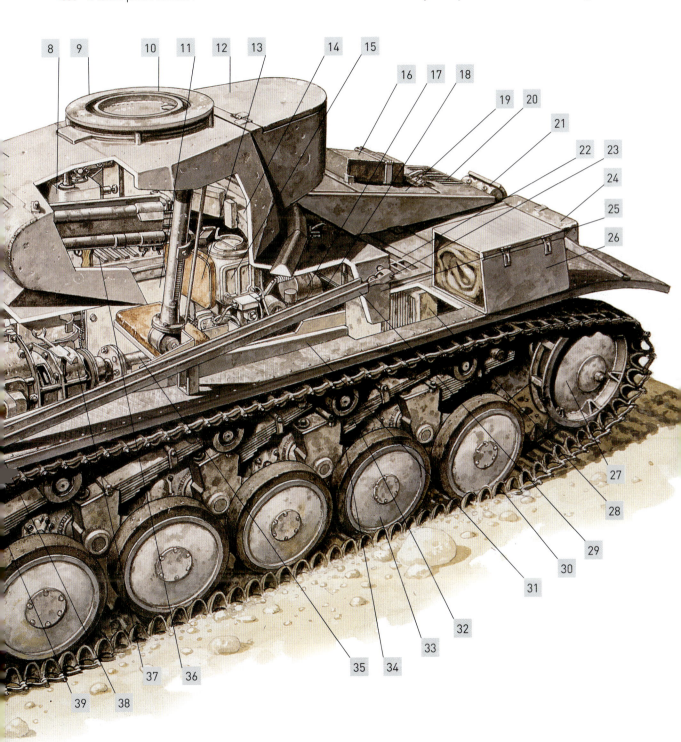

Both Hitler and Mussolini observe the drive-past of a unit of German Kleiner Panzerbefehlswagen light command vehicles. By the end of 1941, the utility of these poorly protected vehicles was marginal, and most ended up as training vehicles. (AirSeaLand/ Cody)

The fighting compartment, surrounded by an open-topped superstructure of armour plate, was located at the rear. A total of 32 rounds of ammunition were stowed, and the vehicle was manned by a crew of five. The L/28 howitzer was fitted with a muzzle brake and could be elevated to +42° and depressed to -5°; 17° of traverse were available either side of the centreline. A machine gun was provided for local defence. In spite of its handy appearance, the Wasp was not universally popular with professional artillerymen, who considered it to be cramped, too high at 2.33m and too poorly protected for its forward fire-support role. Within these limitations, however, the vehicle performed well. A further area of criticism, namely that it carried too little ammunition, was partly remedied by the production of an ammunition carrier version, in which the howitzer was omitted, capable of stowing 90 rounds.

PANZERKAMPFWAGEN 35(t)

During the 1930s, the Czech armaments industry was one of the most highly developed in Europe, and its exports made a substantial contribution to the wealth of the country. In 1935 the two fighting vehicle manufacturers, Ceskomoravska Kolben Danek (CKD) and Skoda, decided jointly to produce a light tank, the designation of which was LT vz. 35, although in German service it was to be known as PzKpfw 35(t). Unlike the German light tanks, the vehicle's armament was comparable to that of the PzKpfw III, consisting of a 3.7cm gun and co-axial 7.92mm machine gun, with a further machine gun in the front plate. The 25mm frontal armour also exceeded by a wide margin that planned for the first models of the PzKpfw III and IV, yet in spite of this the designers had succeeded in producing a compact vehicle weighing only 10.5 tonnes and capable of a maximum speed of 35km/h.

The PzKpfw 35(t) was crewed by a commander/gunner, loader, driver and hull gunner/operator. The commander was located on the left of the turret beneath a rudimentary cupola incorporating four episcopes and a one-piece circular hatch. The loader occupied the opposite side of the turret. In the driving compartment the hull gunner was seated on the left and the driver on the right.

Much priceless internal space had been conserved by the designers' decision to employ a rear drive sprocket, which dispensed with the need for bulky transmission units inside the driving and fighting compartments. The vehicle was powered by a four-cylinder 120hp Skoda T/11 engine, and the gearbox provided six forward and six reverse gears. A planetary steering system was employed, both steering and gear changing being assisted by compressed air. This made the PzKpfw 35(t) a pleasure to drive in normal conditions, although the low temperatures encountered during the Russian winter adversely affected the pneumatic equipment.

The suspension consisted of two sets of double bogie wheel pairs, each set hanging from a large leaf spring bolted to the hull side. This system equalized wear to such an extent that daily road journeys in excess of 160km could be achieved, provided the speed remained moderate, and in some cases a quite remarkable track life of 8,000km was recorded. A further point of interest concerning the suspension was a small track tensioning wheel located between the forward bogie and the front idler.

The hull and turret were constructed from riveted plates, and in this respect the vehicle fell below the specification of its German contemporaries. It was not widely appreciated at the time that the effect upon a rivet head of a high velocity round was to sheer off the shank, which, having absorbed much of the strike's terminal velocity, would then fly round the inside of the hull, killing and maiming.

These PzKpfw 35(t)s, bearing a camouflaged paint scheme and the company tactical numbers on the sides of their turrets, are serving on the Eastern Front in 1941. (AirSeaLand/Cody)

41

A combat image of a PzKpfw 35(t) on the Eastern Front. This tank had little in the way of crew comforts, with little space, poor internal temperature control and high levels of noise, all contributing to crew fatigue. (AirSeaLand/Cody)

The vehicle's main armament was an adapation of the Skoda A3 3.7cm anti-tank gun, fitted with a very simple perforated muzzle brake, and with a semi-automatic falling-block type breech. The recoil cylinder projected some way beyond the mantlet and was protected by a prominent armoured sleeve. The gun fired armour-piercing (AP) shot at a muzzle velocity of 675m/sec and was capable of penetrating 30mm armour at approximately 550m.

The two 7.92mm machine guns were belt-fed air-cooled weapons developed by Česká Zbrojovka of Erno; interestingly, a licence to manufacture this gun was sold to the BSA organization's Birmingham plant in 1937 and it evolved into the BESA machine gun, which was mounted by British tanks throughout World War II and beyond. Stowage consisted of 72 rounds of main and 1,800 rounds of secondary armament ammunition.

In many respects the PzKpfw 35(t) was an advanced design for its day and was always popular with its crews, its best-known users being the 6. Panzer-Division. It was, however, unable to cope with the fearsome cold encountered during the first winter on the Eastern Front, which rendered the vehicle's pneumatic transmission inoperable. The division's sole remaining PzKpfw 35(t), symbolically named 'Anthony the Last', gave up the ghost near Klin on 10 December 1941 during the final abortive advance on Moscow. Thereafter, as far as the German Army was concerned, the vehicle was finished as a gun tank.

Some standard versions of the tank had been equipped as command vehicles, Panzerbefehlswagen (PzBefw) 35(t), for the 1939 campaign in Poland, with extra radios installed and a collapsible frame aerial erected over the engine decks. In general, however, the vehicle's configuration rendered it unsuitable for conversion to specialist roles, so that when chassis did become available through the obsolescence of the gun tank, the German Army used them simply as turretless towing vehicles: one, the

Zugkraftwagen 35(t), was employed by vehicle recovery sections, and another, the Moserzugmittel 35(t), served in the artillery's heavy mortar batteries.

The PzKpfw 35(t) also saw service with some of Germany's Romanian and Slovak allies, and a few were supplied to the Bulgarian Army. The Romanian version of the tank, designated the R-2, differed from the original only in comparatively minor detail and formed the principal equipment of the Romanian 1st Royal Armoured Division. It remained in service until the Stalingrad campaign, but was only able to engage the Soviet light tanks on anything approaching even terms. During 1941 the Romanians sought to rectify the deficiency in firepower by fitting the PzKpfw 35(t) chassis with a larger turret mounting a captured Soviet M1941 7.62cm L/46 gun, the vehicle being designated the TACAM R-2. Only 21 of these conversions were made, and as they were only effective against the T-34 at about 500m range they were relegated to the assault gun role.

PANZERKAMPFWAGEN 38(t)

Notwithstanding its ultimate popularity, the PzKpfw 35(t) suffered an initial unreliability that caused adverse comment within the Czech Army. This reflected a somewhat impatient lack of understanding that a certain amount of modification to detail is inevitably required to perfect a design, even after it has entered service. Nonetheless, in 1937 the Staff requested competitive tenders for a new battle tank from Skoda and CKD (which became known as Bohmisch-Mahrische Maschinenfabrik AG after the German takeover) after the latter's TNHP design was accepted following trials.

A restored PzKpfw 35(t) on display in the United States. The co-axial 7.92mm machine gun is shrouded with a cover next to the main armament, the 3.7cm gun. (AirSeaLand/Cody)

This PzKpfw 38(t) is mounted on the platform of a German Panzerträgerwagen. This specialized rail car had a folding ramp on the front that allowed the tank to disembark and support the train's infantry detachment. The Panzerträgerwagen was lightly armoured to protect the tank's suspension. Armoured trains were allotted two of these, usually at either end of the train. (AirSeaLand/Cody)

In German service the TNHP was designated PzKpfw 38(t). The vehicle was similarly armed and armoured to the PzKpfw 35(t) and was driven by a 125hp Praga EPA six-cylinder water-cooled engine that produced a maximum speed of 42km/h; on later models the engine was fitted with twin carburettors, which raised the output to 150hp and the top speed to 48km/h. A front drive sprocket was employed, power reaching this through a five-forward/one-reverse Praga-Wilson gearbox. The suspension consisted of four large Christie-type road wheels per side, hanging in pairs from horizontal leaf springs bolted to the hull. The steering system was similar to that installed on the PzKpfw 35(t) but lacked pneumatic assistance. Fuel capacity was 151 litres, contained in two double-skin petrol tanks mounted on either side of the engine compartment. An electric starter was provided, as was an inertia starter operated from the rear of the vehicle: in emergencies the engine could be started manually from inside the fighting compartment by a device located on the flywheel housing. The position of the rear idler, which controlled track tension, could be adjusted through hatches in the stern plate.

Hull and turret construction was again of riveted plate, although rather fewer rivets were used than in the PzKpfw 35(t). Internally, the position of the four crew members was identical. The commander's cupola contained four episcopes, and immediately forward of these was a panoramic periscope.

The tank's main armament was the improved Skoda A7 3.7cm gun, known in German service as the KwK 37(t). It was a semi-automatic falling block weapon which fired AP shot at a muzzle velocity of 750m/sec and could penetrate 32mm armour at

1,100m; an HE (high explosive) round was also developed for this gun. The piece was slightly breech-heavy and the recoil cylinder projected a little way beyond the mantlet. Elevation was obtained either by an inconvenient horizontal handwheel to the gunner's right, or by means of a curved crutch that fitted his right shoulder: the latter system could be engaged by removing a worm from the elevating arc, but was extremely tiring. The traverse handwheel was badly sited on the gunner's left, requiring awkward bending of the wrist. Both the main and co-axial armament could be fired from a trigger on the elevating handwheel, which also incorporated a safety button; a gun selector lever was located under the 3.7cm gun, giving four positions: main, main and co-ax, safe, and co-ax. The sighting telescope included both 3.7cm and machine-gun range scales, and in the event of it being rendered inoperable a small open sight for emergency use had been drilled through the armour below. The co-axial mounting could be unlocked and the weapon used independently of the main armament with 10° of traverse, 20° of elevation and 10° of depression. The bow machine gun could be fired either by the hull gunner or the driver, the latter having an additional trigger fitted to his left tiller bar. Ninety rounds of 3.7cm and 2,700 rounds of machine-gun ammunition were stowed, the majority in the bulge at the turret rear. The radio was mounted on the hull wall to the left of the bow gunner.

The PzKpfw 38(t) ran to several models, of which the Ausf A was the standard version taken over upon the occupation of Czechoslovakia. The majority differed only in minor detail, such as the installation of a smoke grenade rack at the rear (Ausf B), but with Ausf E the armour thickness was doubled by bolting 25mm plates to the

A PzKpfw 38(t) rolls across a pontoon bridge over a canal in France, 1940. Overall PzKpfw 38(t) strength on 10 May 1940 was 91 PzKpfw 38(t) and eight Befehlspanzer 38(t) in 7. Panzer-Division, and 116 PzKpfw 38(t) and 15 Befehlspanzer 38(t) in 8. Panzer-Division. (AirSeaLand/Cody)

The PzKpfw 38(t) proved well suited to a campaign of rapid movement, but it was not ideal for tank-vs-tank combat. Its 3.7cm gun was poorly suited to fighting against the thickly armoured French tanks. (AirSeaLand/Cody)

front of the vehicle and 15mm plates to the side. The Ausf G was the last production model before chassis were built exclusively for self-propelled mountings, while Ausf S was a version built for Sweden but confiscated by the German Army before delivery could be made.

Altogether, 1,414 PzKpfw 38(t)s were built. Its reliability and ease of maintenance made it a very attractive acquisition, so that in addition to widespread use by the German Army it was also exported to Iran, Romania, Bulgaria, Hungary, Sweden, Switzerland and Peru. Even the British Army's Royal Armoured Corps (RAC), in the throes of rearmament and desperately short of equipment, was sufficiently interested to arrange for CKD to deliver a demonstration model to the Gunnery School at Lutworth on 23 March 1939, and firing trials took place the next day. The following extract from the report prepared after the trials reflects the RAC's thinking on crew practice in what was evaluated as a medium tank turret, and these, of course, coincided with those of the Panzerwaffe. They also reflect the professional user's view that in achieving their equation of mobility, firepower and protection, tank designers frequently ignore the human element: 'On the whole the machine is almost equivalent to our cruiser tanks, but little experience or experiment has gone into the design of the fighting compartment and performance has been obtained at the expense of the crew and general fight-ability.'

The commander-gunner had plenty of room, and with ammunition in the turret bulge he could easily turn and load the 3.7cm gun. He could not, however, load and clear stoppages on the co-axial 7.92mm machine gun. His foothold on the floor was insecure and in certain positions of the turret he had to crouch owing to the height of the propeller shaft. The report continues:

A sling seat suspended by three chains (one between the gunner's legs) was provided. The adjustment, though simple, could not be altered without standing up. The seat was unsuitable for firing on the move and the gunner could not lift his body up and down to follow the relatively large arcs travelled by the telescope eye-piece and the shoulder-piece, both of which were some distance from the trunnions. The seat could not be used by the gunner when loading for himself.

Without the seat it was easy to change from the position of commander to that of gunner and vice versa, but it must be emphasized that once the commander of a tank becomes a gunner, he ceases to command.

The loader's position was very cramped and uncomfortable. The floor offered a very poor foothold and there were no handholds. He is liable to get part of his body caught between the 37mm gun [spent case] deflector plate and the turret roof – particularly dangerous if the elevation lock becomes jammed.

The hull gunner's position for horizontal fire was very comfortable for a short man. By pressing with his feet on the cross-shaft casing, the gunner could brace himself against the back of the seat, which had a sliding backward and forward adjustment. The shoulder-piece on the gun was also comfortable.

When firing at targets above or below the horizontal, however, the gunner found himself unable to follow the rather extensive movement of the telescope eye-piece and shoulder-piece. It was necessary for the gunner either to contract and extend his body like a caterpillar or, what is only slightly easier, to slide his bottom backwards and forwards by pressing with his feet or pulling on the gun.

When travelling the gun could be released and the mounting locked but the gunner could not sit back comfortably as the wireless set was in the way of his left shoulder.

Seen here in action at Kharkov in the summer of 1943, a Panzerjäger 38(t) für 7.5cm PaK 40, Ausf M (Marder III) rolls past a burning Ukrainian building. (AirSeaLand/ Cody)

The driver had a good seat and satisfactory controls. The position, however, was tiring for a long march as his view through the episcope was limited and he could not open any flaps. Headroom was insufficient and there was no vertical seat adjustment.

While the author's comment had obvious validity, it must also be mentioned that in German service the commander-gunner's sling seat was replaced by a stool suspended by a bar from the turret ring, and that a firmer footing was provided for both him and the loader. Curiously, the author describes the tank as being comfortable to ride in, adding that there was little chance of the crew sustaining injury when travelling over unknown country. One cannot agree with this, as the suspension actually provided an extremely hard, jerky, unpredictable ride. Obviously his comment has to be taken in the context of its time, but he did concede that the judder made it impossible to lay the guns on the move and that even at 1mph (1.6km/h) shooting was poor.

The report contains numerous additional points of minor criticism, some of them trivial, and as the vehicle left Lutworth the morning alter the trial shoot it can safely be assumed that the decision had already been made not to proceed with the purchase. This is hardly surprising, for March 1939 was the month that Hitler consolidated his hold over the whole of Czechoslovakia, and the RAC's equipment requirements could scarcely have been left to the whims and fancies of the Führer.

PzKpfw 38(t) derivatives

The standard PzKpfw 38(t) could quickly be converted to the command role by installing extra radios and fitting a frame aerial above the engine deck, and in this version the vehicle was known as Panzerbefehlswagen 38(t). Once the T-34 had been encountered on the Eastern Front it was obvious that the PzKpfw 38(t)'s days as a gun tank were numbered, although many continued to serve with Germany's satellite armies well into 1942.

Obsolete though the vehicle might be, its robust chassis was capable of conversion to a variety of roles and remained in production until 1944. Perhaps the simplest conversion of all was the Aufklärungspanzer 38(t), in which the original turret was replaced by that of a SdKfz 222 armoured car. Seventy of these vehicles were built in 1944 and issued to favoured armoured reconnaissance battalions. The most common conversions, however, were to the role of self-propelled gun carriage. The Marder III tank-destroyer appeared in three forms, one of which mounted the Russian model 36 76.2mm anti-tank gun, while the other two carried the German 7.5cm L/46 PaK 40/3 anti-tank gun, one with a conventional rear-mounted engine and the other with the engine moved forward. A more advanced, fully armoured tank-destroyer design was the low-slung Hetzer, which was equipped with a 7.5cm L/48 PaK 39 anti-tank gun. A small number of Hetzers were built with a disguised flame gun in place of the 7.5cm

PZKPFW 38(t) AUSF D, 7. PANZER-DIVISION

Crew: 4
Weight: 9.8 tonnes
Length: 4.61m
Width: 2.14m
Height: 2.25m
Main gun: 3.7cm KwK 38(t) gun
Main gun ammunition: 90 rounds
    3.7cm
Secondary armament: two 7.92mm
    MG 37(t); one machine gun on
    platoon command tanks
Machine-gun ammunition: 2,700
    rounds 7.92mm
Radio: Fu 5 and Fu 2 transceiver
    (platoon commander)
Hull front armour: 25mm
Hull side armour: 15mm
Turret front armour: 25mm
Maximum speed: 42km/h
Cross-country speed (track): 15km/h
Road range: 250km
Terrain range: 100km
Fuel capacity: 220 litres
Engine type: Praga TNHPS/II
Transmission: Praga-Wilson CV
Horsepower: 125

(Jim Laurier © Osprey Publishing)

2.25m

2.14m

4.61m

Clad in their distinctive black Panzer uniforms, PzKpfw 38(t) tank crewmen rush to man their vehicles in France, 1940. The Czech tanks amounted to about 13 per cent of German tank strength, but accounted for about half of the tanks armed with a 3.7cm gun. AirSeaLand/Cody)

main armament, their official title being Flammpanzer 38(t). The flame gun had a range of 60m, and 580 litres of fuel were carried for it. These vehicles were used in the 1944 Ardennes offensive.

The PzKpfw 38(t) chassis also provided two carriages for the 15cm sIG 33/1. Both were designated SdKfz 138/1 and sometimes referred to as the Bison, but while the Ausf H version retained the central fighting compartment and rear engine, the Ausf M saw the engine moved forward and the fighting compartment relocated at the back of the vehicle. Both models served in the heavy gun companies of Panzergrenadier divisions, together with an ammunition carrier based on the Ausf M.

The Flakpanzer 38(t) was a stop-gap anti-aircraft vehicle, of which 162 were built in 1943. Like the Bison Ausf M, its engine was mounted forward and the fighting compartment overhung the rear of the chassis. Armament consisted of a single 2cm cannon, for which 540 rounds of HE tracer and AP tracer ammunition were stowed. The gun had a maximum rate of fire of 480rpm, but was usually governed to half this output. The vehicle was manned by a crew of five, and served in the anti-aircraft platoons of armoured regiments until replaced by Flakpanzer IV models.

Altogether, the PzKpfw 38(t) was used as the basis for nearly 3,700 self-propelled carriages and 102 ammunition carriers. With the exception of the Hetzer series, fighting compartments were all open-topped structures of thin armour plating. In addition, some chassis were used as mobile smokescreen layers (PzKpfw 38(t) mit Nebel Ausrastung), while others were sent to tank driving schools where they were converted to burning wood gas generated in a bulky apparatus installed at the rear of the vehicle. From August 1944 a small number of unarmed Hetzers were converted to the Bergepanzer (armoured recovery vehicle) role, a 2-ton derrick being mounted on the vehicle's roof.

The PzKpfw 38(t) chassis was also widely used on experimental projects, very few of which left the drawing board. Some would have employed a German redesign which was driven by a more powerful 210hp Tatra diesel engine located beside the driver. This development was known as the PzKpfw 38(d) ('d' standing for 'Deutsch'), but the war ended before it entered production.

It speaks volumes for the chassis' reputation that it was still actively employed until the 1970s, being used by the Swedish Army for its armoured personnel carrier (APC) as well as the SAV 101, an assault gun mounting a 105mm howitzer in a fixed, angled superstructure.

OPERATIONAL HISTORY

Hitler's resolution to support Franco during the Spanish Civil War led to the despatch of the 'volunteer' Legion Condor, incorporating air force and army elements, and the Panzerwaffe received its baptism of fire in January 1937. The Legion's tank unit was armed with 180 PzKpfw Is and commanded by the then Major Wilhelm Ritter von Thoma, who was eventually able to form tank battalions, each of three 15-tank companies. Thoma thought so little of the PzKpfw I as a combat vehicle that he offered 500 pesetas for every Russian T-26 captured from the communists, the latter being armed with a 45mm high-velocity gun and a co-axial machine gun. Nevertheless, in Spain the unit was able to develop operational techniques in an active service environment, particularly co-operation with the ground support wings of the Luftwaffe and the forward deployment of an anti-tank gun screen through which the tanks could

A PzKpfw II passes the recovery of a PzKpfw VI Tiger I during operations on the Nettuno–Anzio Front in 1944, the size difference between the two vehicles clearly evident. (AirSeaLand/Cody)

PzKpfw II tanks are mounted on train transport in Croatia in 1941, during the German Balkans campaign. Light tanks were ideal for the mountainous terrain often encountered in this theatre. (AirSeaLand/Cody)

PzKpfw I and II tanks put on an impressive display for the German High Command during a pre-war rally at Nuremberg. (AirSeaLand/Cody)

PZKPFW II AMMUNITION

As the most powerful armour-piercing 2cm round available to the Germans, the Swiss Solothurn 20×13.8cm Pzgr 39 138B (1), a belted round, produced a chamber pressure of roughly 3,000atm – the equivalent of 44,000psi – with 46.5kJ muzzle energy. Travelling at 780m/sec, it offered a penetrative capability of 20mm at 100m, 14mm at 500m and 8mm at 1,000m. It was 204mm tall, had a ZZ 1505 fuse and was painted black, with a yellow band to indicate it contained an explosive element. Its markings – here reading 'Rh.1c38.148g' – indicated the manufacturer's code, the shipment code number, the production year and the projectile weight, plus 'Ph' (phosphorus). The Sprgr 39 HE round (2) was painted yellow, with a red band. It had an unpainted AZ 5045 nose-detonating steel fuse and 35.9kJ muzzle energy. The labelling here reads 'Rh.S.1a39.115g'. Both projectiles used the same-sized brass cartridge, with a percussion cap for triggering. The powder was housed in a two-section fabric bag, with a smaller and larger compartment respectively containing an igniter and main propellant charge.

1 **2**

(Richard Chasemore © Osprey Publishing)

retire if hard pressed by the much superior Russian T-26s. The concepts of mobility and concentration were also vindicated. Spain, however, was not a representative proving ground for the protagonists of what would become known as *Blitzkrieg*, and no dramatic successes were recorded. Indeed, Thoma's reports suggested that the tank had failed to live up to its promise; yet Guderian, recognizing the fact that this was not a conventional war fought between first-rate national armies, refused to be deflected from his beliefs.

Eastern Europe

Those beliefs were to be tested again during the Austrian Anschluss of March 1938, when up to 30 per cent of the tanks involved in the march on Vienna littered the roadside, broken down, although the major part of Guderian's 2. Panzer-Division succeeded in covering 390km in only two days. Once installed in his Panzer

A Storch reconnaissance aircraft overflies PzKpfw 38(t) tanks from the 7. Panzer-Division in France, 1940. By the time of the 1940 campaign in Western Europe, more than 200 PzKpfw 38(t) tanks had been delivered. (AirSeaLand/Cody)

Inspectorate, Guderian implacably set about eradicating failures in the tank recovery and repair system. The subsequent occupation of the Sudetenland (October 1938) and Czechoslovakia revealed a greatly improved situation, and in this context it is worth remembering that the PzKpfw I and II were light enough to be ferried long distances on unadapted lorries into their operational zones, so saving critical track mileage.

Whether Hitler would have continued to play his deadly game of brinkmanship over the Polish question had he not acquired the Czech armoury remains a matter of speculation. In the event his bluff was called, and to its horror the Wehrmacht found itself facing the possibility of war on two fronts. Not even the most enthusiastic officers of the Panzerwaffe could have welcomed the prospect of going to war with their under-strength, badly equipped divisions.

The nominal tank strength of a Panzer division in 1939 was 562 vehicles; the reality was somewhat different. As the senior formation, 1. Panzer-Division received a larger allocation of the few medium tanks available, each of its battalions containing 14 PzKpfw IVs, 28 PzKpfw IIIs, 18 PzKpfw IIs and 17 PzKpfw Is: together with command and headquarters vehicles, the divisional tank strength was 324. The battalion establishments of the remaining Panzer divisions were six PzKpfw IVs, five PzKpfw IIIs, 33 PzKpfw IIs and 34 PzKpfw Is: these, together with command vehicles, produced a tank strength of 328 per division. The l. leichte-Division, with three tank battalions, could muster a total of 221 tanks, including a handful of PzKpfw IIIs and IVs, but was one of the strongest formations in the field since the balance of its tank strength included 112 PzKpfw 35(t)s. Meanwhile 2. and 4. leichte-Divisionen each had less than 100 tanks, and of these the PzKpfw II predominated. The 3. leichte-Division, however, was reinforced with a battalion of 59 PzKpfw 38(t)s, giving it approximately 150 tanks.

It was, therefore, upon the light tanks that the burden of the Polish campaign fell. In this context it must be remembered that in 1939 few soldiers had experienced an armoured attack, and that to the average infantryman a tank was a tank, extremely dangerous and ostensibly invulnerable, whatever shortcomings its users may have felt it had. Again, the Polish Army was organized and trained for operations in the style of 1918, and its own armoured force was small and much of its equipment obsolete: Polish sources are scrupulously honest in stating that as far as their armour was concerned, the battle could never have been won, but it could have been fought better.

The course of the campaign will be known to most. Poland, strategically outflanked by East Prussia in the north and Czechoslovakia in the south, was subjected to concentric attacks in the form of two giant pincer movements, the inner set to close near Warsaw and the outer near Brest-Litovsk. Once the cordon of Polish armies guarding the frontier had been penetrated, the continued advance of the Panzer Korps totally disrupted their command and logistic networks, inducing eventual collapse. The *coup de grace* was treacherously administered by the Red Army, the Soviet government claiming that it had 'intervened' to stop the fighting, but keeping a huge slice of Polish territory as a reward for its benevolence.

The Panzerwaffe emerged from the campaign with its confidence enhanced and its operational techniques sharpened by experience, but it had by no means enjoyed the 'dry run with a little shooting' that was later suggested. In some areas senior commanders had been forced to apply considerable pressure to overcome their formations' natural reluctance to maintain their drive into unknown territory in accordance with the theory of deep penetration. The mechanical failure rate, particularly among the PzKpfw Is and IIs, rapidly rose to 25 per cent and remained there. Above all, whenever possible the Poles had fought back with a desperate bravery, using their few anti-tank guns, anti-tank rifles and field artillery firing over open sights: 4. Panzer-Division alone lost 60 tanks in a single day, trying to fight its way prematurely into central Warsaw.

For the campaign as a whole, the Panzerwaffe admitted a loss of 218 tanks, approximately 10 per cent of the total engaged. The breakdown of total losses was 89 PzKpfw Is, 78 PzKpfw IIs, 26 PzKpfw IIIs, 19 PzKpfw IVs and six PzKpfw 35(t)s. In the light of subsequent strength returns, this figure has been regarded as suspect, and a post-war Polish examination of contemporary German documents reveals it to be so. What actually appears is a reduction in the Panzerwaffe's operational tank strength by 674 vehicles, partly the result of battle damage and partly because of mechanical failure and other causes. If one accepts that a third were immediately

A PzKpfw I Ausf B during operations in Poland in September 1939. A total of 89 PzKpfw Is were lost during the Polish campaign, the highest number of losses of any German tank type involved. (AirSeaLand/Cody)

written off, then one arrives close to the published German figure. A further third should simply be regarded as being beyond local repair, and these would have been rebuilt in Germany. The remainder, whether damaged in battle or suffering from major mechanical defects, fall into the category of being beyond economic repair, and in this respect it is worth remembering that the PzKpfw

1) Kleiner Panzerbefehlswagen, 4. Panzer-Division; Poland, 1939. A command tank, carrying the usual regimental headquarters tactical numbers on the turret side, and 'R02' on the number plate on the rear hull. The 4. Panzer-Division was one of the few formations to display a divisional insignia in Poland, a three-point star or 'caltrop' shape painted here on the rear of the cupola.

2) Pzkpfw I Ausf B, Aufklarungs-Zug, II Abteilung Stab, Panzer-Regiment 36, 4. Panzer-Division; France, 1940. The turret code 'IIL' indicates that the 2nd Battalion was a 'light' battalion; '5' is the individual tank number. (Terry Hadler © Osprey Publishing)

Is and IIs were comparatively frail machines and that the more elderly of them had already reached the limit of their service life. The full extent of the German tank loss therefore almost certainly exceeded 400 vehicles, or 20 per cent of the total; this, balanced against deliveries of new and repaired vehicles, is reflected in the line-up for the offensive in the West the following year. This might be regarded as unduly high for a month's fighting in which no major armoured engagement took place, but the fact remains that in that time the Panzer divisions and the Luftwaffe together defeated an army of 1,500,000 at a cost of only 8,000 German lives.

Western Europe

Hitler's next campaign of expansion was directed at Norway and Denmark under the codename of *Weserubung* (Exercise 'Weser'). This began on 9 April 1940, and although the initial assault was delivered by airborne and air-landing troops, a tank battalion known as Panzer-Abteilung z.B.V.40 was included in the second echelon. This battalion, formed from Panzer-Regiment 35 of 4. Panzer-Division, reflected in its equipment the chronic tank shortage still afflicting the Panzerwaffe, now preparing for what was regarded as its supreme test, the invasion of Western Europe. None of the scarce PzKpfw IIIs and IVs could be spared for *Weserubung*, but in their place were respectively 15 PzKpfw 38(t)s and three Neubaufahrzeug prototypes (the NbFz was an

PZKPFW 38(t) SIGHTS

The Zielfernrohr 38(t) telescopic sight had two different reticle patterns. The early Czech pattern (shown here) had the horizontal deflection scale displayed in mils (a measurement denoting 1 yard at 1,000 yards' distance); the later reticle switched to the German pattern of deflection markings by using a series of small triangles. The unit of measure was a graduation (Strich) equalling 1m at 1,000m range, with the large centre triangle having sides of four graduations and the smaller triangle having sides of two graduations. The Czech style of reticles had the range calibrations as a 'staircase' on either side, with armour-piercing on the left and high explosive on the right. The gunner introduced the superelevation needed to compensate for range by dialling in the estimated range to target.

(Jim Laurier © Osprey Publishing)

abandoned design for a multi-turreted breakthrough tank) which, like the PzKpfw IV, carried a 7.5cm main armament; the remainder of the battalion consisted of PzKpfw Is and IIs, approximately 40 in number.

With the Danes offering only token resistance to the onslaught, the main body of the battalion advanced through Denmark and was then shipped over to Oslo, where it joined the NbFz platoon, which had landed as soon as the city had been secured. The tanks were then employed in spearheading the German drive up the two principal valleys north of Oslo, Gudbrandsdalen and Osterdalen. In Gudbrandsdalen the Panzers' advance was delayed by demolitions and brought to a halt by the stiff resistance offered by the British 15th Infantry Brigade. Two vehicles were destroyed by the brigade's French 25mm anti-tank guns, but the Luftwaffe's intervention and the growing volume of German artillery fire at length caused the British to withdraw. In Osterdalen the tanks faced only lightly equipped Norwegian troops and sustained no major checks. By the beginning of May, southern and central Norway was firmly in German hands.

On 10 May 1940 the long-awaited offensive against France and the Low Countries began. An appendix to Guderian's memoirs contains a memorandum despatched by Army Headquarters (*Oberkommando des Heeres*, OKH) to the Führer's military adjutant on 7 November 1944, and this quotes the German tank strength on the eve of the invasion as being as follows:

PzKpfw I – 523
PzKpfw II – 955
PzKpfw III – 349
PzKpfw IV – 278
PzKpfw 35(t) – 106
PzKpfw 38(t) – 228
PzBefw I – 96
PzBefw III – 39

These figures, prepared four-and-a-half years after the event, were as accurate as possible, although there is good reason to believe that they slightly understate the case as far as the Czech vehicles are concerned. Excluding command vehicles, they give a total of 2,439 gun tanks, of which the 1,478 machine-gun-armed PzKpfw Is and IIs still represented a substantial majority. In contrast, the French Army alone could deploy over 3,000 tanks, many of which were better armed and better protected than the best German machines.

The strategic plan for the campaign was the brainchild of the brilliant Erich von Manstein, who predicted, quite correctly, that a German invasion of Holland and Belgium would draw the best French armies and the British Expeditionary Force north into a trap. Once the Allies had taken the bait, a concentrated drive by the mass of the

Panzerwaffe from the Meuse to the Somme Estuary would isolate the British, French and Belgian armies in the north and ensure their destruction. The course of the campaign itself entirely fulfilled Manstein's concept. It is worth mentioning here the part played by the light tanks in this most sweeping of German victories.

Responsibility for the invasion of Holland and Belgium rested with Fedor von Bock's Heeresgruppe B, which was allotted only three Panzer divisions (3., 4. and 9.), although to compensate for this it received most of the airborne and air-landing formations. In this context it should be remembered that any failure on Bock's part to convince the Allies that his invasion was the main German thrust line would be reflected adversely against Gerd von Rundstedt's Heeresgruppe A in its drive to the coast. One armoured formation upon which much depended was Major General Ritter von Hubicki's 9. Panzer-Division, which had been recruited in Austria. Ironically, this was the weakest of all the Panzer divisions, its Panzer-Regiment 33 having only two battalions equipped with a total of 18 PzKpfw IVs, 36 PzKpfw IIIs, 75 PzKpfw IIs and 100 PzKpfw Is; yet it was expected to drive straight across Holland and relieve the German parachute troops (Fallschirmjäger) holding the Moerdijk bridge over the Maas before the French First Army, approaching from the south, could get there. In the event Hubicki's task was made easier by the French commander who, within striking distance of the objective, split his advance guard into a reconnaissance screen which was easily brushed aside, and then withdrew. The 9. Panzer-Division broke

PzKpfw IIs roll through France in 1940. By 1941, the PzKpfw II was unsuited for front-line combat and was instead used for lighter tasks such as reconnaissance. (AirSeaLand/Cody)

ABOVE This captured German PzKpfw I Ausf B is on display in the United States. The two 7.92mm MG 13 machine guns could be fired either together or independently. (AirSeaLand/Cody)

ABOVE RIGHT A PzKpfw II in the Balkans. The vehicle's good cross-country performance meant it could use movement and terrain to avoid being targeted; its leaf-spring suspension was suited to its light weight and proved to be simple, effective and easy to repair.

through to the Fallschirmjäger on 12 May, and then swung north to Rotterdam, which was entered two days later. Although eclipsed by events elsewhere, the division's achievement was astonishing: it had cut Holland in two and isolated the Dutch Army from Allied aid and reinforcement – the entire Manstein plan in microcosm, in fact. Holland surrendered on 15 May.

Further south, but still under the command of Heeresgruppe B, was Erich Hoepner's XVI. Panzer-Korps, consisting of 3. and 4. Panzer-Divisionen, each of which had a nominal tank strength of 24 PzKpfw IVs, 50 PzKpfw IIIs, 110 PzKpfw IIs and 140 PzKpfw Is. After crossing the Maastricht 'Appendix', Hoepner's divisions motored on across Belgium until they reached the Gembloux Gap, and here they were met by General Prioux's 1er Corps de Cavalerie, covering the flank of First Army as it deployed. Prioux's corps consisted of the 2e and 3e Divisions Légères Mecaniques, and was equipped with 174 of the formidable Somuas, 87 Hotchkiss H35s and 40 AMR light tanks, together with a small Belgian contingent. A fierce tank battle was fought on 12–13 May, with each side suffering losses in excess of 100 vehicles and both claiming a victory. However, while the French retired to prepared positions, the Germans retained possession of the field and were able to recover many of their casualties. The principal effects of this engagement, referred to in German records as the 'Panzerschlacht bei Namur', were to rivet French attention on Belgium and to divert the main Allied counter-attack force away from the real threat that was unfolding in the Ardennes, with disastrous consequences.

The most northerly of Heeresgruppe A's armoured formations was Hermann Hoth's XV. Panzer-Korps, composed of 5. and 7. Panzer-Divisionen, the latter commanded by Major General Erwin Rommel. The former was very similarly equipped to 3. and 4. Panzer-Divisionen, but the 7th's equipment at the outset consisted of

36 PzKpfw IVs, 106 PzKpfw 38(t)s, 40 PzKpfw IIs and 10 PzKpfw Is. However, while Rommel's division was moving up to the Meuse, 5. Panzer was delayed by congested roads and Hoth placed its leading armoured regiment, Panzer-Regiment 31, under Rommel's command, thus making 7. Panzer an extremely powerful division. The attachment was intended to be a temporary one, but Rommel was a thoroughly bad neighbour and it is debatable just when or how much of Panzer-Regiment 31 he returned to its owners: certainly, as late as 21 May he sustained the loss of six PzKpfw IIIs in action and these vehicles were not included in his own order of battle. In the centre of Heeresgruppe A's sector was Georg-Hans Reinhardt's XLI. Panzer-Korps, composed of 6. and 8. Panzer-Divisionen. Both had a similar proportion of PzKpfw Is, IIs and IVs to Rommel's division, but the bulk of 6. Panzer-Division's tank strength consisted of 118 PzKpfw 35(t)s accompanied by ten PzBefw 35(t)s, while 8. Panzer-Division had 116 PzKpfw 38(t)s and seven PzBefw 38(t)s.

On the Army Group's left was the strongest Panzer-Korps of all, Guderian's XIX., consisting of 1., 2. and 10. Panzer-Divisionen. Guderian was to lead the drive to the sea, and because of this his divisions received a generous allocation of medium tanks, their respective strength being 56 PzKpfw IVs, 90 PzKpfw IIIs, 100 PzKpfw IIs and 30 PzKpfw Is each.

These dispositions, both quantitative and qualitative, reflect Manstein's overall strategy in that the best equipment, including the reliable Czech vehicles, was concentrated on the German left. In contrast, the French disposed their armour evenly along the front so that the Panzer-Korps, present in overwhelming strength, found no difficulty in breaking through and out into open country. In both the dash to the sea, completed on 20 May, and the subsequent operations against the remaining French armies south of the Somme, the Panzer divisions acted with a drive and confidence that had been absent in Poland. When the campaign ended on 22 June, the world's two most prestigious armies had been defeated. German casualties in six weeks' fighting amounted to only 150,000, but losses in action and through sheer mechanical attrition had reduced the Panzerwaffe's tank strength by 50 per cent.

North Africa, the Balkans and the Eastern Front

While no Czech gun tanks were sent to North Africa with Rommel, his command did contain a substantial number of PzKpfw Is and IIs. The former soon disappeared, but on the eve of Operation *Crusader* (November 1941), PzKpfw IIIs still constituted almost one third of the total German tank strength of 249. Thereafter, those that survived were withdrawn for conversion.

In April 1941, with planning for the onslaught on Soviet Russia well under way, Hitler launched his invasions of Yugoslavia and Greece. Neither country possessed adequate modern anti-tank equipment, but both believed that their mountainous terrain would inhibit the run the Panzers had had in Poland and

France. This belief proved to be mistaken, for although the terrain did present problems, these were far from insuperable. Like the Polish and French General Staff, their Greek and Yugoslav counterparts were simply not prepared for the speed with which events developed once the Panzer divisions had broken through or bypassed their static defences. Yugoslavia surrendered on 17 April and Greece on the 23rd. About one third of the German armoured force had been engaged. (See Chapter 3 for more details on this campaign.)

Many senior officers believed that the Balkans campaign had been unnecessary and that the time spent in its preparation, execution and the subsequent redeployment contributed to the failure of Operation *Barbarossa*, as indeed did the imposition of substantial track mileage, particularly on older vehicles, when the Panzerwaffe was on the point of being asked to perform the impossible. Manufacture of German medium tanks had been accelerated after the fall of France, but the war against Russia opened with the Panzerwaffe still having a preponderance of light tanks, its grand total of 3,332 vehicles being made up of 410 PzKpfw Is, 746 PzKpfw IIs, 965 PzKpfw IIIs, 439 PzKpfw IVs, 149 PzKpfw 35(t)s and 623 PzKpfw 38(t)s , the Czech tanks forming the principal armament of 6., 7., 8., 12., 19. and 20. Panzer-Divisionen. Altogether, 17 Panzer divisions, with two more in reserve, spearheaded the invasion, organized into four Panzergruppen.

A PzKpfw II Ausf F Command Car in North Africa. The PzKpfw II's battlefield survivability depended on being able to move quickly from one position to another, and make use of terrain to mask its presence and promote surprise. (AirSeaLand/Cody)

The sheer arrogance of Hitler's ambition was terrifying. The Red Army possessed more than 20,000 tanks, unlimited manpower resources and an infinity of space into which it could withdraw. Unlike France, where the strategic objectives were just mechanically attainable but placed serious strain on the repair organization, those in Russia were many times further away; moreover, surfaced roads were the exception in Russia, making the going even more difficult.

Yet the Panzergruppen, now thoroughly experienced and at the peak of self-confidence, performed prodigies. Russian armies were repeatedly encircled and destroyed and Moscow was within their grasp when, at the critical moment, Hitler intervened needlessly to divert the central thrust to entrap the already crumbling Soviet formations retreating before Heeresgruppe Süd (Army Group South). By the time the advance was resumed, the Panzer spearheads had been eroded to mere shadows of their former selves, while Stalin was rushing Siberian reinforcements to the Moscow Front. Worse, the autumn rains created a sea of mud in which only tanks could move, and then only with difficulty: many of the less combat-worthy PzKpfw Is and IIs found themselves towing trains of three or four lorries through axle-deep slime so that communications could be kept open.

With the first frosts the ground hardened, and the advance continued for a while. It was finally halted on 8 December by deep snow and unimaginable cold, crews and their machines having to cope with conditions which exceeded the wildest visions of a Nordic hell. In the low temperatures track pins broke, firing pins shattered, telescopic sights iced over, recoil buffer fluid became solid and so prevented the firing of guns, and sump oil assumed the viscosity of treacle. Fires had to be kept burning beneath tanks, and engines had to be run every four hours throughout the night.

True, the Red Army had sustained the staggering loss of 17,000 tanks and over one million men, but German casualties (excluding the numberless frostbite cases) amounted to 743,000, 25 per cent of those engaged. The Panzerwaffe had lost 2,700 vehicles, the repair and replacement organizations' inability to cope with the scale of the problem being compounded by Hitler's insistence, even in this moment of supreme crisis, on retaining new tanks in Germany with which to form yet more Panzer divisions.

Barbarossa had been the light tanks' swan song. Some of the early encounters with the Russian T-34s led at least one Panzergruppe commander to the conclusion that in future no tank with less than a 7.5cm main armament could hope to survive on the Eastern Front. Symbolically, the departure of the light tanks was accompanied by that of Guderian, dismissed following a violent personality clash with his immediate superior, Field Marshal Günther von Kluge. The years of victory were over.

PzKpfw 38(t) Ausf F, II./Panzer-Regiment 204, 22. Panzer-Division; Crimea, Summer 1942. In June 1940, a general order was issued to stop applying the dark-brown colour to armoured vehicle camouflage, leaving the tanks in a uniform dark-grey colour, eventually redesignated as RAL 7017. The 22. Panzer-Division was the last division to be fully equipped with the PzKpfw 38(t), so its vehicles were delivered in overall dark grey. The conditions in the Crimea were far more arid than most of Russia, and the dark-grey colour was not ideal camouflage. As a result, many of the division's tanks were given a hasty camouflage scheme prior to the summer fighting in the Crimea. Since German tank units were not regularly issued camouflage paint at this stage of the war, the scheme was either improvised using local resources, or applied using mud. The latter seems more likely here, given the sloppy finish.

(Richard Casemore © Osprey Publishing)

CHAPTER 2

THE PANZER III

PzKpfw IIIs in Tunisia in 1942. The spare tracks links were not just for track breakdowns, but also provided a form of additional armour, particularly against shaped-charge rounds. (AirSeaLand/Cody)

During the second half of the 1930s, as the PzKpfw I and PzKpfw II left the production lines they were sent immediately to the newly formed Panzer divisions as temporary expedients, pending the appearance of purpose-built main battle tanks, the plan being that each battalion should consist of one heavy company, equipped with tanks carrying a large-calibre gun for close support, and three medium companies, whose tanks would carry an armour-defeating gun and two machine guns. In due course, the mount of the heavy company would become known as the PzKpfw IV, and that of the medium companies as the PzKpfw III.

DEVELOPMENT AND VARIANTS

The starting point for the PzKpfw III design, as in every main battle tank design, was the gun. Senior tank officers requested a 5cm gun, a sensible provision at a time when the British were beginning to fit a 40mm 2-pdr gun into their new Cruiser tanks, and the Russians were already employing a 45mm gun in their BTs and T-26s. However, the Heereswaffenamt, responsible for procurement, demurred, pointing out with the backing of the Artillery Inspectorate that the infantry was already in possession of the 3.7cm anti-tank gun, which was in quantity production, and the obvious desirability of standardization of armour-piercing ammunition and weapons. An intelligent compromise was reached by which the tank officers accepted the 3.7cm, while the turret ring was to be constructed wide enough to accommodate the 5cm gun if necessary.

A PzKpfw III in Greece, 1941. The PzKpfw III had an advanced suspension that provided a smoother ride due to greater road wheel travel from its torsion-bar suspension. (AirSeaLand/Cody)

An early model of the PzKpfw III moves on a pontoon bridge over the Meuse during the French campaign of 1940. The tank has yet to acquire the rear storage unit on the turret. (AirSeaLand/Cody)

Having settled this question, the next step was to design the hull within the then 24-tonne German bridge-loading specification. (Contemporary British designers were similarly hampered by a mandatory railway loading gauge restriction. This had the effect of limiting the width of their tanks, and thus the turret ring, and so ultimately the size of the weapon that could be mounted.) A standard layout was adopted with the engine mounted at the rear. Inside the turret the commander sat centrally beneath his cupola, with the gunner on the left of the gun breech and the loader on the right. In the forward compartment the driver was located on the left and the radio operator/hull gunner on the right, with the transmission between them. The final drive ran to the sprockets across the front of the forward compartment. This basic arrangement remained unaltered throughout the vehicle's history.

Once the prototypes had been produced and tested, Daimler-Benz was appointed to oversee development and manufacture, the essential requirements being specified as a 15-ton vehicle capable of 40km/h. The true purpose of the vehicle was cloaked under the security title of Zugführerwagen or ZW (platoon commander's vehicle); but military bureaucracy being as self-perpetuating as any other kind, successive Marks carried in addition to their Ausführung letter a progressive ZW number, long after security had ceased to be an overriding consideration.

The Ausf A appeared in 1936. The running gear consisted of five medium-sized road wheels, front drive sprocket, spoked idler and two return rollers. The vehicle was powered by a 250hp 12-cylinder Maybach 108 TR engine, and transmission was by means of a five-speed gearbox, which also provided one reverse gear. The L/45 3.7cm main armament was mounted co-axially with twin 7.92mm machine guns behind a recessed mantlet which was vulnerable to bullet splash, while a further 7.92mm machine gun was carried in a ball mounting in the front plate of the hull. The commander's cupola was starkly simple, consisting of a slotted 'dustbin', and the turret was fitted with one-piece side hatches. Daimler-Benz had hit its weight target by providing a maximum armour thickness of 14.5mm, but the suspension system was more suitable for commercial than military usage and the engine output was comparatively low, so that the vehicle's top speed of 32km/h fell below the required specification.

Ten vehicles of this type were produced. The Ausf B was broadly similar in its concept, but attempted to solve the suspension problem by employing leaf instead of coil springs, eight smaller road wheels being suspended from two horizontal spring units, while the number of return rollers was increased to three. This had the effect of raising the weight slightly to 15.9 tonnes, but achieved a modest increase in speed of 2.7km/h. The chassis is of some interest in that it provided the basis for the prototype Sturmgeschütz. Ausf C was almost identical but provided an alternative method of leaf-spring arrangement, employing one large central unit and two smaller units fore and aft.

Ausf B and C were produced concurrently in 1937, 15 vehicles of each type being built. Ostensibly, Ausf D, which appeared late in 1938, was a further variation on the eight-wheel leaf-spring suspension theme, in which the fore and aft units carried by the Ausf C were angled slightly inwards. However, maximum armour thickness had been increased to 30mm and a more workmanlike cupola introduced, which was not only lower, but also provided latched visors for the protection of the vision blocks. These improvements raised the vehicle's weight to 19 tonnes, but the installation of a better gearbox containing an additional forward gear maintained the maximum speed obtainable on previous models. Some 29 vehicles of this type were built, and the earlier Marks were also up-armoured to the 30mm standard. Ausf A to D all carried 120 rounds of main and 4,425 rounds of secondary armament ammunition.

The Ausf E, which appeared in 1939, finally overcame the difficulties that had been experienced with the suspension. A robust torsion bar system was adopted, employing six small road wheels. The redesign of the running gear also incorporated a new disc idler, and the position of the three return rollers was slightly altered. This Mark was driven by the 300hp 12-cylinder Maybach HL 120 TR engine, and the manual gearbox employed on the earlier models was replaced by the Maybach Variorex pre-selector box which provided ten forward and one reverse gears. Although the vehicle's weight was now 20 tonnes, the more powerful engine produced a top speed of 25mph.

Changes in the turret design included the introduction of two-piece side hatches. Early examples of the production run show the retention of the twin co-axial machine

1) PzKpfw III Ausf M Command Tank, unidentified artillery unit; Russia, 1943–44. By this stage of the war the PzKpfw III was of little use as a main battle tank, but numbers served on as headquarters vehicles with heavy tank-destroyer battalions – a position hinted at by the turret number '001'.

2) PzKpfw III Ausf L, 3. SS-Panzer-Division Totenkopf; Kursk, July 1943. Note the large strap-iron stowage rack welded across the rear hull; these were common, and as they were strictly a unit modification they took many varying forms. (David E. Smith © Osprey Publishing)

guns and an internal mantlet, but as the series progressed the co-axial armament was reduced to one gun and an external mantlet was adopted. Hull escape hatches for the driver and radio operator were installed above the second and third road wheels, although, again, these do not appear on the early versions. Estimates of production figures for the Ausf E vary considerably, the most likely figure being in the region of 100.

The Ausf F also began production in 1939, the early vehicles being almost indistinguishable from the first Ausf Es, mounting a 3.7cm gun and twin machine guns behind an internal mantlet. However, on this model new ventilation ducts for the track brakes had been installed, and the covers for these were visible on the glacis plate. By now the wisdom of the original proposal to fit a 5cm main armament had become apparent, and later vehicles in the series were fitted with the L/42 5cm gun in conjunction with a single co-axial machine gun, the mounting being protected by an external mantlet. This gun was also fitted retrospectively to the Ausf E.

Ausf G, which first appeared in October 1940, presented little external difference from its immediate predecessor, but possessed an improved commander's cupola. The first few vehicles mounted the 3.7cm main armament, but thereafter the L/42 5cm gun was fitted as standard. The Ausf G was modified for service in North Africa by the provision of larger radiators and an additional air filter made from felt.

Experience in Poland and France had indicated that the PzKpfw III was under-armoured. A temporary method of correcting this would have been to add external plating to the vulnerable areas, but the suspension was already considered to be carrying its maximum load and a further increase in ground pressure was not thought to be desirable. It was therefore necessary to redesign the basic running gear to allow for the additional weight, and this resulted in the Ausf H. On this model, the torsion bar suspension was strengthened and the track width increased from 36cm to 40cm. To compensate for this, new sprockets and idlers were introduced, the former having six apertures as opposed to eight circular holes, and the latter being of an eight-spoked

OPPOSITE A PzKpfw III production line in 1941, showing particularly the track rolls and two exposed torsion bar suspension units for the road wheels. The PzKpfw III chassis served as the basis for a number of specialized AFVs. (AirSeaLand/Cody)

A PzKpfw III Ausf G in North Africa, 1941. Later production models of this type were armed with the 5cm KwK 38 L/42 main gun, which had an effective range of up to 2,000m. (AirSeaLand/Cody)

A PzKpfw III crew uses foliage and nearby trees to conceal its position from the enemy. Ideally, a gun engagement with an enemy tank would consist of little more than a one-shot ambush. (AirSeaLand/Cody)

type. Existing stocks of the old sprockets and idlers were also used in conjunction with spacer rings. The opportunity was also taken to replace the complicated Variorex pre-selector gearbox with the simpler Aphon synchromesh, which provided six forward and one reverse gears. Additional 30mm plates were fixed to the bow, driver's and stern plates, but although this increased the vehicle's weight to 21.6 tonnes the ground pressure actually showed a slight decrease, and the maximum speed remained unaltered.

The Ausf H began entering service at the end of 1940 and was fitted with the L/42 5cm gun, for which a total of 99 rounds could be stowed, together with 3,750 rounds for the secondary armament. Like the Ausf F and G, it carried a rack of smoke bombs in a prominent box at the rear, the operation of which is described on page 88.

The addition of appliqué armour could, however, only be regarded as a temporary expedient pending the production of a basic up-armoured design. This appeared in 1941 as the Ausf J, which carried integral 50mm front and rear armour. An internal improvement was the provision of levers in place of the pedals which had activated the steering brakes on previous models.

Following the fall of France, Hitler, with considerable prescience, had given orders that the PzKpfw III's main armament should be the longer L/60 5cm gun. Partly because of supply difficulties, these instructions had been ignored, so that when faced with the 76.2mm weapons of the T-34 and KV-1 in Russia the vehicle was caught badly short. Furious at this disobedience, the Führer flew into one of his rages, unfairly describing the PzKpfw III as an unsuccessful design. After the first Ausf Js had been

produced with the L/42 gun, the L/60 weapon was fitted as standard, and earlier models which were returned to Germany for refit were also up-gunned. Stowage of main armament ammunition for the L/60 gun was limited to 78 rounds.

The Ausf J began reaching regiments at the end of 1941, by which time it was already apparent that a 50mm armour base was inadequate. In order to minimize the weight increase inevitable with the addition of further appliqué armour, it was decided to employ a spaced armour system, 20mm plates being mounted slightly ahead of the front plate and mantlet. This, together with the larger main armament, increased the tank's weight to 22.3 tonnes. In this version the vehicle was known as the Ausf L.

The Ausf M appeared in 1942 and closely resembled the Ausf L. It was, however, fitted with a self-sealing exhaust system which enabled it to wade unprepared to a depth of 1.5m, this being located at the extreme rear of the vehicle. Two batteries of three smoke-bomb dischargers were fitted to the turret sides, arranged so as to drop a pattern ahead of the tank if fired simultaneously.

Between the end of 1941 and the spring of 1943, a total of 1,969 L/60 5cm PzKpfw IIIs were built, but it had long been apparent that the design could not absorb further attempts at up-gunning and up-armouring. The role of the German Army's main battle tank had passed to the PzKpfw IV; the final version of the PzKpfw III, the Ausf N, mounted an L/24 howitzer inherited from the early models of the PzKpfw IV which had once equipped the heavy companies of the standard tank battalions. Stowing 64 rounds, these vehicles, of which some 660 were built, were employed in the fire-support role with Panzergrenadier divisions and the newly formed heavy tank battalions; in the latter case, they lingered on in battalion and company headquarters long after Tigers began reaching their units regularly.

A column of PzKpfw IIIs makes a stop in a Russian village during Operation *Barbarossa*. The tanks belong to the 10. Panzer-Division, which fought on the Eastern Front from June 1941 to mid-1942. (AirSeaLand/Cody)

This PzKpfw III Ausf G, serving on the Eastern Front in July 1943, is crewed by men of the infamous Das Reich Division. Production of the PzKpfw III Ausf G with the 5cm gun was planned to begin in June 1940, but the first tanks were not accepted until July and were not in service use until August 1940. (AirSeaLand/Cody)

Production of the PzKpfw III ended in August 1943, although the chassis continued to be used in the construction of assault guns. Latterly, the development of hollow charge munitions, capable of being fired at comparatively close quarters by infantry from a hand-held projector, meant that the main armour had to be shielded by 5mm side skirts and turret girdles, permitting the worst effects of the explosion to disperse in the space between. At about the same time, a coating of Zimmerit anti-magnetic mine paste was applied.

SPECIAL-PURPOSE VEHICLES

An interesting variation of the PzKpfw III was the Tauchpanzer (diving tank), which was designed in 1940 for the invasion of Great Britain. All openings to the exterior of the vehicle were sealed with a watertight compound, and the gap between hull and turret closed by an inflatable rubber ring. Rubber sheeting covered the commander's cupola, the mantlet and the hull machine gun, but this could be blown away from inside the vehicle by means of an electrical detonator. Air was supplied to the engine by a flexible 18m hose that was held on the surface by a buoy, while exhaust gases were carried upwards through two tall vertical pipes fitted with non-return valves. Maximum safe diving depth was 15m, and the crew's submerged endurance set at 20 minutes.

OPPOSITE A knocked-out PzKpfw III Ausf M, distinguished by features such as the visible bank of smoke dischargers. It also featured a self-sealing exhaust for deep wading operations. (AirSeaLand/Cody)

The intention was for the tanks to launch themselves from lighters and then motor ashore along the seabed, direction being maintained by instructions passed through a radio link from the parent vessel. The design was, on the whole, successful and found a practical application at the crossing of the River Bug during Operation *Barbarossa*. The crews were drawn from volunteer battalions, which were later formed into Panzer-Regiment 18.

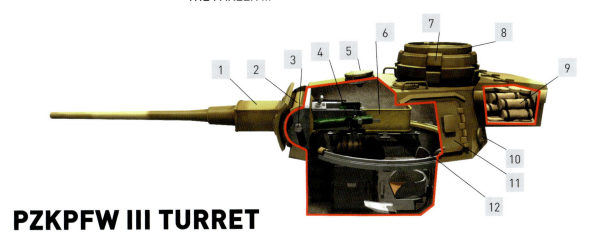

PZKPFW III TURRET

1. 5cm KwK 39 L/60 gun
2. Gun mantlet with add-on spaced armour shield
3. 5cm gun trunnion
4. Gun traverse handwheel
5. Turret air ventilator
6. Gun shield
7. Cupola vision blocks (× 5)
8. Commander's cupola with hatch
9. Add-on equipment bin
10. Pistol port
11. Turret escape hatch with pistol port
12. Commander's seat and bracket

(Ian Palmer © Osprey Publishing)

A StuG III Ausf B makes fast progress cross-country during training in Poland. The Ausf B was initially fitted with the L/24 7.5cm howitzer, but later acquired longer-barrelled guns with better velocities. (AirSeaLand/Cody)

A demonstration of the unusual PzKpfw III Tauchpanzer (diving tank). Air to the inflatable parts of the system came from the 18m-long flexible hose, visible here running around the turret. All being well (which it often wasn't), the vehicle could be submerged for up to 20 minutes. (AirSeaLand/Cody)

The Ausf M formed the basis of a flame-throwing tank, the official designation of which was PzKpfw III (Flam). The flame projector tube replaced the conventional 5cm gun in the mantlet, and was recognizable by being somewhat thicker. One hundred litres of flame liquid were stored inboard and driven through the projector tube by a two-stroke engine. By restricting bursts to 2 or 3 seconds' duration it was possible to obtain up to 80 flame-shots with a maximum range of 55m. The crew consisted of a commander/flame gunner, radio operator/hull gunner and driver. One hundred of these conversions were made, serving in specialist battalions 20 to 30 strong and employed at the discretion of senior commanders.

A slightly offbeat development was the fitting of an Ausf N onto a railway mounting to which the line of drive was passed by means of spindles. The vehicle was intended to patrol railways in Russia and keep them free from partisan interference, but the idea offered little that an armoured train did not, was extremely expensive and did not proceed beyond the prototype phase.

The PzKpfw III was widely used for conversion to the role of Panzerbefehlswagen (command tank). Versions were produced on the Ausf D, E and H chassis, and all followed the same pattern with a fixed turret (usually bolted to the hull) mounting a dummy gun and an unmistakable 'bedstead' loop aerial over the engine deck. A report by Britain's School of Tank Technology on a captured example based on an Ausf H chassis notes that the turret roof was reinforced by an extra 15mm plate, presumably as a defence against mortar fire. The mantlet was moulded in light alloy and modelled on that of the Ausf D. Radio equipment consisted of two sets mounted at the rear of the command compartment, directly above the propeller shaft and connected to the loop aerial. Two further sets were fitted to the forward hull wall, and a further two above the gearbox. Additional vision ports had been provided, and the report also noted the provision of cushioned seats and backrests of a more 'luxurious standard' than those employed in gun tanks, but the term is entirely relative.

The captured example did not contain a map table, but this would normally have been a standard fitting. Originally the Panzerbefehlswagen III was classed as a large command vehicle for use by regimental commanders and above, and there is good reason to believe that vehicles used by certain higher formation commanders contained the Enigma portable trans-coding device. Later in the war, as more vehicles became available, large ACVs were issued to battalion commanders.

One problem with the Panzerbefehlswagen was the easy identification provided by its distinctive loop aerial, which was replaced in 1943 by more conventional rods. Again, command vehicles were just as subject to breakdown as any other and their loss at a critical moment could have serious consequences. To provide immediate first-line replacement, regiments were from the autumn of 1942 issued with a basic PzKpfw III gun tank with additional radio facilities, this being known as the Panzerbefehlswagen III Ausf K.

Until 1943, Panzerartillerie forward observation officers (FOOs) performed their duties from a light half-track which, because of its vulnerability, was not entirely suitable for the task. However, in that year numbers of PzKpfw III gun tanks were specially converted for the role, their title being Panzerbeobachtungswagen (armoured observation vehicle) III. In this version the main armament was stripped out and replaced by a single ball-mounted machine gun in the centre of the mantlet, a dummy gun being installed to its right. The interior contained an artillery board and duplicate radios, one netted to the main operational frequency, the other providing a rear link to the guns. The crew consisted of the FOO, his technical assistant, two radio operators and the driver, all of whom would have been artillery personnel.

PZKPFW III AUSF J

Key

1. 50mm front lower armour plate
2. Spare track links
3. Steering brake inspection hatch
4. 20mm glacis plate
5. Towing bracket
6. 50mm front upper armour plate
7. 50mm superstructure main armour plate
8. 20mm spaced armour plate
9. 7.92mm MG 34 machine gun
10. Kugelblende armoured ball mount
11. Radio rack (rear side)
12. 5cm KwK L/42 main gun
13. Turret ball race bullet splash guard
14. Armoured sleeve for supporting gun during recoil
15. Armoured covers for recoil brake and recuperator
16. Muzzle of 7.92mm MG 34 co-axial machine gun
17. 20mm spaced armour on 50mm gun mantlet
18. 57mm front armour on turret
19. 30mm side armour on turret
20. TZF 5f (2.5 × 24°) telescopic gun sight
21. Travel lock stay
22. 7.92mm MG 34 co-axial machine gun
23. Handwheels for gun elevation and turret traverse
24. Fume extractor fan
25. Breech
26. Recoil guard
27. Rear right ammunition stowage bin
28. Commander's seat
29. Split hatch
30. Commander's cupola with vision blocks
31. Stowage bin for crew belongings
32. Motor inspection hatch and access to fuel tank
33. Antenna stowage tray
34. 2m rod antenna folded down
35. Maybach HL 120 V-12 300 PS petrol motor under armoured inspection hatch
36. Radiator fan inspection hatches
37. Tow cable
38. Cooling air intake
39. Cooling air exhaust (under rear cover)
40. Spare wheel
41. Pistol port
42. Adjustable idler wheel
43. Fire extinguisher
44. Bumpstop
45. Jack
46. 30mm superstructure side armour
47. Six double road wheels, tyres 520/95
48. Crowbar (shortened to allow cutaway)
49. Toolbox

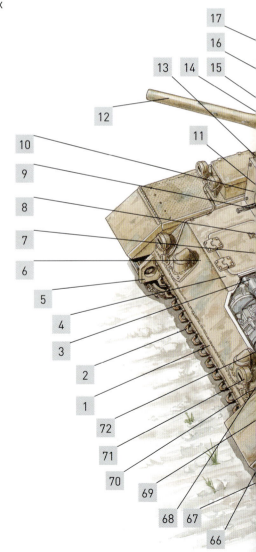

50. Rubber tyred return rollers
51. Flange for bolting superstructure to hull
52. Turret ball race
53. Side escape hatch
54. 30mm side armour
55. Gunner's seat
56. Torsion bars (under floor)
57. Gunner's foot rest and pedal
58. Swing arm connected to transverse
      torsion bar spring
59. Driver's seat
60. Gas mask container
61. Shock absorber

62. Dry pin cast steel track Typ Kgs
      61/400/120 (99 links centre guide tooth
      400mm wide, 120mm pitch)
63. Steering levers
64. Gear shift lever
65. Notek blackout lighting system
66. ZF S.S.G. 77 gearbox
67. Drive sprocket
68. Instrument panel
69. Steering brake
70. Brake cooling air intake
71. Headlights with blackout covers
72. Final drive

(Mike Badrocke © Osprey Publishing)

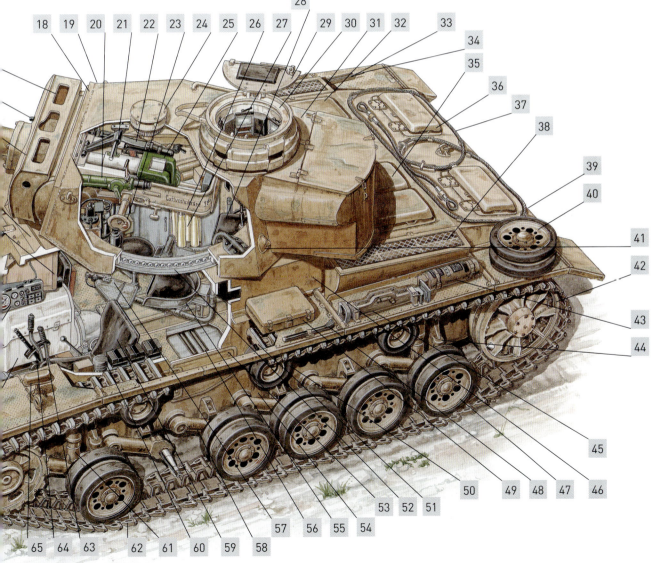

The PzKpfw III's most enduring offspring was, without doubt, the Sturmgeschütz (StuG) or assault gun. This consisted of the standard PzKpfw III chassis on which a low, fixed superstructure was built well forward, mounting first the L/24 7.5cm howitzer carried by early models of the PzKpfw IV and, later, the L/43 or L/48 7.5cm high-velocity guns or a 10.5cm howitzer. The StuG formed the principal equipment of the Sturmartillerie, an elite branch of the artillery dedicated to close infantry support, which considered itself to be every inch the equal of the Panzertruppen. A total of 10,500 StuGs were built on the PzKpfw III chassis, mainly by Alkett of Berlin, and accounted for more than three times their number of enemy fighting vehicles. Latterly, as a result of the general shortage of equipment, Panzer regiments were glad to supplement their few remaining tanks with assault guns, so in that form at least the PzKpfw III can be said to have served throughout the war.

This PzKpfw III at Arnhem has been positioned under cover by the side of a house. A British parachute canopy and its cords hang from a nearby tree. (AirSeaLand/Cody)

On the Eastern Front, the crew of a StuG III quickly take on more 7.5cm ammunition. Ammunition capacity was about 55 rounds, depending on the model. (AirSeaLand/Cody)

In 1942 fighting within the built-up areas of Stalingrad indicated that a heavier weapon was needed than the 7.5cm howitzer carried by the assault gun. First choice fell on the 15cm Infantry Gun 33, which at that time was fitted to the chassis of the PzKpfw I, PzKpfw II and 38(t), some of which were grossly overloaded; moreover, the open-topped superstructures of these vehicles made them unsuitable for street-fighting.

In an attempt to overcome these difficulties, the chassis of the PzKpfw III was used as the basis for an experimental vehicle known as the Sturm-Infanteriegeschütz 33. Layout followed that of the assault gun, the weapon being mounted in

a fixed enclosed superstructure with 80mm frontal armour. The vehicle weighed 22 tonnes, was manned by a crew of five and had a maximum speed of 19km/h; 30 rounds of main armament ammunition were carried. In the event the design was overtaken by the heavy assault gun Brummbär, which was based on the PzKpfw IV chassis. Production of the Sturm-Infanteriegeschütz 33 terminated in November 1942, by which time only 24 vehicles had been produced. They are reported as having equipped the 9. Kompanie of Panzer-Regiment 201 during the summer of 1943.

Other PzKpfw III variants included a very simple recovery vehicle, the Bergepanzerwagen III, which consisted of a turretless hull, fitted with towing attachments; and a supply carrier, the Schlepper III, which carried a large wooden box superstructure in place of the turret.

Turretless versions also carried ammunition in the forward zone, and the heavy equipment required by the Panzer divisions' assault engineer units. Experiments were carried out with a prototype mine-clearing vehicle, which achieved extra ground clearance by means of extension arms, but very few details are available.

At Arnhem in September 1944, British POWs limp off to captivity past a StuG III Ausf G, heavily camouflaged and with additional side armour plates added. The vehicle belonged to the SS-Panzer-Division Hohenstaufen. (AirSeaLand/Cody)

Armour

In April 1943, Messrs William Beardmore & Co Ltd of Glasgow analyzed several samples of the armour plate used to construct the PzKpfw III, the consultants drawing the following conclusions: 'All the material has been made in the electric furnace and the compositions vary considerably, possibly because of different sources of supply. In every case the Carbon content is higher than is used here, whilst the combination of high Silicon and high Chromium is rather an unusual feature. The physical properties approximate to our own bullet-proof material but as a whole it does not show any improvement over this. With regard to the welding which is present at various points, this is extremely poor in all cases.'

These comments were amplified by the Ministry of Supply following detailed examination of the hull and turret of a captured Ausf J: 'The problem of making a battle-worthy structure in this comparatively high carbon armour, using hard-surfacing and austenitic electrodes and at the same time giving assistance to the welds by means of riveted plate edges, was not overcome. The extent of cracking suggests that pre-heating was not adopted. Judged by any standards, the behaviour of the welding is unsatisfactory.'

Automotive

The Maybach engine had been designed to operate in temperate climates, in which it performed satisfactorily. However, in tropical or dusty conditions it was subject to breakdown and overheating, and a British intelligence summary dated 18 February 1942, prepared after examination of abandoned vehicles, commented on the number of failures due to engine and bogie problems: 'The engine trouble was due chiefly to sand blocking oil supply pipes damaging crankshafts and pistons, and sand in the distributor, dynamo and starter. The air filter is entirely inadequate. Bogie trouble was due to the disintegration of tyres due to high speed or heat.'

A formation of PzKpfw IIIs prepare to move through Kharkov. The hatch just behind the commander's cupola provided access to a space for storing crew belongings. (AirSeaLand/ Cody)

In this interesting photograph, we see a StuG III Ausf G optimistically modified with a white US star insignia in the hope that it might pass off, temporarily, as a US armoured vehicle. The presence of the US soldiers indicates the optimism was largely unfounded. (AirSeaLand/Cody)

The user handbook recommended a maximum engine speed of 2,600rpm for normal usage, but in hot climates, which included southern Russia as well as North Africa, it was suggested that employment of a lower gear than was necessary would produce cooler running. Use of the engine as a brake was permissible at 2,200–2,400rpm, but was to be avoided in the 2,600–3,300rpm band. Overheated engines tended to 'diesel' after being switched off, a fault that could be corrected by switching on again and either opening the throttle or idling until the temperature dropped. The principal components in the cooling system were two radiators, through which air was dragged by two fans.

The Variorex pre-selector gearbox was considered to be effective up to seventh gear, after which the tractive effort fell away sharply. The eighth gear was suitable for level road running, but the ninth and tenth gears were regarded as overdrives and seldom used. The Aphon synchromesh gearbox drew favourable comment, although once again the tractive effort in top (i.e. sixth) gear was low, and this was largely reserved for road use. For both systems it was recommended that 'when changing to a lower gear on turnings, hills or bad roads, two gears lower than the one already engaged should be selected'.

The final drive and steering brake assembly was extremely complicated. An excessive number of ball races were incorporated and, as already mentioned, considerable care was taken to provide an air-cooling system for the track brake drums. Even so, there was no automatic equalization of the torque on the two output shafts, and the mechanism did not provide positive steering when both steering brakes were released.

The torsion bar suspension was adequate, although in sandy areas grit tended to penetrate the shock absorbers, shortening their life. Track tension was achieved by means of a bell crank. On the Eastern Front, track extensions known as Ostketten were fitted to increase traction during the winter months, usually to one track only – a most dangerous practice in any sort of hilly country.

An electric self-starter was provided, but this was for use in emergencies only, and never with a cold engine. The normal method of starting was by means of an inertia system, the starting handle entering the engine compartment through the tail plate. The handle was swung by two men until the flywheel had reached 60rpm, when the power was tripped to turn the main engine. The inertia starter was geared, but its operation in the depths of the Russian winter, with sump oil chilled to the consistency of treacle, required a great deal of initial effort, although the driver could eliminate the additional drag of the gearbox oil by depressing his clutch. Cold starting was assisted by a starter carburettor, which was not to be used in conjunction with the accelerator. Minimum unassisted working temperature for the engine was 50°C at 2,000rpm with an oil pressure of not less than 4.2kg/cm^2.

Gunnery and optical

Elevation of the main and co-axial armament was by means of a handwheel operated with the gunner's left hand. Immediately to the right of this was the traversing handwheel, which included a release latch and which was sometimes linked under the gun to a hand crank which could be turned by the loader. The traverse mechanism incorporated two gears, one requiring 88 turns of the handwheel to achieve a complete revolution of the turret, and the other, used for fine laying, 132 turns. The main armament was fired electrically and its recoil was controlled by a hydro-pneumatic buffer system containing a filling liquid which was simply known as Braun.

The 5cm guns carried by the PzKpfw III were muzzle-heavy in their mounting. In the case of the L/42 model, this was easily corrected by the addition of a lead weight to the rear of the spent case deflector shield. However, the imbalance became even more pronounced when the longer L/60 model was fitted, and to compensate for this a small compression spring in a cylinder was mounted on the forward offside corner of the turret ring and attached to the gun. This arrangement was found on the Ausf J, but on later Marks a torsion bar was bolted across the turret roof and connected to the upper part of the gun mounting. On later Marks, too, the recoil shield arms were 11.4cm longer, providing additional compensation but reducing clearance to the turret ring to 44.5cm.

The sighting telescope was more complicated than its British counterpart, which employed a simple graticule pattern and contained two movable plates. The first or range plate rotated about its own axis, the main armament and machine-gun scales being marked on opposing quadrants; the 5cm scale was marked from 0 to 2,000m,

PZKPFW III GUN SIGHT

Range 200m: the 5cm gun has been fired and the tracer is en route to the half-track driver's compartment.

The round passes through the driver's compartment and explodes in the rear, igniting ammunition.

(Ian Palmer © Osprey Publishing)

and the machine-gun scale from 0 to 800m. The second or sighting plate moved in a vertical plane and contained the sighting and aim-off markings. The two plates moved simultaneously, the sighting plate rising or falling as the range plate turned. To engage at a selected range, the range wheel was turned until the required marking was opposite the pointer at the top of the sight, and the sighting mark laid onto the target by the traverse and elevation controls.

Ammunition stowage in vehicles fitted with the L/42 5cm gun was as follows:

- under gunner's seat: 5 rounds;
- in locker situated at right/rear of fighting compartment: 22 rounds;
- in locker immediately above: 12 rounds;
- in locker situated at left/rear compartment: 36 rounds;
- in locker immediately above: 24 rounds;
- total: 99 rounds.

With the exception of the rounds under the gunner's seat, all ammunition was stowed vertically, the case fitting into a recess in the locker floor while the nose was held in

A British Stuart light tank passes the remains of a PzKpfw III that has been utterly obliterated by a catastrophic ammunition explosion, which has thrown the turret several metres away from the hull. (AirSeaLand/Cody)

place by a spring clip. The arrangement was neat, but made withdrawal of certain rounds difficult. The right lower locker and two left/rear lockers were closed by sliding doors, which tended to jam with sand particles; the right upper locker was fitted with a hinged door. On L/60 5cm vehicles a horizontal stowage pattern was adopted for ready-use rounds.

Whatever system was employed, the loader laboured under something of a disadvantage in that the turret floor was fixed and he was forced to 'walk after' the gun breech whenever the turret was traversed. The commander and gunner were more fortunate in that their seats were attached to the turret itself. Machine-gun ammunition was distributed along the walls of the fighting and hull gunner's compartments in bags, each bag containing a 150-round belt. The bag system was less efficient than the British metal box 'liner' and required one hand to assist passage of the belt into the gun. In consequence, while the hull gunner could traverse by using the pistol grip of his weapon, elevation and depression were extremely difficult. The problem was resolved by the novel method of the hull gunner inserting his head into a moulded rubber cap which was linked to the butt of the machine gun by a bar; he could then lower his head to obtain elevation and raise it for depression.

Some mention has already been made of the smoke-bomb rack, which was prominent on the rear of Ausf F, G and H. On later models, pending the introduction of turret dischargers, this device was concealed beneath the engine air-outlet cowling. The rack carried five bombs, held in position by spring-loaded catches. The vehicle commander released the bombs singly by a wire control, which operated a ratchet wheel coupled to a camshaft. Each pull of the wire rotated the camshaft one-fifth of a turn, releasing a bomb, the pin of which was drawn by a fixed chain, and the ratchet was returned by a

PZKPFW III

Panzer-Regiment 7 tanks were painted yellow-brown (RAL 8000), sometimes with the original dark grey (RAL 7027) showing through. Sometimes about 20 per cent of the tank was splotched with grey-green (RAL 7008). Sometimes continental-painted tanks were merely coated with used oil and dusted with sand. The company number was painted in black on the turret side, 4. Kompanie, with the tank number in smaller characters. The regimental insignia is seen on the equipment bin behind the turret. The *Balkenkreuz* (beamed cross) is on the hull and was often partly obscured by mud or lightly sprayed paint.

(Ian Palmer © Osprey Publishing)

2.49m

2.95m

5.53m

second spring. Thus, five pulls on the control wire would release all the bombs in succession, enabling the tank to reverse out of sight into its own smokescreen.

The design of the commander's cupola incorporated armoured shutters which could be latched in the open, intermediate or closed positions to protect the safety-glass vision blocks. Some commanders had a clock code painted round the inside of their cupolas to remind them of the turret's position in relation to the hull, a thing sometimes forgotten in the heat of action.

PZKPFW III AMMUNITION

1. 3.7cm Sprgr 18
2. 3.7cm Sprgr 40
3. 3.7cm Pzgr
4. 5cm Pzgr (KwK 38)
5. 5cm Pzgr 39 (KwK 38)
6. 5cm Pzgr 40 (KwK 38)
7. 5cm Sprgr 38 (KwK 38)
8. 5cm Pzgr 39 (KwK 39)
9. 5cm Pzgr 40 (KwK 39)
10. 5cm Sprgr 38 (KwK 39) 7

The German 7.92mm MG 34 mounted in tanks was the same as the standard infantry machine gun. In February 1941 a tank version with a heavier barrel jacket lacking ventilator holes was authorized for installation in new production tanks. Standard combat ammunition was the 'bullet with steel core' (black tip, red-rimmed primer) as opposed to lead cores to achieve better penetration. The recoil-operated gun fired at 800–900rpm.

(Ian Palmer © Osprey Publishing)

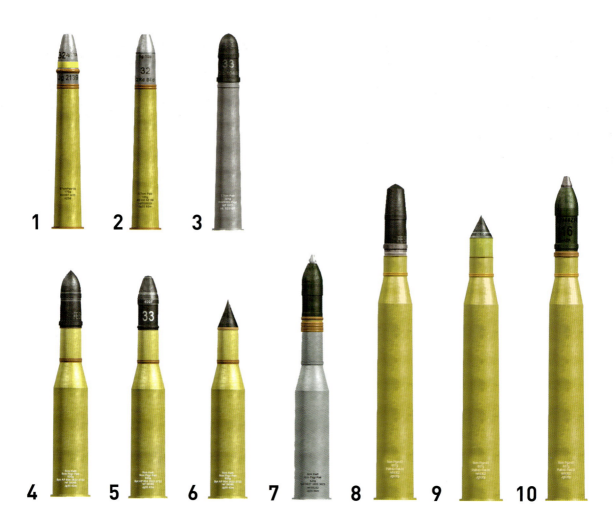

In normal circumstances the driver employed a direct-vision safety-glass block. In action this could be covered by a latched slab, its place being taken by a pair of periscopic binoculars, the two ports for which were visible directly above the visor. The German safety glass of the period had a slightly greenish tinge.

OPERATIONAL HISTORY
France and the Low Countries

The numbers of PzKpfw IIIs available for Hitler's Western European campaign have already been noted in the previous chapter. Opposing the Panzerwaffe were 3,285 first-line French tanks of various designs, manned by an army that contemporary world opinion considered to be the true experts in armoured warfare. However, over one-third of these vehicles were distributed along the front in direct support of infantry and horsed cavalry divisions, rather like beads on a string, and could be excluded from any plan involving concerted reaction en masse. The French did in fact possess a number of armoured formations, of which the most experienced were the three Divisions Légères Mécaniques (DLM), composed of mechanized cavalry regiments, and the

ABOVE LEFT A PzKpfw III Ausf M is readied for action by its crew in Russia in 1943. Note the bank of smoke dischargers on the side of the turret, used to lay down a smokescreen either to shield an escape or obscure the vision of enemy gunners. (AirSeaLand/Cody)

ABOVE A PzKpfw III approaches the outskirts of Stalingrad in the autumn of 1942. Many Panzermänner preferred the PzKpfw III over the PzKpfw IV owing to its higher speed. (AirSeaLand/Cody)

PZKPFW III LAYOUT

The bow of the PzKpfw III was blunt and boxy with a vertically stepped front compartment. The driver was on the left and the radio operator on the right with a ball-mounted machine gun. On the forward horizontal deck over their knees were small break servicing hatches that could be used as escape hatches. The driver had a shuttered vision port with 'armoured' binoculars, and small vision/pistol ports were on both sides of the forward portion of the superstructure. A small escape hatch was set in the lower hull sides above the bogie wheels and between the first and second return rollers. These were deleted with the Ausf M. The three-man turret had a heavy gun mantlet mounting the main gun with two co-axial machine guns to the right in the Ausf A to C and the sight to the left. Later versions had one co-axial gun. The turret sides were gently sloped and the back slightly rounded. There were vent/pistol ports on the forward sides and split-door escape hatches on both sides of the turret's rear sides, each with a vision port. The vision ports/slits were protected by bulletproof glass blocks. In the rear centre of the turret top was the raised commander's 'dustbin-type' cupola with a split hatch on top. Five vision slits provided 360° observation. The gunner sat to the gun's left, and the loader, who also operated the co-axial machine gun by a foot-pedal trigger, sat to the right. The gunner manually rotated the turret, and the loader had an auxiliary traverse handle. The commander and gunner had seats mounted on the turret wall, but the loader did not. There was no turret floor, so the loader had to walk on the hull floor as the turret traversed.

A version of the PzKpfw III capable of driving underwater, the Tauchpanzer (diving tank), was supplied with air via a snorkel hose and its hull was made completely waterproof by sealing all sighting ports, hatches and air intakes. (AirSeaLand/Cody)

lessons of the Polish campaign had led to the hasty formation of four armoured divisions known as Divisions Cuirassées (DCR), which had barely settled down as integrated formations. The functions of the DLMs and DCRs each covered certain aspects of the Panzer divisions' potential, the former performing the traditional cavalry role of reconnaissance and advanced screen, while the latter's primary task was breaching the enemy's defensive crust; but neither had been designed, nor were mentally prepared, for continuous fast-moving operations in the German manner. Their principal armament consisted respectively of the Somua medium tank with its 47mm gun, 56mm armour and top speed of 40km/h, and the Char B heavy tank with a 37mm gun in the turret, a 75mm in the hull, 60mm armour and a speed of 28km/h, both backed by Hotchkiss H35 light tanks, which were armed with a 37mm gun and carried 34mm armour.

At the time, the only armoured formation serving with the British Expeditionary Force was 1st Army Tank Brigade, equipped with 74 Mark I and II Matilda infantry tanks, protected by 60mm and 78mm armour, the latter being armed with a 2-pdr gun which was marginally superior to the German 3.7cm. The remainder of the British armour consisted of the thin-skinned light tanks of the infantry's divisional cavalry regiments.

A PzKpfw III is loaded onto a merchant ship for transportation to the North African theatre. The three-digit numbering system worked as follows: the first digit designated the company, the second the platoon and the third the specific tank. (AirSeaLand/Cody)

Thus, save in the area of light tanks, the Germans were outnumbered, outgunned and under-armoured, and it was clear from the outset that in the inevitable tank-versus-tank fighting the burden would fall heavily on the 3.7cm-armed vehicles, and specifically on the PzKpfw IIIs, which carried slightly heavier armour than the Czech tanks. On the other hand, the apparent technical superiority of the French tanks was more than offset by the adoption of a one-man turret system. This meant that the vehicle commander was something of a one-man band, directing his driver, selecting ground on which to fight, loading, laying and firing the main armament and, if an officer, trying to control the other vehicles under his command as well.

Few men can cope successfully with such uncompromising and simultaneous pressures, which presented a marked contrast to the smoothly efficient drill being executed in the turrets of the PzKpfw IIIs, and in consequence the standard of French tactical performance was well below that of the Germans.

General Heinz Guderian was one of the pioneers of German armoured warfare tactics, and largely responsible for rebuilding the Panzerwaffe after the catastrophic defeat at Stalingrad in 1942–43. (AirSeaLand/Cody)

For the designers of the PzKpfw III the campaign in the West represented their greatest triumph, and entirely vindicated the German concept of a main battle tank. Yet the Char Bs and the Somuas had provided some anxious moments. In terms of combat performance, both the Somua S 35 and the PzKpfw III were found deficient in tank-versus-tank fighting in the 1940 campaign. The German reliance on the 3.7cm gun for the main armament of the PzKpfw III was a mistake, both in terms of anti-tank performance and general fire support. The Heer had selected the 3.7cm gun before the start of the arms race in the mid-1930s, and not surprisingly, both the French and British armies designed their tanks to resist this weapon at typical battle ranges. The PzKpfw III had little hope of surviving a face-to-face confrontation with a Somua S 35 at normal battle ranges, and only had a chance of succeeding with a side-shot at close range. Likewise, the armour protection of the PzKpfw III was seriously deficient when facing modern anti-tank weapons such as the French 25mm and 47mm anti-tank guns and the British 2-pdr. The next step forward for the PzKpfw III, the short 5cm gun, was also deficient by the time it entered combat in 1941 in the Soviet Union when confronting the new T-34 tank. Both PzKpfw III weapons were selected prior to 1939 at a point in time where there was some question whether tank-versus-tank fighting would be widespread on the modern battlefield. The Heer showed little appreciation for future threats and made poor choices. The Panzer divisions prevailed on the 1940 battlefield due to better training rather than better technology.

PzKpfw IIIs are driven onto ferries for a river crossing in France, 1940. Note the roll of logs on the engine cover: these were useful for gapping ditches or helping the vehicle get free of boggy ground. (AirSeaLand/Cody)

This PzKpfw III is fitted with the longer 5cm KwK 39 L/60. The gun was an improvement over the the 5cm KwK 38 L/42, but it still struggled to penetrate the armour of heavier Allied tanks. (AirSeaLand/ Cody)

Besides the complaints about the basic PzKpfw III tank, 4. Panzer-Division was especially critical of the Befehlspanzer because of its lack of a gun. During the four days of fighting from 12 to 15 May, the brigade commander, one regimental commander and at least one battalion commander had their command tanks knocked out. At least two other command tanks were also lost, though one or both were normal gun tanks. The German battalion and regimental commanders tended to lead from the front, and the use of an unarmed radio vehicle was poorly suited to such a command style. While early radio networks may have required such a communication vehicle to link battalion and regimental headquarters to brigade and division, such vehicles would have been better suited for the use of someone on the staff other than the commander. This led to the eventual production of a Befehlspanzer on the PzKpfw III chassis with a traversable turret and 5cm gun (the British Matildas had barely been encountered in the tank-versus-tank context).

SPECIFICATIONS: PZKPFW III AUSF L LIGHT TANK

General

Production run: March 1941–late 1942
Vehicles produced: 1,549 (5cm L/42); 1,067 (5cm L/60)
Combat weight: 21,500kg
Crew: Five (commander, gunner, loader, driver, radio operator)

Dimensions

Hull length: 5.56m
Width: 2.95m
Height: 2.50m
Ground contact length: 2.86m

Armour

Hull front: 50mm
Hull sides: 30mm
Hull rear: 50mm
Hull roof: 16mm
Hull bottom: 15mm
Turret front: 50mm
Turret sides: 30mm
Turret rear: 30mm
Turret roof: 10mm

Armament

Main gun: 5cm KwK 38 L/42 kurz or KwK 39 L/60 lang
Machine guns: 2 × 7.92mm MG 34
Main gun rate of fire: 10–15 rpm

Ammunition storage

Main gun: 99 rounds (KwK 38 L/42); 84 rounds (KwK 39 L/60)
Machine gun: 3,750 rounds

Communications

Fu 5 receiver/transmitter

Motive power

Engine: Maybach HL 120 TRM
Power: 300hp at 3,000rpm
Fuel capacity: 320 litres

Performance

Maximum road speed: 40km/h
Operational range: 145km
Trench crossing ability: 2m
Vertical obstacle ability: 0.6m
Fording depth: 0.8m
Ground clearance: 0.38m
Turning radius: 5.85m

British troops advance to capture the crew of a PzKpfw III in North Africa. Note the frame fitted at the back to carry extra fuel jerry cans and other supplies. (AirSeaLand/Cody)

North Africa

That the German Army was present at all in North Africa, an improbable theatre, was due to the shattering defeat inflicted on the Italians by Wavell's 'Thirty Thousand' during late 1940 and early 1941. Sent by Hitler to bolster his shaky ally with strictly limited resources and an equally limited brief, Generalleutnant Erwin Rommel, former commander of 7. Panzer- Division, discovered a weakness in the British dispositions at Mersa Brega and, contrary to his orders, attacked on 3 March 1941. The attack broke through the flimsy defensive screen and the ruthless exploitation that followed compelled the evacuation not only of the Benghazi bulge but of the whole of Cyrenaica, with the exception of the port of Tobruk. By 13 April the Axis forces were on the Egyptian frontier and had taken the strategically important Halfaya Pass.

On 19 April an attempt was made to penetrate the Tobruk perimeter. The Australian infantry let the leading PzKpfw IIIs pass over them and then engaged the follow-up troops, who were compelled to go to ground. The German tanks were then subjected to fire from the hull-down Cruisers of B and C Squadrons 1st Royal Tank Regiment (RTR) and the Matildas of D Squadron, 7 RTR; they lost several vehicles and were bundled back the way they had come.

At dawn on the morning of 15 May, Halfaya Pass fell to a *coup de main* carried out by C Squadron, 4 RTR, a Matilda regiment. Rommel was adamant that the pass should be retaken, and on 27 May no less than 160 tanks, organized in three battle groups and led by PzKpfw IIIs, converged towards its head.

An incredible sight met the eyes of their commanders: nine Matildas, all that C Squadron could muster, were crawling out to meet them, covering the withdrawal of their infantry down onto the coastal plain. Eagerly, the German gunners set their sights and loosed off round after round, only to see the 3.7cm and 5cm shot go flying off the Matildas' thick hides. Unlike the Char B, the Matilda did not have vulnerable radiator louvres, and its tracks were better protected; in addition, the drill in its three-man turret was every bit as efficient as that in the PzKpfw III, and the return fire of the 2-pdrs could penetrate the armour of every German and Italian vehicle present at the normal battle range of 500–750m. German tanks in the leading ranks of the *Keil* (wedge) began to explode and burn without any apparent reduction in the enemy's strength. Those behind, even less capable of engaging on even terms,

The commander of a PzKpfw III Ausf D conducts observation from his turret during manoeuvres. Frontal armour upgrades were implemented on the Ausf D and later models. (AirSeaLand/Cody)

Note the large number of fuel jerry cans on the rear; it would take 16 of these cans to perform one fuel fill-up on a PzKpfw III. Operations in North Africa were extremely demanding on fuel supplies. (AirSeaLand/Cody)

started a retrogressive movement which soon took an entire battalion out of range. Satisfied, the three surviving Matildas retired down Halfaya Pass, picking up the crews of the six which had been immobilized by track damage.

Such an event was unparalleled in the history of the Panzerwaffe, and Rommel was beside himself with rage at the propaganda victory handed to the British. The unfortunate battalion commander was court-martialled, his immediate superior dismissed out of hand and the commander of 5. leichte-Division removed from his post. That there existed among Panzer crews a very real fear of the Matilda was quite understandable, for the only effective defence at the time was the 8.8cm anti-aircraft gun firing in the anti-tank role. However, '88s' were only to be had at a premium, and an immediate request was made for Panzerjäger anti-tank forces to be despatched to Africa to restore the balance.

In June the British mounted their first major offensive to relieve Tobruk, Operation *Battleaxe*, capturing Fort Capuzzo on the 15th. At first light the following day, 15. Panzer-Division launched a counter-attack, but drove into an ambush laid by A and B Squadrons, 7 RTR. Fifty of the division's 80 fighting vehicles were lost before it was able to extricate itself. The divisional commander, mindful of the fate of his colleagues following the Halfaya debacle, quickly regrouped and bypassed Capuzzo, hoping to isolate it from the east; his only reward was to be stalled yet again by Matildas, this time manned by B Squadron, 4 RTR, at a ridge known as Point 206.

Further south, 5. leichte-Division was fighting a successful offensive/defensive battle against the Cruisers of 7th Armoured Brigade, whose two regiments (2 and 6 RTR) had blunted their potential against an anti-tank gun screen at Hafid Ridge. The 5. leichte-Division's Panzers had then sallied forth to engage the 'Desert Rats' in a running fight, during which 6 RTR's new Crusader tanks broke down at an alarming rate. The German intention was to sweep north to the coast, thus trapping the British troops in the Capuzzo area; but before this could be achieved, *Battleaxe* was cancelled and an escape corridor held open by two Matilda squadrons, each of which held off an entire German division for a day.

During the tank battles the British had knocked out more than 100 German tanks, but only 12 of these were completely written off, the rest being recovered and repaired.

Their own loss had been 91 vehicles, many of them simple breakdowns which could have been recovered had it not been for high-level muddle and misunderstanding. This time it was the heads of senior British officers which rolled. It was not until November that a further attempt was made to relieve Tobruk. Operation *Crusader* was a much larger affair than *Battleaxe* and included three armoured brigades (4th, 7th and 22nd) as well as two tank brigades, the 1st covering the northern flank with XIII Corps, and the 32nd the Tobruk garrison's breakout. British first-line tank strength was 756; that of the Axis 320.

But while Rommel fought with both his Panzer divisions concentrated (5. leichte-Division had been restyled as 21. Panzer-Division), the British armoured brigades each pursued their separate objectives, with the result that within days of the start of the offensive 7th Armoured Brigade was removed from the board while the 4th and 22nd were left confused and dispersed. However, Rommel's brief foray into Egypt, by which he hoped, unsuccessfully, to destroy the British commander's nerve, provided just sufficient time for a reorganization to be carried out. Tobruk was relieved by XIII Corps, isolated again, and finally relieved for the last time, while sheer attrition, both tactical and mechanical, reduced the German strength to such a dangerous level that Cyrenaica had to be evacuated. Some 300 Axis tanks had been destroyed as opposed to a British loss of 187. In addition to the casualties sustained by the Panzer divisions in actions with the British armour, other causes of loss included breakdowns induced by the PzKpfw III's inefficient air filters, and tanks destroyed by 2-pdr portees and 25-pdrs firing over open sights, a reminder that the British did not hold a monopoly in charging unshaken gunlines.

Rommel's remarkable resilience was demonstrated in January 1942 when, having received a meagre reinforcement of tanks, he riposted so unexpectedly that much of the

As this photograph indicates, the PzKpfw III was not a large vehicle in relation to its human occupants, and here we see only three members of the five-man crew. (AirSeaLand/Cody)

1) PzKpfw III Ausf G, DAK; Libya, 1941. There is a definite 'early days' look about this Ausf G; the original Panzer grey is starting to show through the hastily applied sand-yellow 'slap'.

2) PzKpfw III Ausf J, ex-21. Panzer-Division; North Africa, 1942. This tank seems to have enjoyed a spell in British service, perhaps after abandonment due to a breakdown, for on the offside front is the rhinoceros sign of 1st Armoured Division, and on the nearside the tactical number 86, indicating 9th Lancers.

3) PzKpfw III Ausf N, 15. Panzer-Division; Tunisia, 1942–43. The track links draped over the turret roof of this Ausf N reflect the growing Allied air superiority of this period. (David E. Smith © Osprey Publishing)

lost ground was recovered, the line eventually being stabilized at Gazala. Here both sides began to build up their strength for the next round. Panzerarmee Afrika eventually accumulated 228 Italian tanks, 50 PzKpfw IIs, 40 7.5cm howitzer PzKpfw IVs, 223 L/42 5cm PzKpfw IIIs and 19 L/60 5cm PzKpfw IIIs, a total of 560 tanks. Opposing them would be 843 British tanks, of which the most significant were the 167 Grants, new arrivals in the desert, which, with their sponson-mounted 7.5cm guns, put the British ahead for once in tank-killing potential.

The Axis got in the first and vital blow on 27 May. The Grants tore great holes in the ranks of the Panzer divisions, but the British fought in the same uncoordinated fashion they had employed during *Crusader*, missed priceless opportunities and ultimately suffered a disastrous defeat that cost them most of their armour and which was followed almost immediately by the surrender of Tobruk. It was the PzKpfw III's crowning achievement in Africa and earned Rommel his field marshal's baton.

The Afrika Korps had also suffered severely, and the pursuit of the beaten Eighth Army was carried out with a mere handful of tanks. These succeeded in turning the British out of their defensive position at Mersa Matruh, but lacked the necessary clout to penetrate the newly forming line at El Alamein.

By the end of August, Rommel had been reinforced sufficiently to attempt a repeat of the right hook with which he had begun the Gazala/Knightsbridge battle. In addition to 243 Italian M13s, he had 71 L/60 and 93 L/42 PzKpfw IIIs, ten of the older PzKpfw IVs and a handful of light tanks. Of greater significance was the arrival of 27 PzKpfw IVF2s, armed with an L/43 7.5cm gun, which would become his cutting edge – a clear indication that the PzKpfw III was now falling below battlefield requirements. In the event, the offensive was severely checked at Alam Halfa ridge and the Axis army thrown onto the defensive by an acute shortage of fuel.

This was a factor which the Eighth Army's new commander, Lieutenant-General Bernard Montgomery, intended to exploit to the full in the planning for the second battle of Alamein. Eighth Army would fight a 'crumbling' battle, attacking first in one place and then another, forcing the Panzer divisions to burn irreplaceable petrol driving between sectors in the counter-attack role. It was a strategy against which Rommel had no effective defence, since a breakthrough would spell annihilation for his army.

When the battle began on 23 October, Eighth Army could deploy over 1,000 tanks, including 170 Grants and 252 Shermans, with more in reserve. Axis tank strength was 278 MI3s, 85 L/42 and 88 L/60 PzKpfw IIIs, 8 old PzKpfw IVs and 30 PzKpfw IVF2s. During major tank engagements such as Tel el Aqqaqir the British lost the greater number of vehicles, but Rommel's strength was effectively whittled away until defeat became inevitable. By the time the battle ended the Italian armoured divisions had ceased to exist and all but a handful of German tanks had been destroyed or abandoned on the battlefield, while the Afrika Korps began its long withdrawal to Tunisia.

Most of the subsequent fighting took place in mountainous country. With the Anglo-American First Army closing in on their last African bridgehead, the Germans hastily shipped over 10. Panzer-Division, sufficient tanks to re-equip 15. and 21. Panzer-Divisionen, and a Tiger battalion. A notable success was gained against the US 1st Armoured Division at Kasserine Pass, but the end could not be long delayed, and on 12 May 1943 the war in Africa was officially over.

During the final phase the PzKpfw III remained the most numerous tank in the German order of battle, but an increasing number of those reaching the front were the 7.5cm-armed Ausf N, a weapon that offered better delivery of AP shells.

Combat Case Study

Panzeroberschütze Baldur Köhler was a *Funker für gepanzert Kraftwagen* (radio operator) of a PzKpfw III in Tunisia in 1943. Interestingly, he knew his tank only as a '*Panzer drei lang*' (Panzer III long), and he had no idea which variant it was. With a 5cm long gun it may have been an Ausf J, L or M, but he was not familiar with the Ausführung term. He was assigned to 5. Kompanie Abteilung II, Panzer-Regiment 7, 10. Panzer-Division.

On the morning of 14 February 1943, the troops were awake and manning their tanks hours before dawn. The evening before, they had cleaned the air filters and guns. Breakfast was preserved bread, marmalade and ersatz coffee or tea. Knowing this was a major action, they were keyed up and confident not only in their years of experience, but also knowing that the Americans were inexperienced, slow to respond and thinly spread. Their confidence was increased by their many recent small victories, and their commanders were plainly disdainful of the *Amis* (Americans).

It was not without a sense of excitement that the Panzermänner sparked the electric primer igniters in their guns to test them, adjusted engine chokes and pressed starter

A PzKpfw III Ausf J, which compared to previous models had upgraded armour (50mm front and rear) and better driving controls. (AirSeaLand/Cody)

buttons. They started off at 0400hrs with a strong sandstorm blowing from the north-west – an excellent condition. Moving slowly, the Germans advanced along the Faïd-Sidi Bou Zid road. They had been briefed that there were some American tanks blocking the road between the hills on either side. The hills were held by American infantry. Köhler, manning his machine gun in the tank's bow, was surprised to see they were turning off the road and starting north on what appeared a route to attack Djebel Lessouda. He was concerned because tanks did not attack hills. He knew they were being followed by trucks of Panzergrenadier-Regiment 86.

His tank commander reported other tanks were swinging to the south toward the town. It made sense now that they were going to cut off the enemy on the hill. The sandstorm abated, but a thick haze hung low on the plain. Slowly crawling across the broken ground, their turret traversed to the left and began cracking off occasional rounds at the hill. In return they received sporadic mortar rounds and inaccurate anti-tank fire. Even though the platoon leader occasionally sent instructions to fire on hillside targets over the radio he was manning, Köhler was no more aware of what was going on than anyone else in the tank. When German aircraft came over they would throw orange smoke signals out of the tank to identify themselves. Eventually they rounded the hill and found abandoned artillery positions, some still containing artillery pieces – even trucks and equipment had been left behind. The area appeared to have been heavily blasted by their artillery and bombs.

Reaching the road behind the hill again late in the morning they could see many columns of black smoke and clouds of dust in the direction of Sidi Bou Zid and to the south. Their force split yet again, with part moving toward Sidi Bou Zid. They turned right on to the road and continued for several kilometres before turning on to a southbound road at which time they spread out into a broad wedge. They soon halted in a wadi with engines idling. They were in a *Beobachtungsstellung* – an observation position in which the commander's cupola was exposed over the lip of the wadi. The radio suddenly crackled a warning that American tanks were approaching from the north-west and that large clouds of dust were visible. The crew concluded that it must be a massive force to raise so much dust.

It was soon realized that the American M4 Sherman tanks were charging in a 'V' formation across the plain toward Sidi Bou Zid. Their formation was scattered, and the dust they were raising was blinding the following tanks. German anti-tank guns concealed in an olive grove opened fire on the lead tanks. Word came over the radio to hold fire until ordered, then not to advance until ordered. The anti-tank guns continued to fire on the charging Americans. The Germans could admire their courage, but the tank commander, the only long-time African veteran among the crew, kept yelling how foolish they were.

Shortly the platoon leader ordered his tanks to assume a *Feuerstellung* – a fire position in a *Halbverdeckte* or *Randstellung* (hull defilade). They knew they would soon be in action and that a *Panzerwarte* (armour ambush) was about to be executed against the exposed American flank. With green flares arcing into the sky and the radio

A dead crewman lies atop the hull of his wrecked PzKpfw III Ausf L. The reason for the tank loss is unknown, but there appears to be damage around the turret ring. (AirSeaLand/Cody)

command '*Feuer*!', Köhler and the crew opened up at a rapid rate. The tank bucked slightly and dust leaped off the ground as rounds were pumped out and cartridge cases clanged in the turret. Seated in the hull with the tank squatting in a wadi, Köhler could see little and he felt helpless that he was not even contributing to the fight. '*Anfahren*!' crackled over the radio, and the Panzers crawled out of the wadi, creeping slowly toward burning tanks.

The Americans were running. Tanks and half-tracks were pulling back. Some tanks were moving in reverse, attempting to cover others. Burning vehicles were scattered all about, some in clusters with their rear ends facing them. The gunner later said he had not seen anything like this since Russia. The Germans pursued the Americans, threading their way through burning tanks and scattered bodies. They did not see any knocked-out Panzers. It was difficult to detect targets through the smoke and dust, and the Panzers crawled even slower. There were shouts over the radio that the *Amis* were getting away. It was then that the radio went dead, as did the intercom. The commander ducked down and yelled at Köhler, ordering him to fix it as though it was his fault. Köhler pulled the radio out from its case. It was so hot he could barely touch it. Nothing else was obviously wrong. They pulled up beside another tank so that it could be relayed to the platoon leader that they had lost their radio. In frustration Köhler began machine-gunning abandoned American trucks, resulting in the commander yelling '*Feuerpause!*' ('Cease fire!'). The *Amis* trucks would be recovered for their own use.

Feeling worthless, Köhler spotted movement behind a pile of rocks, and through drifting smoke he made out an anti-tank gun. He swung his machine gun and pressed on the trigger, hammering out a long thread of white tracers that ricocheted in all directions but peppering the gun shield. The commander yelled at him again, but then realized what Köhler's target was. The co-axial machine gun opened up, smothering the target in a shower of tracers as other Panzers joined in. Köhler lost all track of time. His tank had halted, moved, halted again. At dusk they were ordered into a wadi to *laager*. It was not long before word spread that over 30 tanks had been knocked out, along with many half-tracks and trucks. Their own losses were light. They did not expect a counter-attack that night, and none materialized in the morning. An American counter-attack failed on the 15th, and during the night of 16–17 February, the infantry cut off on Djebel Ksaira and Garet Hadid were ordered to exfiltrate. Destroying heavy weapons and equipment, they struck across the plain 15 miles to Djebel Hamra. They were caught in the open at dawn by motorized units and 1,400 were captured.

THE PZKPFW III IN *BARBAROSSA*

During the opening months of Hitler's campaign into the Soviet Union, when tank had met tank the PzKpfw IIIs dealt easily with the elderly T-35s, T-26s and thin-skinned BTs; but the KV provided an unpleasant surprise. Squatting on a causeway, a single KV could hold up an entire Panzer division for a day, shrugging off rounds from every gun that could be brought to bear, and in such circumstances the only effective answer was for German infantry to stalk the brute with explosive charges. The 3.7cm gun was useless against these monsters, and although the L/42 5cm could score a kill this was usually achieved at a range of 50m or less, and preferably from the rear.

The superb T-34 was an even greater headache for Panzer crews who sincerely believed at the start of the campaign that they held a wide lead in technology over their Russian counterparts, and as far as the PzKpfw III was concerned not even the fitting of the L/60 gun could bridge the gap; the balance was redressed, bloodily, by inept Russian tactics opposed to German expertise and initiative.

For the Wehrmacht, the major event of 1942 was the great drive into the Caucasus in pursuit of the Baku oilfields. Once more the tank columns motored across the steppe under cloudless skies, and as the miles disappeared beneath their tracks it seemed as though the Panzer divisions were to enjoy a second 'Happy Time'. There was, in fact, very little fighting, for the Red Army had learned its lesson and had sidestepped the principal thrust.

But on the eastern flank of the advance lay Stalingrad, concerning which Hitler developed a total megalomania. All available reserves were diverted to the capture of

On the Eastern Front, a PzKpfw III advances through burning grassland. The commander's hatch is open to improve ventilation in the hot summer conditions. (AirSeaLand/Cody)

the city, a fact duly noted by the Russian Supreme Command (Stavka), which responded with a gigantic double envelopment, trapping the German 6. Armee, and part of 4. Panzerarmee as well, which had been forced against its better judgement to take part in the street-fighting. The bitter struggle continued until 2 February 1943, when the newly created Generalfeldmarschall Friedrich Paulus surrendered with 200,000 of his men.

Stalingrad had been a disaster which not only shook the German Army to its core, but also opened the door on the even more horrendous possibility of the Red Army encircling those forces now hastily withdrawing from the Caucasus; all that was needed was a determined thrust south-west to the Sea of Azov, and their fate would be sealed.

Stavka detailed two armies for the task, Vatutin's South-West Front and Golikov's Voronezh Front, and for a while they had a free run. This was permitted as a matter of deliberate policy by Manstein, the Commander-in-Chief of Heeresgruppe Süd, who was fully aware of Soviet intentions. He appreciated that because of Russian inexperience in deep-penetration operations and poor logistics back-up, both Soviet

1) PzKpfw III Ausf H, 10. Panzer-Division; Russia, 1941–42. The national cross, in white outline, is painted on a supplementary bin which has been welded to the track-guard.

2) Pzkpfw III Ausf J, 24. Panzer-Division; Russia, 1942. In common with many tanks of this division photographed in Russia, this L/60 Ausf J has a large stowage bin fixed across the rear of the engine deck, and on this can be seen the black and white national cross and the division's distinctive sign. (David E. Smith © Osprey Publishing)

1) PzKpfw III Ausf M, thought to be of 3. SS-Panzer-Division Totenkopf; Kursk, 1943. The new standard overall colour scheme of dark yellow, with added camouflage in the form of red-brown blotches, covers even the spare track links on the tank's nose and the large wooden stowage crate on the rear deck.

2) PzKpfw III Ausf J, 1. SS-Panzer-Division Leibstandarte Adolf Hitler; Russia, 1943. Photographed, possibly near Belgorod, towards the end of Manstein's 1943 offensive, this tank still wears basic Panzer grey, but has been heavily overpainted with white snow camouflage. (David E. Smith © Osprey Publishing)

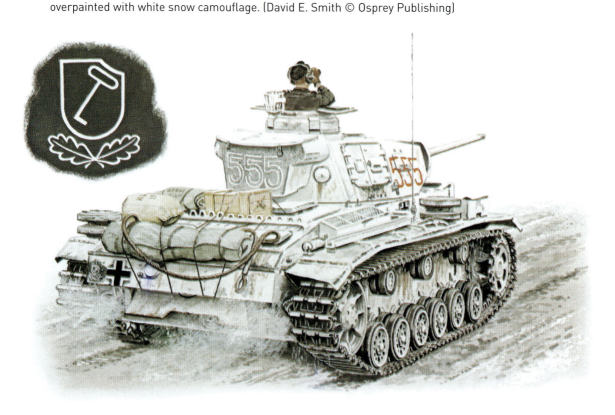

A famous image of a
PzKpfw III, framed against
the backdrop of a burning
vehicle during Operation
Barbarossa in 1941.
(AirSeaLand/Cody)

An SdKfz 251 half-track and a PzKpfw III Ausf L lead a formation of vehicles on the Eastern Front. The Ausf L, armed with a 5cm gun, was the tenth PzKpfw III model produced. Production began in July 1942. It was almost identical to the much more numerous Ausf J. (AirSeaLand/Cody)

armies would quickly outrun their supply echelons, and that the inevitable breakdowns would steadily drain away the strength of their tank formations. Conversely, he did not wish to launch his own counter-offensive until the German armour had been sufficiently concentrated for a knock-out blow, for Stalingrad had cost the Army 800 Panzers and the average strength of his Panzer divisions was now just 27 tanks.

On 20 February 1943, he moved at last, slicing into Vatutin's flank and finding most of the Russian columns stalled for want of fuel. South-West Front was routed and forced into a precipitate retreat, losing 615 tanks, 400 guns, 23,000 men killed and 9,000 captured. Golikov, hastening to his stricken comrade's aid, was caught while still deploying and handled even more severely. Voronezh Front was thrown back across the Donets, leaving behind 600 tanks, 500 guns and 40,000 casualties. Only the *rasputitsa*, the great thaw which turned hard-frozen ground into impassable mud, brought an end to Manstein's runaway progress.

This operation completely restored the integrity of the Eastern Front, and was the last occasion on which the PzKpfw III played the major role in a successful strategic offensive. Indeed, it was the Panzerwaffe's last strategic success of the war, for in July its potential was irrevocably blunted against the interminable defensive belts of the Kursk salient, and then written down in the great tank battle of Prokhorovka, the largest of World War II, in which machines rammed each other or fought murderous duels at point-blank range. Kursk cost the Germans 1,500 tanks, which could not be spared, and the Russians about the same, which were replaced almost at once from factories safe beyond the Urals. Thereafter, the PzKpfw III soldiered on in decreasing numbers, its place as the Panzer divisions' main battle tank being taken by the PzKpfw IV and the Panther, and its last actions being fought during the great defensive battles of 1944.

Technically the PzKpfw III was, despite minor faults, a well-balanced basic design which left provision for up-gunning and up-armouring, but by 1942 it was incapable of further modification that would enable it to keep pace with the spiral of the gun/armour race. During the high years of *Blitzkrieg* it was the only weapon in the German tank arsenal that really counted, and thus it did not merely witness history in the making – it made it, from the Channel to the Volga and from the Arctic to the North African desert. This achievement has, perhaps, been overshadowed in recent years by the study of later and more dramatic German designs, but the fact remains that it was the PzKpfw III that brought Hitler closest to achieving his wildest dreams.

German tanks, including a PzKpfw III in the foreground of the picture, sit on a transport train captured by Soviet forces in 1945. Both radiator inspection covers have been opened at the rear. (AirSeaLand/Cody)

CHAPTER 3

THE PANZER IV

Waffen-SS PzKpfw IV Ausf Es on the move on the Eastern Front. In 1942, the PzKpfw IV, originally conceived as support tank for the PzKpfw III, became the principal battle tank of the Panzer divisions. (AirSeaLand/Cody)

The design of the PzKpfw IV dated from January 1934, when the specification for the new close-support tank was put to the manufacturing industry by the Army, together with the overall weight limitation of 24 tonnes. During the next 18 months three firms – Rheinmetall-Borsig, Krupp and MAN – each produced their own design for the project under the deception title of Bataillonsführerwagen ('battalion commander's vehicle'), generally shortened to BW. Of these the Krupp design, designated VK (*Vollketten*, 'fully tracked') 20.01 (K), was most acceptable, having some resemblance to the contemporary PzKpfw III in its hull and turret. However, the VK 20.01 (K) did not go into production. The Army had requested, and been given, a six-wheeled interleaved suspension, but by the time the plans had been completed it had changed its mind in favour of a torsion bar system, which provided a better ride and which permitted the road wheels a greater degree of vertical lift. At this point Krupp took issue with the Heereswaffenamt, the Army's procurement agency, agreeing to dispense with the interleaved suspension but insisting on employing the leaf-spring double bogie unit that had been a feature of their unsuccessful design for the PzKpfw III; the Army gave way, since a production run of PzKpfw IVs was urgently required, and appointed Krupp to oversee the project.

A PzKpfw IV tracks down a road in Normandy in 1944. Open movement such as this became almost impossible as the campaign went on, on account of the endless predations of Allied fighter-bombers. (AirSeaLand/Cody)

DEVELOPMENT

As finalized, therefore, the PzKpfw IV design combined many features of the VK 20.01 (K) hull and turret with the Krupp suspension. A standard layout was adopted with the engine mounted at the rear. Inside the turret the commander sat centrally beneath his cupola, with the gunner on the left of the gun breech and the loader on the right. In the forward compartment the driver was located on the left and the radio operator/hull gunner on the right, with the transmission between them. The final drive ran to the sprockets across the front of the forward compartment. A point of interest is that the turret was offset 50.6mm to the left of the vehicle's centreline and the engine 152mm to the right, thus permitting the torque shaft connecting the engine with the gearbox to clear the rotary base junction, through which power was supplied to the turret's electrical systems. The effect of this was to provide a greater internal stowage area on the right than on the left, this being usefully absorbed by the installation of generous ready-use ammunition lockers for the loader.

The suspension and running gear consisted of eight small-diameter road wheels suspended in pairs from leaf-spring units, front drive sprocket, rear idler and four top return rollers. Throughout the PzKpfw IV's long service life, the vehicle's basic layout and suspension system remained essentially unchanged, save for minor details.

The Ausf A, or first production version of the vehicle, appeared in 1936 and was powered by a 250hp 12-cylinder Maybach 108 TR engine. The transmission was by means of a five-speed gearbox, which also provided one reverse gear. The 7.5cm main armament was mounted co-axially with a 7.92mm machine gun, while a further 7.92mm machine gun was carried in the front plate of the hull, the hull gunner's position being stepped back slightly from that of the driver. A simple cupola, consisting of a slotted 'dustbin', rose from the rear wall of the turret, which was also fitted with one-piece side hatches. Electrical power traverse was available to the gunner, and an advanced feature of the design was the provision of a DKW 2-stroke auxiliary generator, located at the left-hand side of the engine compartment, which enabled the vehicle's batteries to be kept charged without recourse to the main engine. The Ausf A was protected by 14.5mm hull and 20mm turret armour, weighed 17.3 tonnes and had a maximum speed of 30km/h. A total of 35 vehicles of this Mark were produced.

The Ausf B entered production in 1937 and incorporated a number of improvements, the most notable of which was the installation of the more powerful 320hp Maybach HL 120 TRM engine, together with a new gearbox with six forward gears and one reverse gear. A straight 30mm front plate was introduced, and some vehicles were fitted with a cupola of more sophisticated design, the vision slits now being protected by latched visors. The Ausf B weighed 17.7 tonnes, but the extra power available produced an improved top speed of 39.4km/h.

The Ausf D variant, as seen here, had an added shield for the gun mantlet and returned to the use of a hull machine gun, which had been deleted in the Ausf B and C. (AirSeaLand/Cody)

A PzKpfw IV B or C. The main difference between the two was that the Ausf C had thicker turret armour, measuring 30mm depth. (AirSeaLand/Cody)

In contrast to the 42 vehicles of this type manufactured, the Ausf C, which appeared in 1938, had a production run of 140. Superficially, Ausf B and C were almost identical, although on the latter the thickness of the turret armour had been increased to 30mm, raising the overall weight to 20 tonnes without impairing performance; and the hull machine gun had been replaced by a covered carbine port. The Ausf A, B and C had each been fitted with an internal mantlet that was found to be vulnerable to bullet-splash, and this was remedied in 1939 by the fitting of an external mantlet to the Ausf D, on which the hull machine gun was also reintroduced. Only 45 vehicles of this type were built before the outbreak of war.

If the Polish campaign vindicated the concept of *Blitzkrieg*, it also demonstrated that the armour basis of existing German tank designs was entirely inadequate, although this was by no means apparent to the world at the time. The Polish anti-tank guns had torn great holes in the ranks of the thin-skinned PzKpfw Is and IIs, and the larger PzKpfw IIIs and IVs suffered severely as well. Thus the next step in the development of the PzKpfw IV, the Ausf E, saw an increase in the thickness of the bow plate to 50mm, while an additional 30mm plate was fixed to the front plate and 20mm plates to the hull sides, raising the overall weight to 21 tonnes. These modifications were also carried out retrospectively to earlier Marks which had been returned to the manufacturers for refitting. The Ausf E additionally saw the cupola moved forward into the body of the turret.

The Ausf E production run commenced in December 1939, but the system of fitting appliqué armour to existing models could not be regarded as anything but a temporary expedient. However, some 280 vehicles of this type had been built by the time a redesigned model, the Ausf F, began entering service in the spring of

A carefully stage-managed photograph of a PzKpfw IV Ausf B or C. The Ausf B was introduced in April 1938, while the Ausf C followed in September that year. (AirSeaLand/Cody)

1941. This vehicle had single-thickness 50mm hull and turret frontal armour, the effect being to raise the weight to 22.3 tonnes. As this would have increased the ground pressure to an unacceptable figure, the track width was increased from 380mm to 400mm, necessitating wider drive sprockets and idlers; older vehicles fitted with the new track retained their original sprockets and idlers, supplemented by spacer rings. On the Ausf F the earlier one-piece turret hatches were replaced by split hatches, and a large stowage bin was mounted across the turret rear.

In the months directly preceding Operation *Barbarossa*, plans were being made for the PzKpfw IV to be fitted with the 5cm L/42 gun already in service in the PzKpfw III. Hitler was greatly interested in the project, evincing his prescience concerning weapon development, and was fully convinced that the PzKpfw IV should change its role from close-support to main battle tank. Events in Russia were to prove that the L/42 gun was not only outranged by the Soviet 76.2mm weapons, but also that it was incapable of defeating the stout Russian armour. Interest therefore turned to the 5cm L/60 gun, and an experimental PzKpfw IV fitted with this weapon was eventually produced.

PZKPFW IV AUSF D, 7./ PANZER-REGIMENT 8, 10. PANZER-DIVISION, MAY 1940

Crew: 5
Length: 5.92m
Width: 2.84m
Height: 2.68m
Combat weight: 20 tonnes
Main gun: 75mm KwK 37 L/24, 80 rounds
Elevation: -8/+20°
Machine guns: one co-axial MG 34,
    one hull-mounted MG 34
Radio: FuG 5 transceiver
Engine: Maybach HL 120 TRM, 265hp
Fuel capacity: 470 litres
Range: 130–210km
Top speed: 42km/h
Armour: 35mm gun mantlet, 30mm front,
    20mm side, 20mm rear

(Richard Chasemore © Osprey Publishing)

2.68m

2.84m

5.92m

This was, of course, symptomatic of the German Army's having prepared for a short war without adequate consideration being given to longer-term considerations such as the design of a second generation of tanks. Moreover, with the Panzerwaffe's morale jolted off-balance by the discovery that the Red Army had better tank designs, the problem of restoring parity had acquired a desperate urgency. It was pointed out that the L/60 was already being fitted to the PzKpfw III, and since the PzKpfw IV's turret ring was larger, if the same weapon was fitted it would produce, in simple terms, a case of too much chassis for too little gun. By the greatest of good fortune, however, the PzKpfw IV's wide turret ring was not only capable of accommodating much greater recoil movement than

that of the L/24 howitzer, but would also permit the handling of larger rounds of ammunition, and as the vehicle already carried a 7.5cm mounting it was decided to adapt this to take a high-velocity gun. The choice of weapon fell upon the 7.5cm L/43 KwK 40, with a basic muzzle velocity (AP) of 740m/sec and the ability to penetrate 89mm armour set back at 30°. This gun, fitted with a spherical single-baffle muzzle brake, was mounted on an Ausf F to produce PzKpfw Ausf IVF2, the original Ausf F vehicles that retained their L/24 howitzers being known thereafter as Ausf IVF1s.

A PzKpfw IV Ausf F2 serving with the 9. Panzer-Division. The full title of the vehicles was the PzKpfw IV (7.5cm KwK 40) (SdKfz 161), 7./B.W., Ausf F2. (AirSeaLand/Cody)

The Ausf IVF2 entered service early in 1942 in Russia and proved to be a match for the Soviet T-34 and KV, although it remained under-armoured by Eastern Front standards, and the increase in weight to 23.6 tonnes brought about a slight reduction in performance. An attempt to remedy the deficiency in armour led to the appearance of the Ausf G later the same year. The designers were conscious that they were very close to the chassis' viable weight limit and were therefore forced to produce a compromise solution, removing the 20mm plates which had been added to the hull sides from Ausf E onwards and increasing the thickness of the basic side armour to 30mm. The saving thus made was transferred to the vehicle's front armour in the shape of 30mm appliqué plates.

In addition, the single-baffle muzzle brake of the Ausf IVF2 was replaced by a more efficient double-baffle system. However, the improved 75mm L/48 gun, with a basic AP muzzle velocity of 750m/sec, became available towards the end of the Ausf G's production run and was thereafter fitted as standard.

In one way the longer 7.5cm guns were a very mixed blessing. In spite of the designers' efforts to conserve weight, the new weapons made the vehicle nose-heavy to such an extent that the forward suspension springs were under constant compression, with the result that the tank tended to sway about even when no steering was applied. The effect of this was compounded when the Ausf H was introduced in March 1943, as this model not only had

RIGHT A captured PzKpfw IV Ausf G, featuring the earlier ball-shaped muzzle brake, which was eventually replaced by the squarer multi-baffle design. (AirSeaLand/Cody)

BELOW A PzKpfw IV embarked for transportation aboard a train. A German combat report from North Africa noted regarding the tank: 'Because of its distinctive form, it drew concentrated fire down on itself from aircraft, artillery and anti-tank guns.' (AirSeaLand/Cody)

integral 80mm armour on the bow, front plate and mantlet, but also had 5mm side skirts and a turret girdle as a defence against hollow-charge ammunition. The Ausf H weighed 25 tonnes, and in spite of a new six-speed transmission borrowed from the PzKpfw III its performance was inferior to earlier models, cross-country speed dropping as low as 16km/h on anything but good, hard, level going. An experimental version of the Ausf H was fitted with a hydrostatic transmission, but was not proceeded with.

The PzKpfw IV was now the mainstay of the Panzerwaffe, and as production had been greatly accelerated it was leaving the factories in some numbers, over 900 Ausf Gs being completed in 1942 and 3,000 Ausf Hs in 1943. In spite of this, sectional interests within the Third Reich almost succeeded in persuading Hitler to abandon PzKpfw IV manufacture in favour of its Panzerjäger derivative; fortunately for Germany, General Guderian, now Inspector General of Armoured Troops, was on hand to point out forcefully and with irrefutable logic that as mass production of the Panther was still some way off, the loss of the PzKpfw IV would mean that the only new tanks reaching the German Army in the field would be the handful of Tigers that were being built each month. The PzKpfw IV thus remained in production until the war ended.

The final production version of the tank, the Ausf J, entered service in 1944, and in design terms must be regarded as a retrograde step induced by necessity. The electrical power traverse was discarded in favour of a purely manual system, the additional space available being filled by an auxiliary fuel tank of 200-litre capacity. This increased the vehicle's theoretical road range from 201km to 300km (cross-country from 132km to 182km) at a time when the Panzer divisions were conducting a mobile defence along the Eastern Front in the face of supply difficulties. Some attempt to reduce weight was evident in the substitution of wire mesh side skirts for solid plate, although this did not apply to the turret girdle.

By 1944 there was general acceptance that the design had reached the limit of its development potential, and an attempt by Krupp to fit a Panther turret, complete with 7.5cm L/70 gun, simply confirmed that the chassis was already overloaded. As a result of the German system of thoroughly updating vehicles returned for refit, a number of hybrid types were produced, so that it was by no means unusual to find, for example, an Ausf D chassis carrying an Ausf G turret and main armament. No system of classifying these sub-Marks was adopted, and they are generally referred to by the standard up to which they had been refitted.

SPECIAL-PURPOSE VEHICLES

Following the Wehrmacht's complete victory over the British and French armies in 1940, plans were made for the invasion of Great Britain. It was appreciated that no landing could hope to succeed unless it was supported by armour at a very early stage, and, as we saw in the previous chapter, submerged wading experiments were carried out with the PzKpfw III, the converted vehicles being known as Tauchpanzer or 'diving tanks'. The PzKpfw IV was similarly adapted using the same fittings and principles, with similar performance. Once submerged, a PzKpfw IV could maintain a speed of approximately 5km/h along the bottom.

By September 1941, PzKpfw III and PzKpfw IV were performing a similar battlefield role; and as the two designs had much in common it was felt that numerous benefits, including the standardization of parts, would accrue if they were to be merged. The composite vehicle was given the title of PzKpfw III/IV, and several prototypes were constructed in which the parentage of the hull and turret were clearly identifiable, although the suspension now carried six large interleaved wheels, so

The 3.7cm Flak auf Fahrgestell Panzerkampfwagen IV (sf) (SdKfz 161/3) Möbelwagen (Moving Van) mounted a single 3.7cm Flak 43 L/89. Here note the crewmember on the right using an EM 34 coincidence rangefinder. (AirSeaLand/Cody)

The Jagdpanzer IV (SdKfz 162) used a modified Panzer IV Ausf H chassis, with 80mm-thick sloped armour. With its long 7.5cm PaK 42 L/70 gun, the vehicle was very nose-heavy. (AirSeaLand/Cody)

that the finished product bore a startling resemblance to the original VK 20.01 (K) plan. The design was ingenious but became a casualty in the accelerating gun/armour race, and was finally abandoned in 1944.

Unlike the PzKpfw III, the PzKpfw IV was not widely converted for use as a Panzerbefehlswagen (armoured command vehicle), but several Ausf Hs were fitted with a second radio, which was operated by the loader, and additional antennae bases, so that they could if necessary assume the command role. In this version the vehicle was known as the Panzerbefehlswagen IV.

Again, the requirements of the Panzerartillerie's FOOs were successfully met by the PzKpfw III until mid-1944, when existing stocks began to run down. After this they used a PzKpfw IV, more often than not an Ausf J, which had been very simply converted by the installation of a tall, thin periscope to the left of the commander's cupola, and by the provision of additional radios for communication with the tank as well as the artillery net. The crew consisted of the FOO, his technical assistant, two radio operators and the driver, all of whom were artillery personnel. Between September 1944 and March 1945, some 96 PzKpfw IVs were also converted to the role of Panzerbeobachtungswagen (armoured observation vehicle).

The chassis of the PzKpfw IV was eminently suitable for employment in a variety of tasks and formed the basis for a number of other first-line combat vehicles, including the Sturmgeschütz (StuG) IV, armed with a 7.5cm L/48 gun. The StuG IV equipped the elite Sturmartillerie, supplementing the more numerous StuG III; the Brummbär

(Grizzly Bear), also known as Sturmpanzer IV, a heavy assault gun designed for street-fighting and mounting a 150mm L/12 howitzer which, from April 1943, served with the heavy infantry gun companies of Panzergrenadier regiments and in 45-strong assault battalions at the disposal of senior commanders; the 8.8cm first-generation heavy tank-destroyer Nashorn (Rhino); and the Panzerjäger IV, which carried first an L/48 and later an L/70 7.5cm gun.

A notable development in the Panzerartillerie field was the Hummel (Bumble-bee) 15cm self-propelled howitzer which, like the Nashorn, employed a PzKpfw IV chassis incorporating the final drive of the PzKpfw III. The engine was located amidships so as to leave the rear of the vehicle clear for the gun mounting, and the fighting compartment was enclosed by a fixed, open-topped superstructure of 10mm plate. Early models of the vehicle were fitted with a muzzle brake and had an angled driver's cab, but as the series progressed the former was dispensed with as being unnecessary, and the latter was extended across the front to include the radio operator's compartment. The Hummel weighed 23.5 tonnes, had a maximum speed of 40km/h and carried a crew of six. It entered service during 1943 and equipped the six-gun heavy battery of the Panzer division's artillery regiment; such an allocation was far from universal, as the total production run was only 666, and only the most favoured divisions would have received their full quota. The 15cm howitzer threw a 44kg shell 15,000m. Only 18 rounds of ammunition could be stowed, but immediate replenishment was generally available from a Munitionsträger Hummel, an amunitions carrier with the same layout but without a gun, several of which formed part of the battery establishment.

A PzKpfw IV Ausf G, preserved at the Aberdeen Proving Ground in Maryland, United States. In June 1942 an order was made that all PzKpfw IV with the KwK 40 gun were to be referred to as Ausf G. (AirSeaLand/Cody)

The Jagdpanzer IV – here we see one being destroyed by a Red Army T-34 – was another of the PzKpfw IV derivatives, being essentially a modified Panzer IV Ausf H chassis with sloped 80mm armour plate on the front and fitted with either the 7.5cm PaK 39 L/48 or, later, the 7.5cm PaK 42 L/70. Note the absence of muzzle brake; crews often removed these owing to the heavy kick-up of dust produced by the muzzle brake gun flash. (AirSeaLand/Cody)

Like any branch of the service, the Panzerartillerie possessed its reactionary elements, and these expressed themselves as being far from satisfied with the designs for the Hummel and its lighter companion, the 10.5cm self-propelled howitzer Wespe (Wasp). Their principal complaints were that the mountings had insufficient traverse and were too high and too poorly protected, and some effort was made to produce a gun carriage which would remedy these defects.

The simplest of the new designs went by the cumbersome title of 1eFH 18/1 (Sf) auf GW IVb (Self-propelled Light Field Howitzer 18/1 on Gun Carriage IVb) and employed a shortened PzKpfw IV chassis carried on six slightly increased-diameter road wheels per side, the number of return rollers being reduced to three. On this was mounted a better-shaped but still open-topped turret of 20mm plate, the total traverse available being 70°. The 10.5cm howitzer had a heavy muzzle brake and could be elevated to +40° and depressed to -10°. Eight of these vehicles were built and saw active service in Russia, but it was felt that manufacturing capacity could not be diverted for a purpose-built artillery chassis, and the Wespe continued quantity production, employing the obsolete PzKpfw II chassis.

A more complex design for use with the same weapon was the Heuschrecke (Grasshopper), which was based on a slightly lengthened version of the standard PzKpfw IV chassis. The turret was of similar pattern to that of the vehicle described immediately above, but had all-round traverse. In addition, by using a crane-rail gantry that formed an integral part of the design, the turret could be lifted bodily from its seating and lowered over the tail onto a ground mounting, leaving the vehicle itself free to act as an ammunition carrier. The Heuschrecke, which did not proceed beyond the prototype stage, formed part of a whole series of projected artillery equipment known collectively as Waffenträger (weapon carriers), the majority of which never left the drawing-board. Guderian thought they were interesting, but hardly worth the disruption of tank production.

By 1943 the Luftwaffe had lost its overall command of the air and could no longer guarantee the Army protection against hostile aircraft. As the situation in the air continued to deteriorate, the ground troops were forced to rely to an ever-increasing extent on their own resources. For the Panzer divisions this meant acquiring more powerful mobile anti-aircraft equipment than the single 2cm automatic cannon carried by the Flakpanzer 38(t), and the chassis of the PzKpfw IV offered an obvious alternative for the installation of heavier weapons.

Hitler's own preference was for a twin 37mm mounting, but a quadruple 20mm equipment was immediately available and went into production on Ausf H and J chassis, the first examples reaching the divisions in the autumn of 1943. The mounting was protected by four hinged rectangular flaps which earned the vehicle the title Möbelwagen (Furniture Van), but a major disadvantage of this system was that these had to be lowered when the weapon was in action, reducing the crew's protection to a simple gunshield. An alternative type of mounting carried a single 3.7cm cannon. A total of 211 Möbelwagen of both types was eventually built.

A much improved Flakpanzer, the Wirbelwind (Whirlwind), appeared in December 1943, consisting of a 2cm quadruple mounting in an open-topped fully rotating turret with 16mm armour. This was joined in March 1944 by the Ostwind (East Wind), which was almost identical in layout but had 25mm armour and carried a single 3.7cm cannon. Both Wirbelwind and Ostwind used the Ausf J chassis, and production figures

The Flakpanzer IV Wirbelwind (Whirlwind) took the chassis and hull of a PzKpfw IV and topped it with an anti-aircraft turret mounting four 2cm Flak cannon. The maximum practical rate of fire was 800rpm, although standard operating realities usually dropped the figure to around 400rpm. (AirSeaLand/ Cody)

The Sturmpanzer IV Brummbär mounted the wall-smashing 15cm L/12 howitzer, and was principally deployed as a heavy assault gun, breaching obstacles and defences in support of infantry assaults. (AirSeaLand/Cody)

A StuG crew carefully take aboard 7.5cm shells for their KwK 40/StuK 40 anti-tank gun, one of the most effective German anti-tank weapons. Total shell capacity for the StuG IV was 63 rounds. (AirSeaLand/Cody)

for each model were respectively 140 and 40. The maximum rate of fire of the quadruple 2cm system was 1,800 rounds per minute, but a lower rate was generally set; the 3.7cm's maximum output was 160 rounds per minute.

The last of the PzKpfw IV anti-aircraft series was the Kugelblitz (Fireball), which was armed with twin 3cm cannon enclosed in a domed turret. This required only 25 seconds for a complete traverse of 360° and provided an elevation of +80°. The Kugelblitz was a most efficient design and had a rate of fire of 900 rounds per minute, but only half a dozen or so had been built by the time the war ended. Like the other Flakpanzer IV mountings it was powered by an improved performance version of the standard engine.

It had originally been intended that each Panzer division's assault engineer battalion should be issued with three Bruckenlegepanzer (armoured bridge layers), and in 1939/40 such a vehicle was constructed in small numbers using the PzKpfw IV Ausf C and D chassis. The 9m bridge, which had a 28-ton capacity, was launched over the bows, but the complete

equipment so overloaded the suspension that the design was not taken up, and in fact bridge-layer production was officially terminated in 1941.

Another assault engineering device which employed the PzKpfw IV chassis was the Infanterie-Sturm-Steg (Infantry assault bridge). This consisted of a telescopic catwalk launched rather like a fire-engine ladder from the back of the carrying vehicle, and dropped into place over an anti-tank ditch or small river for the infantry to swarm across and secure a bridgehead. Not many of these vehicles were built, but several were used during the 1940 campaign in the West and again during the early days of Operation *Barbarossa*. Because of the roomy interior of the hull, a turretless PzKpfw IV was chosen as an ammunition carrier for the enormous 60cm Karl mortars which saw service at the siege of Sebastopol and during the Warsaw Uprising. Only three of the huge 2.2-tonne shells could be stowed, and a 3-ton electric crane was installed over the radio operator's compartment to effect the transfer of these. A further supply version was the Land-Wasser Schlepper (amphibious tractor), which performed the same function as the American Buffalo LVT, and which it closely resembled. Also known as the Panzerfähre, it consisted of a large pontoon fixed to the upper hull of the tank with a control cabin mounted forward and a small cargo space amidships.

Some PzKpfw IVs were fitted locally with recovery equipment to become Bergepanzer (armoured recovery vehicles), and the fitting of a dozer blade was not unknown. In addition to the tank's hull and chassis finding such diverse employment, the turret was also used to provide the main armament of the armoured trains which patrolled the German rear areas in Russia.

PZKPFW IV DESCRIBED
Armour

In 1942 the consulting engineers Messrs Merz and McLellan performed a detailed evaluation of a captured Ausf E, including an analysis of the armour plate. They reported:

> Hardness tests were carried out on a number of armour plates and it was concluded that they were all of machinable quality with the exception of the spaced armour plate over the hull machine-gun mounting. The port armour covers and the hull machine-gun mounting were found to be face hardened. The hardness of the inside and outside surfaces of the machinable quality plates lay between 300 and 460 Brinell [standardized hardness test for metals]. The additional 20mm plates which form the reinforced side armour are of homogenous quality and have a Brinell hardness of about 370 on the front surface. Resistance of reinforced side armour will not withstand 2-pdr attack at 1,000yd at normal impact.

PZKPFW IV AUSF H

Key

1. 80mm front armour plate
2. Spare track links
3. 20mm armour glacis plate
4. Final drive inspection hatch
5. Brake cooling air intake
6. Steering brake inspection hatch
7. Tow bracket
8. Headlights with blackout covers
9. Schürzen 5mm armour plate protection against anti-tank rifle fire
10. Stowage clips for axe
11. Brackets for stowage of spare track links
12. 7.92mm MG 34 machine gun
13. Kugelblende, armoured ball mount
14. Radio operator's roof escape hatch
15. 80mm superstructure armour plate
16. Muzzle brake
17. Kill rings painted on gun
18. 7.5cm KwK 40 L/48 main gun
19. Forward ammunition bin, 23 rounds
20. Turret ball race bullet splash guard
21. Armoured sleeve for supporting gun during recoil
22. Armoured covers for recoil brake and recuperator
23. 30mm side armour on turret
24. 50mm front armour on turret
25. TZF 5f (2.5 x 24°) telescopic gun sight
26. Handwheels for gun elevation and turret traverse
27. Breech
28. Electric turret traverse motor
29. Fume extractor fan
30. Travel lock stay
31. Single piece hatch
32. Commander's cupola with vision blocks
33. Spare glass vision blocks
34. Recoil guard
35. Pistol port
36. Stowage bin for crew belongings
37. 5mm Schürzen armour surrounding turret
38. Maybach HL 120 V-12 300 PS petrol motor (hatch in firewall removed)
39. Cooling air outlet
40. 2m rod antenna for FuG 5 radio system
41. Gun cleaning rods
42. Cooling air intake
43. Sheet metal covers for sealing off air intake in cold weather
44. Column distance light
45. Crowbar
46. Cast idler wheel, adjustable for track tensioning
47. Quarter elliptic sprung two-wheel bogie
48. Air exhaust outlet from steering brakes and gearbox
49. Eight double road wheels, rubber tyres 470/90
50. Bogie bumpstops
51. Jack
52. Fuel tanks under floor
53. Gunner's seat
54. Side armour upper, 30mm
55. Side armour lower, 30mm
56. Steel tyred return rollers (rubber saving)
57. Hooks for use with towing cable
58. Fire extinguisher
59. Base socket for headlight (removed for combat)
60. Dry pin cast steel track Typ Kgs 61/400/120 (99 licentre guide tooth 400mm wide, 120mm pitch)

61. Drive sprocket

62. Driver's seat

63. Steering levers

64. Instrument panel

65. ZF S.S.G. 76 gearbox

(Jim Laurier © Osprey Publishing)

On the other hand, firing trials carried out in the Middle East during June 1941 showed that 500yd (457m) could be considered as the maximum effective range for the 2-pdr when engaging the PzKpfw IV's frontal armour, and this was confirmed by similar trials at the Royal Arsenal, Woolwich, the report on which noted that 'the armour is 10 per cent better than British machinable quality plate, and in some respects better than our homogenous hard'.

However, the method of joining plates drew unfavourable comment from Leyland Motors: 'The quality of welding did not, at first sight, appear to be very good. In two or three places, near the regions where the plates had been damaged by shellfire, the welded joints had broken and the plates separated.' The danger of bullet-splash penetrating the vehicle's hatches was removed by incorporating channels to catch the molten metal as it forced its way through the apertures.

ABOVE A PzKpfw IV Ausf F sits hidden amongst the trees of the Ardennes in 1940, waiting to drive into France. The Panzer IV was at this stage still armed with the short 7.5cm L/24 howitzer. (AirSeaLand/Cody)

RIGHT PzKpfw Ausf Hs, serving with the Das Reich Division, advance through the forests of Russia in February 1943. The Ausf H was essentially the same as the late-production Ausf G except for a series of small changes, including a new planetary drive cover and thicker turret-roof armour. (AirSeaLand/Cody)

Automotive

The Maybach engine and the Variorex pre-selector gearbox on the PzKpfw IV suffered from the same constraints and limitations as those on the PzKpfw III (see previous chapter). As already described, the later models of the tank tended to overload the leaf-spring suspension, although replacement of complete bogie units, damaged in action, was a fairly simple matter. Track adjustment was achieved by movement of the rear idler, the mounting of which included an eccentric axle with a splined end. The axle could be rotated by a suitable tool and the adjustment retained by ratchet rings, the whole being secured by locking nuts.

The Ostketten were also fitted to increase traction during the winter months. An extremely simple but efficient track repair device was tested experimentally on the PzKpfw IV. This consisted of a length of industrial belting the same width as the track, with perforations along its edges to match the teeth of the drive sprocket. One end of the belting was clipped to the rear end of the broken track, while the other was led forward over the return rollers and married to the sprocket. The engine was then started and a gear engaged; the sprocket turned, hauling the belting forward until the track itself engaged the teeth. This performed effortlessly and in minutes a task which otherwise involved the whole crew in the back-breaking job of lifting and pulling forward the track by hand, with the aid of a wire hawser.

The vehicle was equipped with a 24-volt electric self-starter, and because the auxiliary generator kept the batteries fully charged this could be used more consistently than that fitted to the PzKpfw III. If the self-starter failed, or if it was inadvisable to use it because extreme cold had chilled the sump oil to a semi-solid state, thus increasing resistance, the crew used an inertia starter, in the same position as on the PzKpfw III.

A further aid to cold-starting on the Eastern Front was a system known as the Kühlwasserübertragung (cold water exchanger). When one tank had been started and had reached its normal operating temperature, the warm coolant was pumped from it to the next vehicle by the exchanger, in return for cold coolant. In due course the rise in temperature would permit the second vehicle to be started. The system required slight modification to the tank's cooling system by the provision of inlet and outlet valves.

Gunnery and Optical

The 7.5cm L/24 howitzer was rifled clockwise with 28 grooves 0.85mm deep, its breech being closed by a semi-automatic vertical sliding block. Its artillery origins were evident in that a clinometer remained fitted to those PzKpfw IV models equipped with the gun, providing the vehicle with an indirect-fire capability. The recoil cylinders projected beyond the mantlet and the barrel was covered for most of its length by a steel protective jacket to which a deflector guard was attached, its function being to

RIGHT A PzKpfw III Ausf G on the Eastern Front, *c.* 1944. The entire vehicle has been given a coating of whitewash snow camouflage; the tankers themselves have white padded winter uniforms. (AirSeaLand/Cody)

BELOW A good close-up of the front hull and turret of the PzKpfw IV Ausf H, this particular one serving with the Hohenstaufen Division in France in 1944. Note the Zimmerit paste applied around the hull machine gun and driver's vision block. (AirSeaLand/Cody)

sweep the tank's aerial out of the line of fire when the gun was traversed to the right. The gun cradle was heavier than was strictly necessary, putting the turret slightly out of balance. A full range of ammunition was developed for the howitzer, including HE shell, AP shot, smoke and canister, but essentially it remained a HE weapon system with a lazy muzzle velocity of 385m/sec and a sharply curved trajectory.

The PzKpfw IV's firing trials were conducted concurrently with those of the StuG III, which mounted the same weapon, and the Sturmartilleristen took a certain amount of malicious pleasure in noting that the tank crews were a lot slower getting onto the target. (Perhaps such feelings were understandable, as the Panzerwaffe had attempted to strangle their own branch of the service at birth!) However, once they had mastered the idiosyncrasies of the high-angle weapon, the tank men quickly perfected their own three-round bracketing technique which, given an experienced crew, could be considerably shortened.

Elevation of the main and co-axial armament was by means of a handwheel operated with the gunner's left hand. Traverse could be either manual or powered, and a selector lever switched in whichever system was required. The traversing handwheel was located immediately to the right of the elevation control and included a release latch. It was sometimes linked under the gun to a hand crank which could be turned by the loader; if the turret was being traversed manually the gunner could produce 1.9° per turn of his wheel and the loader 2.6°. If the power traverse was engaged, power was supplied via the rotary base junction to a motor located on the left of the turret, the speed of the motor being controlled by the traverse handwheel through a chain and sprocket. Using this system, the maximum rate of traverse obtainable was 14° per second (about half that available in British tanks) and the minimum 0.14° per second. As the motor's response to control signals was generally abrupt, this made the tracking of moving targets extremely difficult. The main armament was fired electrically by a trigger on the traverse handwheel, and its recoil was controlled by a hydro-pneumatic buffer system. A number of safety devices were installed, including a loader's safety switch and a misfire lamp.

The substitution of the longer L/43 and L/48 guns for the short L/24 howitzer produced the same situation as that of the PzKpfw III, in which the tank's main armament was muzzle-heavy in its mounting. Similarly, to compensate for this a compression spring in a cylinder was fitted to the right/forward segment of the turret ring and connected to the gun. The more powerful weapons naturally produced recoil forces well in excess of those of the L/24, and this was allowed for by extending the mounting cradle and providing recoil buffers that were both wider and longer – so long, in fact, that part of the breech-ring had to be cut away to accommodate them. Even so, the recoil of the long guns was 50mm greater than that of the L/24. A recoil indicator with a scale of 430–520mm was fitted, and this was marked *Feuerpause* at 505mm. During road marches or for transit by rail, the L/43 and L/48 guns could be locked at +16° by means of a quick-release internal crutch, mounted along the underside of the turret roof.

TZF 5B TELESCOPIC GUN SIGHT

The 7.5cm KwK 40 gun on the PzKpfw IV Ausf H was aimed using the Leitz TZF 5b (*Turmzielfernrohr*) monocular telescopic gun sight. This telescope operated at a single magnification of 2.5× with a 25° field of view. The sight contained two engraved reticles. The centre reticle consisted of an aiming triangle in the centre with smaller triangles on either side. The gunner placed the target at the apex of the centre triangle. This reticle provided a limited stadiametric ranging capability which allowed a well-trained gunner to estimate the range based on the size of the target compared to the large triangle. The unit of measure was a graduation (Strich) equalling 1m at 1,000m range, with the larger triangle having sides of four graduations and the smaller triangle having sides of two graduations. Such calculations were too difficult in the heat of battle, so a gunner had to be so well trained that the procedure became instinctive. In actual practice, the gunners often used the co-axial machine gun to determine range. The series of triangles was intended to provide the gunner

with a method to gauge the speed of a crossing target. The second reticle provided the graduations visible around the periphery of the reticle and was used to adjust the weapon depending on the weapon and the range. In the case here, the reticle has been turned to the setting for the 7.5cm gun at a range of 200m. The two reticles were mechanically linked and by rotating the reticle, the gunner moved the centre aiming reticle, forcing him to elevate the gun to compensate for range.

(Richard Chasemore © Osprey Publishing)

The telescopic sight for the long 7.5cm possessed all the same complexity as that discussed in Chapter 3. On the PzKpfw IV, however, the HE scale (Gr34) and the machine-gun scale were common and were marked from 0 to 3,200m, while the two AP scales (Pzgr 39 and Pzgr 40) were marked respectively from 0 to 2,400 and from 0 to 1,400m.

In many ways, the PzKpfw IV was a very sophisticated vehicle for its day. Around the inside of the commander's cupola was a scale marked from 1 to 12, with 24 sub-divisions. When the turret was traversed a pinion which engaged the teeth of the turret rack drove the scale in the opposite direction but at the same speed, so that the figure 12 remained in constant alignment with the hull's centreline, looking directly forward. This enabled the commander to determine the bearing of his next target and inform the gunner accordingly. To the gunner's left was a repeat target position indicator in the form of a dial identically marked to the cupola scale, and also driven from the turret rack. Upon receiving the order, the gunner would quickly traverse the turret to the bearing indicated, e.g. 10 o'clock, using his own indicator, and find the gun approximately on line for the target. Early models had a single-dial target – or more precisely, turret-position indicator – but this was subsequently replaced by a two-dial system, the left-hand dial showing 1–12 with 64 sub-divisions each of 100 mils (a measurement denoting 1 yard at 1,000 yards' distance), the right-hand dial being divided into mils with 100 divisions. It is, perhaps, a little surprising to find that having gone to so much trouble to install an accurate traverse indicator, the authorities decided to dispense with the clinometer on vehicles fitted with the long 75mm gun.

The driver was provided with a gun warning indicator in the form of two blue lamps mounted on either side of his compartment. When the gun was traversed over the side of the vehicle a switch was tripped automatically and the corresponding lamp lit up, warning him to allow extra room if the tank was passing between trees or buildings. Failure to do this could result in the barrel striking an obstruction and causing damage to the gun mounting. This device was not fitted on later production models.

Vehicles fitted with the L/24 howitzer stowed 80 rounds of main armament and 2,700 rounds of machine-gun ammunition; those with the longer gun, 87 and 3,150 rounds respectively. The majority of ammunition lockers and racks were within easy reach of the loader, the open racks being protected by canvas covers secured by press-studs. Evidence suggests that the secondary armament was drum-fed up to Ausf E and employed belts thereafter, each belt containing 150 rounds and being housed in a bag. Like the PzKpfw III, however, the hull machine-gun operator of the PzKpfw IV was also obliged to use the moulded rubber cap to perform weapon elevation and depression. For emergency use a 17in-diameter escape manhole was sited in the floor of the radio operator's compartment.

Presenting a vision of armoured power, PzKpfw IVs of the Hitlerjugend Division are gathered for inspection on the Western Front in 1944. Note how each tank has a top-mounted 7.92mm machine gun for air defence. (AirSeaLand/Cody)

The earlier models of the PzKpfw IV were fitted with a smoke-bomb rack mounted on the stern plate, operated in the same way as described for the PzKpfw III. The system was abandoned following the introduction of turret smoke-bomb dischargers.

Crew

The PzKpfw IV crew consisted of five men: three in the turret and two in the hull. The PzKpfw IV had a turret basket with rotating floor. The tank commander (*Kommandant*) sat on 'the throne' in the rear centre of the turret behind the main gun. Above the throne was an armoured cupola with vision ports that were shielded externally by armoured visors and 50mm-thick bullet-resistant glass. In addition, the cupola had an overhead hatch that allowed the commander to operate with his head out of the tank for better situational awareness. The commander communicated with the crew via a throat microphone and intercom system. The gunner (*Richtkanonier*) was located in the left side of the turret. The main gun was aimed using a TZF 5b telescopic sight. The gunner could traverse the turret either with a mechanical handwheel or an electric drive powered off an auxiliary motor that could turn the turret 360° in 23 seconds. A British report concluded that, 'the maximum speed [of the electric traverse] is relatively low, but the response is quick and the braking good … The number of resistance steps is too small with the result that the characteristic is noticeably stepped, making it impossible to follow moving targets accurately particularly at low angular speeds.' The hand-gear required 190 turns for a complete rotation of the turret. The loader (*Ladekanonier*) had a seat on the right side of the turret but in action the seat would be folded and the loader would stand on

This PzKpfw IV of the Waffen-SS Wiking Division, being serenaded by the local military band, displays a swirling camouflage pattern, rendered in browns and greens ideal for operations in the summer months. (AirSeaLand/Cody)

the turret basket floor. The ammunition was distributed around the PzKpfw IV's interior in several bins scattered around the fighting compartment; those in the driver's compartment were accessed with the assistance of the radio operator. The loader was also responsible for loading the co-axial machine gun, which was directly in front of him. The driver (*Fahrer*) was located in the left front of the hull. Steering was a conventional Wilson clutch-steering type manufactured by Krupp, with the transmission in the front centre of the hull and the steering brakes forward of the driver. The driver had a direct-vision port with armoured cover immediately in front of him protected by thick glass; he lacked the binocular telescope found in earlier versions of the PzKpfw IV. The radio operator (*Funker*) sat in the right front hull opposite the driver. The FuG 5 radio transmitter-receiver was mounted centrally above the transmission to the left of the radio-operator. This was a voice/telegraphic AM radio with two preset channels and an effective range of about 2km in voice mode. It suffered from the inherent shortcomings of AM radios in tanks, namely the susceptibility to static noise which made the set useless during travel. It was also less powerful than US tank radios, with only 10 watts of forward power versus 30 watts.

OPERATIONAL HISTORY

As already indicated, the primary function of the L/24 PzKpfw IV was the close support of the other tanks within the Panzer regiment by suppressing the fire of strongpoints and anti-tank guns that were causing loss and delaying the advance. Although in theory they formed a heavy company of their own, in practice battalion commanders could, and frequently did, distribute their PzKpfw IVs among the other companies so that each would have its own platoon of close-support vehicles immediately available and at the company commander's disposal. In such circumstances, PzKpfw IV commanders who were unable to identify their targets at first glance would have them indicated either by radio, by a burst of tracer fired from another vehicle or by a smoke marker shell. The heavy company or platoon would then set about their systematic destruction.

The Panzer regiment fought its tank-vs-tank battles in a concentrated *Keil* or wedge. The PzKpfw IIIs and PzKpfw 38(t)s would form the front ranks of the wedge, while the lighter PzKpfw Is and IIs retired to the flanks. The PzKpfw IVs tended to lie back, choosing their targets and sending their low-velocity shells over the vehicles in front. During the early war years, a direct hit from a 75mm shell was a serious matter for all but the most stoutly armoured tanks, and even these could have their tracks blown off or turrets jammed by splinters.

By no means every operation carried out by the Panzer divisions required the full presence of their tank element. Numerous secondary operations could be undertaken by their motor rifle regiments, known after 1942 as Panzergrenadiers, and for these the

PZKPFW IV TURRET

1. Commander's seat
2. Gunner's seat
3. Gunner's elevating and traverse handwheels
4. Gunner's azimuth indicator
5. Gunner's TZF 5b telescopic sight
6. 75mm KwK 37
7. Turret ventilator
8. 7.92mm MG 34 co-axial machine gun
9. Loader's seat
10. Turret basket floor

(Richard Chasemore © Osprey Publishing)

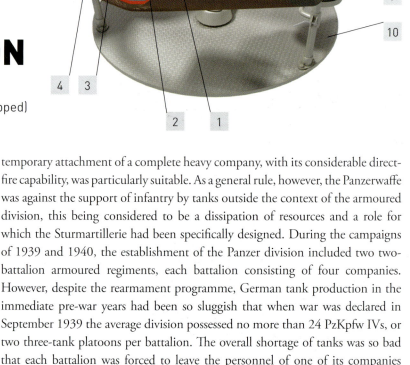

PZKPFW IV AMMUNITION

1. 7.5cm High-Explosive
2. 7.5cm Armour-Piercing (Capped)

temporary attachment of a complete heavy company, with its considerable direct-fire capability, was particularly suitable. As a general rule, however, the Panzerwaffe was against the support of infantry by tanks outside the context of the armoured division, this being considered to be a dissipation of resources and a role for which the Sturmartillerie had been specifically designed. During the campaigns of 1939 and 1940, the establishment of the Panzer division included two two-battalion armoured regiments, each battalion consisting of four companies. However, despite the rearmament programme, German tank production in the immediate pre-war years had been so sluggish that when war was declared in September 1939 the average division possessed no more than 24 PzKpfw IVs, or two three-tank platoons per battalion. The overall shortage of tanks was so bad that each battalion was forced to leave the personnel of one of its companies behind in their depots.

By May 1940 the situation had improved sufficiently for each of the three divisions of Guderian's XIX. Panzer-Korps to have been allocated 36 PzKpfw IVs, or three three-tank platoons per battalion. Other divisions, however, had to be content with the original allocation of 24. Following the startling success achieved in France, Hitler decided to double the number of Panzer divisions. This was achieved by halving the tank element, which was generally reduced to a single regiment of two battalions, although six of the regiments had a three-battalion establishment. In June 1941 Operation *Barbarossa* was mounted with 17 Panzer divisions, equipped with a total of

3,200 tanks, of which 517 were PzKpfw IVs. The average division therefore possessed 30 close-support tanks, or enough to equip three five-tank troops per tank battalion. The ratio of PzKpfw IVs to other tanks had now risen to 1:6, but this still fell a long way short of the original intention of approximately 1:4.

The appearance of the superb T-34 and the thick-skinned KV-1 was directly responsible for the re-equipment and internal reorganization of the Panzer battalions. The few remaining PzKpfw Is and IIs disappeared, and for a while battalions were equipped with a mixture of 5cm L/42 and L/60 PzKpfw IIIs and 7.5cm L/24 PzKpfw IVs. However, as the 7.5cm L/43 and L/48 PzKpfw IV models

This PzKpfw IV is towing a fuel trailer, to reduce its dependency on other logistics troops. Note also the Nazi flag draped on the rear hull; this was not an act of patriotism, but helped identify the tank to German attack aircraft. (AirSeaLand/Cody)

began reaching the front they gradually replaced both types, automatically assuming the role of main battle tank as opposed to close-support vehicle. The concept of the integral heavy company therefore became obsolete, and battalions operated with three similarly equipped companies.

The major problem facing the Panzerwaffe was that tank production remained sluggish, and in consequence there were never enough PzKpfw IVs to go around. The situation was aggravated when in 1942 Hitler ordered a further increase in the number of Panzer divisions, in spite of the fact that the serious equipment losses of the previous year had to be made good. On the Eastern Front the northern and central sectors remained relatively quiet, and Panzer regiments there were reduced to a single battalion: on the active southern sector regimental strength was increased to three battalions, but in practical terms this meant a mere 170 tanks, a sharp contrast to the 320 tanks with which regiments had begun the Polish campaign of 1939.

At this stage it was decided to increase the number of battalion companies to four, the old pre-war figure, but in the majority of cases the equipment was simply not available to implement the directive. Indeed, following the disastrous Stalingrad campaign and the withdrawal from the Caucasus, the average Panzer division on the southern sector possessed about 27 tanks.

With the Panzerwaffe sliding rapidly into a state of administrative chaos, Hitler recalled Guderian to active duty and appointed him Inspector General of Armoured Troops on 1 March 1943. At the same time the energetic Albert Speer was made Minister of Production. One result of these appointments was that the number of completed PzKpfw IVs leaving the factories began to rise sharply. The new main battle tank, the PzKpfw V Panther, also made its first appearance in 1943, but although it was to play an increasingly important part in events, it never replaced the PzKpfw IV.

From the middle of 1943 onwards, Germany was on the defensive, the role of the Panzerwaffe becoming more and more that of the spearhead of the strategic counter-attack. Favoured or more fortunate Panzer regiments might be able to equip one of their battalions with the PzKpfw V and the other with PzKpfw IVs, but this was not the common experience. Indeed, the equipment shortage remained so serious that assault guns were supplied to replace the missing tanks, so that by 1944 most Panzer regiments contained one or two companies so armed, if not a complete battalion. Because of the limited traverse of their weapons the assault guns could not be substituted for tanks in the attack, although they could supply direct fire support, providing a curious reversion to the purpose for which the PzKpfw IV had originally been designed.

During the closing months of the war the Panzer regiments employed any vehicle that they could lay their hands on, provided it could move and shoot. Formal organization disappeared and ad hoc battle groups, based on a few tanks or assault guns, became the order of the day.

WESTERN EUROPE, THE BALKANS AND NORTH AFRICA

Turning the clock back to 1939–40, the Polish campaign confirmed that the architects of the Panzerwaffe had been absolutely right to include a close-support tank within the battalion establishment Although the PzKpfw IVs, stretched painfully thin on the ground, were unable to prevent their comrades' serious losses, it was their presence, aided on occasion by the Luftwaffe, which enabled the Panzer divisions to break the Polish anti-tank gun screens and maintain an advance which might otherwise have stalled. For their subsequent campaign in the West, the Germans fielded a total of 2,439 tanks, of which 278, or slightly more than 10 per cent, were PzKpfw IVs, their useful firepower capabilities rather offset by their limited numbers.

A SdKfz 252 half-track passes a PzKpfw IV Ausf F2 in Tunisia, 1942/43. The PzKpfw IV Ausf F2, later designated as Ausf G, used a ball-shaped muzzle brake on its L/43 main gun. (AirSeaLand/Cody)

The PzKpfw IV found more useful employment in the short but successful campaigns that resulted in the conquest of Greece and Yugoslavia. The Yugoslav Army, riven as it was by racial, religious and political differences, was in no condition to fight a war, let alone one against as experienced and efficient a foe as the German Panzerwaffe, which quickly broke through the cordon of frontier defences and advanced along the principal valleys to carve the country into sections. In this way the major cities were taken by simultaneously converging attacks from different directions, long before the enemy high command could establish a coherent defence. There was little fighting, and on 17 April 1941, only 11 days after the invasion commenced, Yugoslavia surrendered unconditionally. No fewer than 345,000 of its soldiers marched into captivity; German personnel casualties amounted to a mere 558. Greece proved to be a tougher nut to crack, but with 15 of its 21 divisions already engaged with the Italians in Albania, and the left flank of its defence lines fronting Bulgaria wide open to attack from Yugoslavia, an Axis victory was a virtual certainty. In places, however, the Panzer divisions encountered the toughest imaginable opposition, nowhere more so than in the famous Pass of Thermopylae, where 19 tanks of I./Panzer-Regiment 31 (5. Panzer Division) unwisely tried to batter their way through the defile occupied by British troops despatched from Egypt; every one was set ablaze or knocked out. When the campaign ended on 28 April, Greek casualties amounted to 340,000, including 270,000 captured, British to 12,000 plus a great deal of heavy equipment lost, and German to 12,000 plus an acceptable number of tanks. On the one hand, the Balkan campaigns had demonstrated beyond doubt that the Panzerwaffe was a formidable weapon system honed to perfection; on the other, these easy victories had cost irreplaceable time and been won in difficult terrain which imposed mechanical wear and tear on the Panzer division's vehicles Both these factors would produce baleful consequences during the months to come.

In North Africa, the PzKpfw IV with the 7.5cm KwK L/43 was first employed in a major offensive during Operation *Venezia* – Rommel's pre-emptive strike against the British Eighth Army in Libya in late May 1942. Known in the Deutsches Afrika-Korps (DAK) as the 'PzKpfw IV Spezial', only nine of the ten sent to North Africa had arrived by May, and most arrived at front-line units a few days after the start of the offensive. At the same time there were 416 Allied Grant tanks in the Middle East, of which 138 were at the front with the Eighth Army. German Army intelligence had discovered a photograph of the pilot model of the Grant medium tank with the caption 'Pilot', and mistakenly thought that this was its name.

On 11 August 1942, the DAK reported on their tactical experience with the PzKpfw IV with the 7.5cm KwK 40 L/43, along with suggested improvements:

From the first time it was used, the 7.5 cm KwK 40 tank gun with its higher armour-penetrating power and accuracy showed that it was superior to all weapons that had previously been mounted in a Panzer. At ranges up to 1,500

German Panzers knocked out in Tunisia in April 1943. Note how the entire turret ring of one tank lies in the foreground. In such terrain, German tanks would be very exposed to long-range fire from anti-tank guns. (AirSeaLand/Cody)

metres the armour-piercing shell penetrates the front of all of the American and British tank types (including the 'Pilot') that have been used in the African theatre of war. Accuracy decreases at ranges exceeding 1,500 metres because observation of the target is hampered by the shimmering atmosphere. Lighter tank types have been destroyed at ranges up to 2,000 metres when the view was clear.

The opponent quickly recognized the PzKpfw IV Spezial as being especially dangerous. Because of its distinctive form, it drew concentrated fire down on itself from aircraft, artillery and anti-tank guns. It is therefore necessary to screen the PzKpfw IV Spezial with several PzKpfw III. In general, the PzKpfw IV Spezial should join in the firefight only after the appearance of targets that were worthwhile such as the 'Pilot'. Then flank protection is especially important. It therefore appears not to be useful to always employ the PzKpfw IV Spezial as a concentrated group. It should not be employed in reconnaissance troops or for flank defence. It should only be assigned to *Schwerpunkt* [the point of main emphasis] tasks. It is usually incorrect to fire more than a few rounds from one position. The muzzle flash and the especially large dust cloud very quickly draw concentrated fire from the opponent's artillery.

The PzKpfw IV Spezial should not be used as a command vehicle. However, it should be outfitted with both transmitting and receiving radio sets.

As long as the PzKpfw IV Spezial is only available in small numbers, during combat it is necessary to resupply them with ammunition brought to them in armoured vehicles. The divisions are testing the possibility of delivering ammunition by using armoured carriers, armoured half-tracks or other armoured vehicles.

It is difficult to observe fire due to the muzzle flash and dust, especially in the desert.

Up to now, the long gun tube extending far past the front has not been a problem even in terrain cut through with many gullies.

Softer springs are desired for the suspension to reduce the rough impacts when driving in stony terrain.

Strengthen the armour plate on the turret roof and strengthen the superstructure. Install a shot deflector on the turret roof to protect the commander's cupola.

Mount a travel lock on the front of the PzKpfw IV to hold the gun barrel in a depressed position. If possible, this travel lock should be releasable from inside the Panzer so that up to the last moment, the Panzer can be driven with the gun supported by the travel lock. Rearward impacts cause the gun tube to vibrate so strongly that the guide rings inside the armour sleeve are knocked out.

Install ammunition racks on the turret floor in front of and behind the foot rest for the commander.

Install another fume exhaust fan for improved and quicker discharge of burnt propellant fumes. Because of burnt propellant fumes, it is almost impossible to see out of the vision slits. In addition, the biting stench of the burnt propellant severely taxes the crew. For this same reason, it is necessary to quickly throw spent cartridges out of the fighting compartment.

A Canadian soldier in Italy in January 1944 proudly stands atop a Nashorn tank-destroyer, holding the weapon he used to destroy it, the Projector, Infantry, Anti-Tank (PIAT) Mk I. (AirSeaLand/Cody)

Problems with spent propellant fumes in the turret and difficulty observing due to the muzzle flash and dust cloud were not unique to the PzKpfw IV. The same problems occurred with all of the high-velocity guns used by the Germans and Allies in World War II. In fact, these problems were worse with the British 17-pdr and the American 76 mm M1A1; these both lacked smokeless propellant, which made it almost impossible for gunners to observe the tracers.

An additional 37 PzKpfw IV Spezials were sent as replacements to North Africa between July and October 1942, but this number was insignificant compared to the 318 Shermans and 426 Grants and Lees among 2,670 tanks in the Middle East at the start of the British Eighth Army offensive at El Alamein on 23 October. After Panzerarmee Afrika was almost wiped out at El Alamein, British and American forces landed in neutral countries in north-west Africa. Germany responded by sending units to Tunisia, including Panzer-Abteilung 190 with ten PzKpfw IVs in November 1942, Panzer-Regiment 7 in 10. Panzer-Division with 20 PzKpfw IVs (although 12 were sunk in transit) in November and December 1942, and 3. Kompanie/Panzer-Regiment Hermann Göring with eight PzKpfw IVs in 1943.

The East, 1942–45

On the Eastern Front, some units had to wait a very long time before they received an allocation of the new PzKpfw IVs. Panzer-Regiment 35 of 4. Panzer-Division, for example, did not receive theirs until the spring of 1943, the occasion being recalled by Gefreiter Rudolf Meckl of 2. Kompanie:

> Shortly before the attack on Ssewsk the great day arrives for us – general issue of the long-barrelled PzKpfw IVs! The term 'general issue' meant in fact that each company was given six or eight of these vehicles, but in spite of this we feel that this is worthwhile. Near Ssewsk, the Ic of our division monitors the radio traffic on the Russian command frequency. As our 'Hams' move forward a Russian commander is heard calling for help: 'German heavy tanks are advancing towards me!' With these heavies we have long looked forward to challenging the Snow Kings. Sometimes we wish we had a little more armour. Our own tank is fitted with armoured side skirts, and as a matter of fact these give us a rather menacing appearance. Now we have the long gun, it is the start of a 'Happy Time' for us Panzer crews. Even when the company was sometimes reduced to three or four vehicles, this did not bother us unduly.

The German operations of 1942–43, which swung widely between victories and defeats – including the cataclysmic failure at Stalingrad – nevertheless proved that the PzKpfw IV was more than capable of taking on the T-34. The tank's greatest single test, however, would come in and around the Kursk salient. The elimination of that salient,

Hitler decided, would be the major objective of the 1943 summer campaign. His plan called for converging attacks by Army Groups Centre and South against respectively the northern and southern flanks, which, if successful, would trap so many divisions that the Red Army would be decisively weakened. The idea found few supporters among senior German commanders, but Hitler insisted that it be implemented, using the bulk of the Panzerwaffe which Guderian and Speer had so painstakingly rebuilt.

The German preparations did not escape Russian notice. The walls of the salient were fortified to a depth of several kilometres with successive defended zones, each stiff with anti-tank guns and protected by deep mine belts, while most of the Russian armour was held back in the counter-attack role. Save in artillery, in which the Red Army had a superiority of two to one, the two sides were fairly evenly matched, 3,300 Russian tanks being opposed by 2,700 German, the latter including Tigers, Panthers, PzKpfw IVs and PzKpfw IIIs. Since the Tigers were few in number and the Panthers not yet fully cured of their teething troubles, the mainstay of the German effort would be the newer models of PzKpfw IV.

The great offensive, codenamed *Zitadelle* ('Citadel'), began on 5 July. On the northern sector the Germans advanced only 16km; in the south the figure was 40km, bought at a terrible price. The battle reached its climax on 12 July when the 700 tanks of II SS-Panzer-Korps, attempting to break out of the last of the defended zones, were met head-on by the 850 tanks of Fifth Guards Tank Army at the village of Prokhorovka. The Russians were aware that their 76.2mm guns no longer provided a decisive advantage, and had been ordered to close the range. This they did with a vengeance, driving right into the German ranks to engage in a murderous close-quarter melee in

OPPOSITE A late-model PzKpfw IV rumbles past German troops in an anti-tank ditch around Stalingrad in late 1942. In June 1942 an extended radio antenna deflector was fitted on the 7.5cm KwK 40 L/43 PzKpfw IV Ausf G but this was dropped again in July 1942. (AirSeaLand/Cody)

A Soviet soldier cautiously inspects two PzKpfw IV tanks destroyed in fighting in the Bobruysk pocket in late June 1944. Both tanks are fitted with the 5mm Schürzen armour around the rear turret. (AirSeaLand/Cody)

ABOVE A snow-camouflaged PzKpfw IV of the Waffen-SS Wiking Division. In 1942 a single Panzer-Abteilung with a medium tank company was created and assigned as an integral part of the 3., 16., 29. and 60. Infanterie-Divisionen (mot), as well as the Wiking Division. (AirSeaLand/Cody)

RIGHT A PzKpfw IV Ausf J of the Leibstandarte Division on the Eastern Front. The interlocking side and front hull plates were characteristic of the Ausf J, but were introduced with some of the final Ausf H. (AirSeaLand/Cody)

which tanks resorted to ramming each other. In the end Fifth Guards Tank Army drew off, leaving 300 of its tanks behind. The SS-Panzer-Korps lost about the same, but the Germans had shot their bolt: *Zitadelle* was over.

The Red Army went over to the offensive almost immediately, grinding away at the Wehrmacht in a series of massive set-piece attacks which pushed the German line steadily away to the west. In August Kharkov was abandoned; in September Army Group South retired across the Dniepr; on 6 November Kiev was recaptured; and by the New Year most of the Ukraine had been liberated.

In this dramatic image, a PzKpfw IV is literally ripped apart in a massive explosion during fighting on the Eastern Front. Such blasts were typically caused by the sudden detonation of the ammunition supply. (AirSeaLand/Cody)

The pressure never let up. Tied hand and foot by Hitler's 'no withdrawal' directives, Manstein and Army Group South was unable to offer an effective defence to the Red Army's 1944 spring offensive. Many German formations were surrounded in their defences and overwhelmed, although 1st Panzer Army, isolated at Kamenets-Podolsk, was just able to cut its way out. By the end of March, Army Group South was fighting with its back to the Carpathians.

Farther north, Field Marshal Ernst Busch, the commander of Army Group Centre, realized that he was the Red Army's next target. He could oppose 4,000 Russian tanks with only 900 of his own, and had virtually no reserves as almost all his resources were committed to holding the line. His suggestion that a tactical withdrawal would not only save his own troops but also disrupt Soviet plans was received with outrage by the Führer, who insisted that Army Group Centre should fight where it stood. In July it was ripped to pieces, and 40 Russian tank brigades poured onto the Polish plain through the 250-mile gap that had been torn in the line.

The destruction of Army Group Centre isolated Army Group North in the Baltic States. Here the Red Army opened a fresh offensive in the autumn, culminating in the capture of Riga on 15 October, following which the Army Group's survivors remained blockaded on the Courland peninsula for the remainder of the war.

Throughout these operations the Panzer divisions had fought hard to stem the Russian advance, and had inflicted losses which against any other enemy would have been regarded as crippling. During the last months of the war, the Red Army would pay an even higher price for every kilometre of German territory it occupied, but it was not enough: for every T-34 destroyed there were three more on their way to the front. The PzKpfw IV remained in action to the end, outgunned in the final stages by the 122mm gun of the Russian heavy IS series and by the 85mm gun of the T-34/85. It was the only German tank design to have been in continuous service throughout the entire war.

PZKPFW IV AUSF H, 5./PANZER-LEHR-REGIMENT 130, JULY 1944

Crew: 5
Overall length: 7.02m
Width (without skirts): 2.84m
Height: 2.68m
Combat weight: 26 tonnes
Main gun: 7.5cm KwK 40 L/48, 85 rounds
Elevation: -8/+20°
Machine guns: One co-axial MG 34,
    one hull-mounted MG 34
Radio: FuG 5 transceiver

Engine: Maybach HL 120 TRM,
    195kW (265hp)
Fuel capacity: 470 litres
Range: 210km
Top speed: 38km/h
Armour: 50mm gun mantlet, 80mm hull front,
    30mm side, 30mm turret rear

(Richard Chasemore © Osprey Publishing)

2.84m

2.68m

7.02m

North-West Europe 1944–45

Following the Normandy landings on 6 June 1944, the Allied strategy required incessant pressure to be maintained by the British and Canadian armies on their sectors while the Americans prepared to break out of the beachhead to the south. In the Caen area, a series of operations which had all the appearance of an attempted breakout by the British succeeded in tying down the bulk of the German armour, which was forced to fight defensively for most of the campaign.

Because of total Allied air superiority, Panzer crews had to pay greater attention to their camouflage than at any other time of the war, and most movement took place at night. Here, again, the Germans fought at a numerical disadvantage, counterbalanced to some extent by their more powerful armament and the difficulties experienced by their opponents in the bocage country. On occasion the German armour was destroying four Allied tanks for the loss of one of its own, and a major defensive success was achieved in the repulse of Operation *Goodwood*, when the advance of no less than three British armoured divisions was brought up short east of Caen.

On the other hand, most German counter-attacks ended disastrously. The popular perception of World War II tank combat imagines large-scale tank-vs-tank clashes akin to the battles in the open desert of North Africa or the steppes of Russia. However, the vast majority of tank actions in 1944 were more likely to be tanks against troops, buildings, vehicles and other objectives. The Normandy *bocage* presented much more claustrophobic terrain conditions than in other theatres and relatively short fields of fire. As often as not, tank-vs-tank engagements involved very small numbers of tanks, usually fewer than five on either side. The Panzers found it no easier to attack in the *bocage* than did their foes, and they sacrificed the potential of their superior armament by doing so. In the close-quarter fighting among the hedgerows and orchards, they were vulnerable to the infantry's bazookas as well as the fire of anti-tank guns, tank-destroyers and tanks; they were also strafed mercilessly from the air, pounded by massed artillery and subjected to the terrible ordeal of naval gunfire. During the early days of the campaign the PzKpfw IVs, firing hull-down from carefully concealed positions, received a slightly backhanded compliment from the outranged British crews, whose contact reports frequently described the German vehicles as Panthers. In long-range shooting the only Allied vehicles capable of defeating the PzKpfw IV were the 17-pdr Sherman Firefly and the Achilles and M10 tank destroyers.

Very little statistical evidence from wartime operational research was collected regarding tank-vs-tank fighting in Normandy. A German assessment based on the reports of five Panzer and Panzergrenadier divisions indicates that AFVs accounted for about 54 per cent of the kills against Allied tanks, artillery 26 per cent and infantry anti-tank

A wrecked PzKpfw IV lies amidst the ruins of a building in France, 1944. The greatest dangers to armour in Normandy were usually Allied ground-attack aircraft and heavy field artillery. (AirSeaLand/Cody)

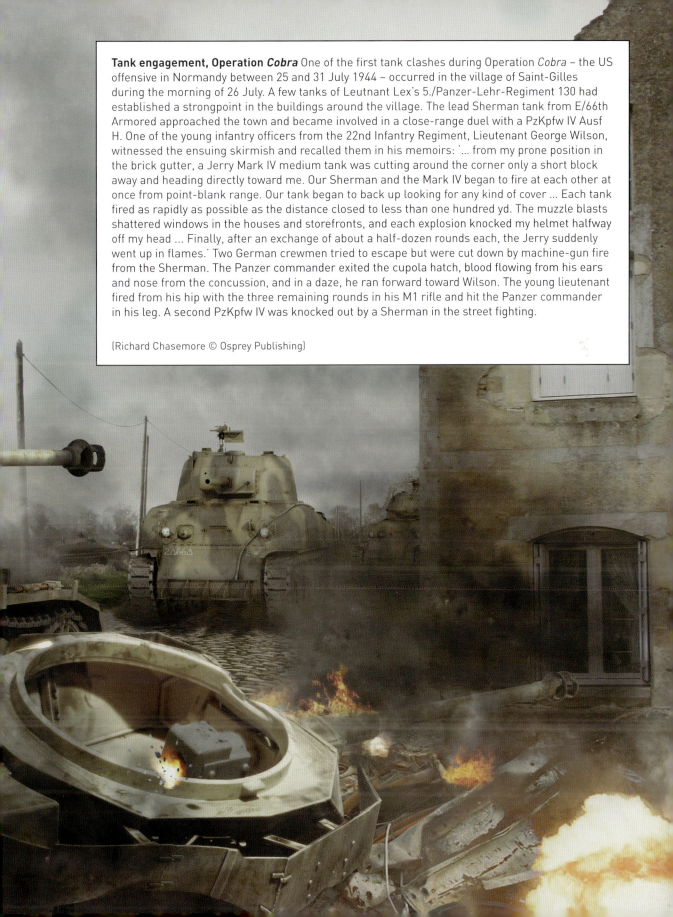

Tank engagement, Operation *Cobra* One of the first tank clashes during Operation *Cobra* – the US offensive in Normandy between 25 and 31 July 1944 – occurred in the village of Saint-Gilles during the morning of 26 July. A few tanks of Leutnant Lex's 5./Panzer-Lehr-Regiment 130 had established a strongpoint in the buildings around the village. The lead Sherman tank from E/66th Armored approached the town and became involved in a close-range duel with a PzKpfw IV Ausf H. One of the young infantry officers from the 22nd Infantry Regiment, Lieutenant George Wilson, witnessed the ensuing skirmish and recalled them in his memoirs: '... from my prone position in the brick gutter, a Jerry Mark IV medium tank was cutting around the corner only a short block away and heading directly toward me. Our Sherman and the Mark IV began to fire at each other at once from point-blank range. Our tank began to back up looking for any kind of cover ... Each tank fired as rapidly as possible as the distance closed to less than one hundred yd. The muzzle blasts shattered windows in the houses and storefronts, and each explosion knocked my helmet halfway off my head ... Finally, after an exchange of about a half-dozen rounds each, the Jerry suddenly went up in flames.' Two German crewmen tried to escape but were cut down by machine-gun fire from the Sherman. The Panzer commander exited the cupola hatch, blood flowing from his ears and nose from the concussion, and in a daze, he ran forward toward Wilson. The young lieutenant fired from his hip with the three remaining rounds in his M1 rifle and hit the Panzer commander in his leg. A second PzKpfw IV was knocked out by a Sherman in the street fighting.

(Richard Chasemore © Osprey Publishing)

weapons 20 per cent. Since infantry divisions were not included in this tally, it is undoubtedly skewed towards AFVs.

German kill claims versus Allied tanks by weapon type, 6 June–3 July 1944

	Number	%
Tanks	227	42.3
Sturmgeschütz and Panzerjäger	61	11.4
Anti-tank and Flak guns	105	19.5
Field artillery	36	6.7
Close-combat weapons	108	20.1
Total	537	100.0

Post-war research of Allied tank casualties in World War II concluded that gunfire was the principal cause of tank losses, amounting to 54 per cent, followed by mines (20 per cent) and accidents/breakdowns (13 per cent each). In the case of the US Army in the European Theatre of Operations (ETO) in 1944, the figures were somewhat different, with gunfire accounting for the greatest proportion of losses (48 per cent) alongside accidents/breakdowns (20 per cent), mines (16 per cent) and anti-tank rockets (12 per cent); the other 4 per cent being attributed to miscellaneous causes. In the Operation *Cobra* sector, there were about 90 German anti-tank guns versus about 155 tanks, including those in the infantry divisions. A rough extrapolation from these figures suggests that US tank losses in Operation *Cobra* might be attributed to German tanks (34 per cent), anti-tank guns (20 per cent), mines (16 per cent) and anti-tank rockets (12 per cent), with the remaining 18 per cent succumbing to other, miscellaneous causes such as accidents, breakdowns and so on.

After World War II, Britain's Army Operational Research Group (AORG) attempted to calculate the technical effectiveness of tanks in tank-vs-tank engagements, using both theoretical parameters and data collected from the 1944–45 campaigns. Effectiveness was defined as 'the reciprocal of the number of tanks required per enemy tank to achieve parity in battle'. A summary of the results is contained in the chart below. The data suggests that the PzKpfw IV Ausf H was about 10 per cent more efficient that the normal 75mm Sherman, and about 10 per cent less efficient in battle than the Sherman 17-pdr Firefly in an engagement at 1,000yd (915m). By the study's definition, this meant that it would take 11 75mm Shermans to reach parity with ten PzKpfw IVs in an engagement at 1,000yd. The study also found that the situation was reversed at a range of 1,500yd (1,375m) where the Sherman would be more effective; this was largely irrelevant in Operation *Cobra*, where engagement ranges were seldom greater than 750m.

Effectiveness of PzKpfw IV Ausf H versus Allied tanks

PzKpfw IV Ausf H	Sherman (75mm)	Sherman (17-pdr)	Cromwell (75mm)
1,000yd (915m)	1.10	0.90	1.35
1,500yd (1,375m)	0.90	n/a	1.5

The AORG analysis suggests that the M4A1 Sherman and PzKpfw IV Ausf H were very close in combat performance. Under such circumstances, performance in a skirmish depended on the quality of the crew and the circumstances of the engagement. In the case of the 66th Armored Regiment versus II./Panzer-Lehr-Regiment 130, crew qualities were similar, with both sides enjoying a high level of training. The German tank crews had an edge in battlefield experience, while the American crews had more prolonged and thorough training.

In view of the similarity of the tactical effectiveness of the two tanks and their crews, the most important factor in deciding the results of the skirmish were the circumstances of the engagement. The 66th Armored Regiment enjoyed significant numerical advantage over II./Panzer-Lehr-Regiment 130, though this seldom translated into a significant numerical edge in the various tank-vs-tank skirmishes.

Operational research about tank-vs-tank fighting in both World War II and the Korean War strongly indicates that the side that spotted the enemy force and engaged first had up to a six-fold advantage. The simplest condensation of the rule of tank fighting is 'see first, engage first, hit first'. Tanks in a stationary defensive position had an obvious advantage against tanks moving to contact, since the stationary tanks were more likely to spot the approaching enemy first. US operational research from tank battles in the Korean War suggests that tanks in well-prepared defensive positions enjoyed a three-to-one advantage against attacking tanks. However, the actual circumstances of individual skirmishes varied widely and did not necessarily correlate to which side was on the defensive at the operational level. For example, in the case of 5./Panzer-Lehr-Regiment 130, most of its tanks were knocked out in direct clashes with tanks of 2/66th Armored while fighting from static defensive positions.

However, the neighbouring 7./Panzer-Lehr-Regiment 130 lost only a few of its tanks in tank-vs-tank confrontations, losing most to misadventures while trying to escape the

Tank crew members of the Hohenstaufen Division pose for a photo op on their PzKpfw IV Ausf J. The Ausf J dropped the auxiliary turret-traverse generator motor in favour of additional fuel stowage. Turret traverse at this point was manual, using a new two-speed hand-crank supplemented with an auxiliary crank in the loader's station. (AirSeaLand/Cody)

1) PzKpfw IV Ausf J, Panzer-Regiment 3, 2. Panzer-Division; France, early 1944. Photographed in Picardy in the early months of 1944, this tank is in a dense, dark-toned camouflage of the standard colours, applied in short, mainly diagonal streaks and blotches.

2) PzKpfw IV Ausf J, Panzer-Regiment 29, 12. Panzer-Division; North Russia, early 1944. This division distinguished itself in the fighting before Leningrad in February 1944. The tank has an overall coat of whitewash snow camouflage over its dark yellow factory scheme; the rough square of dark green left exposed as backing for the divisional sign, at the lower front corner of the turret girdle plate, suggests that it was in multi-colour temperate zone camouflage before being whitewashed. (David E. Smith © Osprey Publishing)

On the Eastern Front in 1943, we here see Panzers of the Das Reich Division. On the right is a PzKpfw IV, replete with Schürzen armour over both the hull and the turret, while on the left is a Tiger I. (AirSeaLand/Cody)

encirclement. Although the US side was on the offensive during Operation *Cobra*, many of the tank kills scored against German AFVs occurred in the night battles when US tanks were in defensive positions while German AFVs were manoeuvring in an attempt to escape encirclement.

The battlefield performances of tanks such as the M4 and PzKpfw IV were shaped less by their technical merits and more by the broad circumstances of the battlefield. Ultimately the Panzer divisions, almost totally lacking in reinforcements and replacement vehicles, were bled white by Hitler's 'no withdrawal' orders, and what remained of them was battered to scrap in the Falaise Cauldron. The PzKpfw IV's last major offensive employment in the West was during the December 1944 Ardennes offensive. Following the failure of this operation, the tank was only encountered again in declining numbers, most of the crumbling German defence relying on small battle groups built around a few assault guns or Panzerjäger.

In this evocative image, a PzKpfw IV grinds its way through deep sand in the North African theatre. When mixed with engine oil, the fine particles of dust and sand produced a grinding paste that wore away mechanical components. (AirSeaLand/Cody)

CHAPTER 4

PANTHER MEDIUM TANK

A PzKpfw V Panther Ausf D. Production of this model began in August 1943 and ended the following September. (AirSeaLand/ Cody)

A PzKpfw V Panther of the Waffen-SS Wiking Division rolls past ground troops. Regardless of a tank's size and combat capability, it always had to operate with infantry support if it were to survive. (AirSeaLand/Cody)

The origins of the Panther tank lay in the shock, already noted in previous chapters, that the German Army experienced during Operation *Barbarossa* – its June 1941 invasion of the Soviet Union. During the first week of combat, the otherwise triumphant German Panzer spearheads experienced fierce encounters with the Soviet T-34/76 medium tank. Although the T-34/76 was in short supply at the front in 1941, it nevertheless outclassed every German tank then in service. With its combination of excellent mobility, mechanical reliability, potent firepower and effective, well-sloped armour protection, the T-34 posed a formidable threat to the success of *Barbarossa*. Several tactical engagements during the campaign demonstrated the superiority of the T-34, particularly the severe blow experienced by the 4. Panzer-Division at Mtsensk, near Orel, on 4 October 1941. This division belonged to Guderian's Panzergruppe 2, which spearheaded the German Heeresgruppe Mitte (Army Group Centre).

In the aftermath of the setback at Mtsensk, Guderian demanded that an inquiry be established into the realities of tank warfare on the Eastern Front. During 18–21 November, senior German tank designers and manufacturers, plus staff officers from the Army Weapons Department, toured Guderian's operational area to study captured T-34 tanks and evaluate the implications that this vehicle posed for future German tank development. Guderian suggested to the inquiry that Germany should simply produce a direct copy of the T-34 tank, as this would be the quickest way of countering the threat that this vehicle posed. The Weapons Department disagreed, however, because Germany would find it difficult to produce steel alloy and diesel engines in sufficient quantities.

DEVELOPMENT

While deliberations on a new tank unfolded, the inquiry recommended that the Army up-gunned its PzKpfw IV tanks and Sturmgeschütz III assault guns. The answer, however, as the inquiry recognized, was to incorporate the best features of the T-34 into a new German medium tank. The inquiry – now known as the Panther Commission – concluded that the T-34's main strengths revolved around three features that to date had been lacking in German tank design. The Soviet tank's main armament overhung the front of the vehicle, which enabled it to have a greater barrel length and thus deliver a higher muzzle velocity to its rounds; consequently, the weapon obtained increased armour penetration capabilities. Second, the suspension on the T-34 featured large road wheels and wide tracks that gave the vehicle excellent off-road mobility and an impressive maximum road speed. Lastly, while the Soviet tank had only modestly thick armour (with 45mm plates), these were well sloped and so gave greater levels of protection than German tanks with vertical armoured plates of similar thickness.

In late November 1941, the Panther Commission contracted the armaments firms of Daimler-Benz and Maschinenfabrik Augsberg-Nuremburg (MAN) to begin development work on a new tank in the 30-tonne class, designated the VK 30.02. Each firm's prototypes were to mount the turret then being developed by Rheinmetall that featured the long-barrelled 7.5cm L/70 gun. On 9 December 1941, the Weapons Department set the specified weight of the VK 30.02 at 32.5 tonnes. During spring 1942, Daimler-Benz completed three slightly different versions of their prototype design, the VK 30.02 (DB). These vehicles had a sloping hull design, forward-mounted turret, overhanging main gun and large square gun mantlet that all bore a strong resemblance to the T-34. In addition, one of these three prototypes had a diesel engine similar to that fitted in the Soviet tank, although here driven through a rear sprocket. However, unlike the T-34, the VK 30.02 (DB) featured the traditional German suspension design based on bogie wheels mounted on external leaf springs that had been used on the previous PzKpfw I–IV tanks.

The VK 30.02 (DB) weighed 35 tonnes, had sloped armour up to 60mm thick and delivered an operational by-road range of 195km. The vehicle's relatively narrow tracks, however, produced an unimpressively high ground pressure figure of 0.83kg/cm². In comparison, the VK 30.02 (MAN)

A PzKpfw V Panther in Germany, the 'clean' nature of the photograph suggesting a training exercise or trial. The Panther design reflected the German industry's penchant for craftsmanship that favoured optimal design over mass production considerations. (AirSeaLand/Cody)

Technical manual illustrations for the PzKpfw V Panther. In the rear view, note the two large stowage bins fitted on both sides of the rear plate, a feature common to all Panthers. (AirSeaLand/Cody)

design represented less of a direct copy of the T-34 and had much in common with earlier German tanks. In terms of the vehicle's overall shape, only its sloped glacis front plate represented design copied from the T-34. The three MAN prototype vehicles in turn used an MB502 diesel engine, or one of two traditional German petrol engines – the 650bhp Maybach HL 210 and 700bhp HL 230 – all with an orthodox drive train that ran under the fighting compartment to the gearbox.

The suspensions on the MAN prototypes, however, owed little to typical German tank design. The vehicles had eight large road wheel bogies that used a sophisticated internal twin torsion bar system instead of the more usual German external leaf spring system. By locating the turret in the centre of the tank, the VK30.02(MAN) design minimized the degree to which the gun barrel overhung the front of the tank. The MAN prototypes weighed the same as the Daimler-Benz vehicles, yet their larger (750-litre) fuel tanks delivered a greater by-road operating range of 270km and their wider tracks a more favourable ground pressure figure of 0.68kg/cm².

After evaluating the designs, Hitler concluded that the Daimler-Benz prototypes were superior, but on 11 May the Weapons Department recommended acceptance of the MAN proposal. This was because the Department feared that friendly-fire incidents would arise because the VK 30.02 (DB) looked too similar to the T-34, and that the long overhang of the main armament might result in vehicles getting their gun jammed into the ground when moving down slopes. Moreover, as the Daimler-Benz chassis possessed a narrower turret ring than the MAN version, this complicated the fitting of the Rheinmetall turret with its 7.5cm gun onto the vehicle.

Consequently, on 15 May 1942, the Army contracted MAN to produce the first pre-production versions of the new tank, now designated the PzKpfw V Panther Ausf A (SdKfz 171), the tank's name deriving from the Panther Commission that had initiated the project back in late 1941. In January 1943, however, the Germans redesignated this first general production vehicle as the Panther Ausf D. The contracts issued in May included several modifications to the vehicle's specifications, most notably a front glacis plate with armour thickened from 60mm to 80mm. But concerns lingered within the High Command that the new Panther tank would be inadequately protected against the weapons likely to appear on the Eastern Front in the foreseeable future. Therefore, on 4 June 1942, Hitler suggested that the frontal armour of the Ausf D be increased to 100mm. Experiments revealed, however, that adding additional bolt-on armoured plates to the existing Panther design (as done previously on the PzKpfw III and IV) would pose enormous technical

Panthers side-by-side at the Aberdeen Proving Ground, United States. The radio operator also manned the bow machine gun, an MG 34 in a ball mount sighted through a KZF 2 cranked sight. (AirSeaLand/Cody)

difficulties. This in turn led the Germans to halt these up-armouring proposals and instead consider the development of a redesigned and up-armoured Panther tank, subsequently designated the Panther II.

During August 1942, MAN produced two prototype Panthers for evaluation, designated Versuchs (Experimental) Panther Vehicles V1 and V2. The V1 was just a chassis without a turret fitted, whereas the V2 was a complete tank. The latter featured an unusual hexagonal turret that mounted the Rheinmetall 7.5cm KwK 42 L/70 gun with a single-baffle muzzle brake – whereas all subsequent Panther tanks featured a double-baffle brake. In addition, the rear left of the vehicle's turret had a distinctive drum-shaped commander's cupola that visibly bulged out beyond the face of the turret's left-hand side plates.

During 8–14 November, the Germans tested the V2 tank at proving grounds near Eisenach in Germany. While these tests showed the design to be sound in general, they nevertheless exposed the many technical problems from which the V2 suffered. Over-hasty design and production work, for example, meant that the V2 vehicle weighed 43 tonnes, well above the target weight limit of 35 tonnes. One reason for this excessive weight was that during the development stage Hitler had insisted that the vehicle's frontal armour be increased from the stipulated 60mm thickness to 80mm. With its 650bhp Maybach engine, the V2 tank delivered a power-to-weight ratio of just 15.1bhp/tonne – 15 per cent lower than the figure for the T-34 tank and 25 per cent lower than that of the original VK 30.02 (MAN). This excessive weight-to-power ratio caused numerous mechanical problems – especially excessive strain on the wheels, engine, gearbox and transmission – that dogged the Ausf D Panther throughout its nine-month production run. The subsequent modifications that the Germans

PANTHER SPECIFICATIONS

Panther Ausf G, II./SS-Panzer-Regiment 1, Kampfgruppe Peiper, La Gleize, Belgium, December 1944

General
Crew: 5 (commander, gunner, loader, driver, radioman)
Combat weight: 44.8 tonnes
Power-to-weight ratio: 15.5hp/T

Dimensions
Overall length: 8.6m
Width: 3.4m
Height: 2.9m

Motive power
Engine: Maybach HL 230 P30 12-cylinder; 700hp at 3,000rpm
Transmission: AK 7-200; seven forward gears, one reverse
Fuel capacity: 720 litres

Performance
Max speed (road): 55km/h
Max speed (cross-country): 30km/h
Range: 70–130km
Fuel consumption: 2.8–7 litres per km (road/crosscountry)
Ground pressure: 0.89kg/cm^2

Armament
Main armament: 7.5cm KwK L/70 with co-axial 7.92mm LMG
Secondary armament: two MG 34 LMG
Main gun ammunition: 82 rounds 7.5cm, 4,200 rounds 7.92mm

Armour
100mm turret mantlet, 45mm turret side, 80mm glacis, 40mm hull side

(Jim Laurier © Osprey Publishing)

3.4m

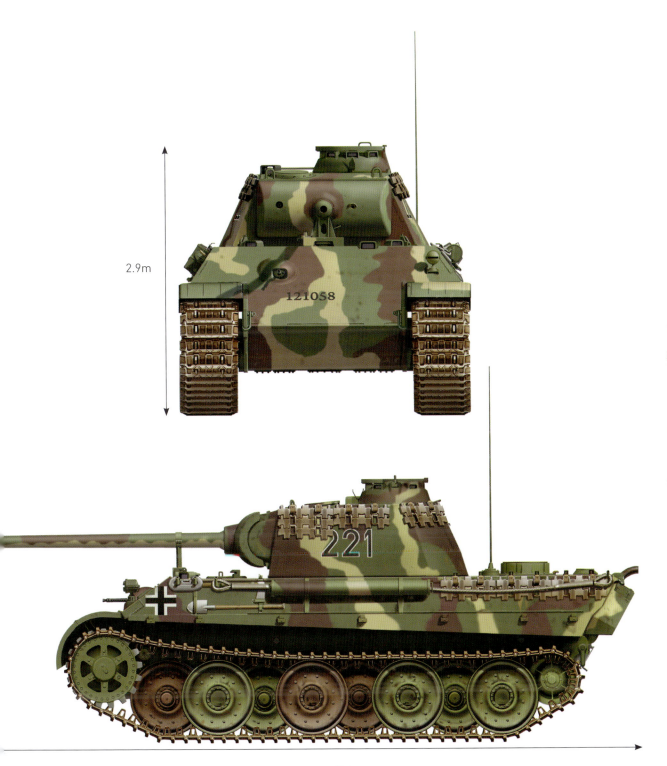

2.9m

121058

221

8.6m

implemented during the Panther Ausf D and Ausf A production runs alleviated these problems, and thus in the Ausf G Panther the Germans arrived at a mechanically more reliable tank. Nevertheless, they never entirely solved these weaknesses prior to the war's end in May 1945, and this unreliability somewhat undermined the tank's obvious benefits – notably the combination of a potent 7.5cm gun and well-sloped armour.

During late 1942, however, the Germans were desperate to get their new Panther tank into combat on the Eastern Front. Consequently, despite the many flaws exposed during the Eisenach trials, the Army rushed the V2 design straight into general production as the Ausf D Panther. With the benefit of hindsight, it is clear that the Germans ought to have ironed out these design problems through a series of modified pre-production vehicles before rushing prematurely into general production. As it was, although significant numbers of completed Ausf D Panthers reached the Army during spring 1943, it remained far from clear that these vehicles were ready for use in combat.

PANTHER AUSF D

During late November 1942, the Germans embarked on general production of the V2 design, now designated the Panther Ausf D. Indeed, as far back as July 1942, the High Command had set a target figure of 250 Panthers to be delivered by 12 May 1943. Consequently, between November 1942 and January 1943, MAN produced the first four production Ausf D tanks. During 24–26 January 1943, three of these vehicles arrived at the Grafenwöhr testing grounds, with the fourth going to Kummersdorf.

The Ausf D production version featured a redesigned turret that lacked the hexagonal shape of the V2 turret, and which incorporated the commander's cupola positioned flush with the surface of the turret's left-hand side. In addition, the Ausf D mounted a modified 7.5cm KwK 42 L/70 gun that sported a double-baffle muzzle brake. In terms of secondary armament, the tank had one 7.92mm MG 34 machine gun co-axially in the right of the turret mantlet, plus a hull machine gun that fired through a letterbox mount in the sloping hull glacis plate. The vehicle carried 79 rounds for the main gun and 4,200 rounds for its machine guns. Finally, the tank mounted a set of three smoke-grenade launchers on the front of each turret side for close-range defence.

The Ausf D Panther had armour similar to the V2, except that the frontal glacis plate was 80mm thick and sloped at 55°, while the hull side plates were 40mm thick and set at 40°. The tank mounted the 650bhp Maybach HL 210 P30 engine and the seven-speed AK 7-200 transmission used in the V2. Thanks to the additional armour protection, the Ausf D weighed 44.8 tonnes, slightly heavier than the already overweight V2 prototype. Nevertheless, the vehicle's torsion bar suspension, which was based on eight pairs of interleaved rubber-tyred road wheels, still delivered an acceptable ground pressure figure of 0.735kg/cm². The tank's by-road fuel consumption was

2.8 litres per kilometre which, given its 720-litre fuel tanks, enabled it to achieve a maximum operational range of 250km by road, yet just 100km off-road.

In terms of communications equipment, the Ausf D mounted the standard German tank device, the Fu 5. This consisted of a 10-watt transmitter with ultra-short wavelength receiver, operating in the frequency band 27.2–33.4MHz, that used a 2m rod antenna fitted onto the vehicle's rear hull decking.

These first four Panthers underwent extensive tests at Grafenwöhr and Kummersdorf during late January and early February 1943, to be joined by further vehicles over the next few weeks. However, these tests – carried out by the crews of two new armoured units, the Panzer-Abteilungen 51 and 52 – revealed numerous minor design faults, as well as shoddy standards of manufacture. The gun, for example, could not be elevated or depressed to the specified degrees, while the corners of the turret often struck the closed driver's and radio operator's hatches on the hull roof. Furthermore, the vehicle's final drive chains tended to break, its transmission frequently broke down, its motors often caught fire and its fuel pumps regularly failed. The unseemly haste to rush the vehicle into general production had resulted, inevitably, in myriad teething problems.

During February 1943, despite these problems, MAN delivered a further 11 completed Panthers to the proving grounds, while Daimler-Benz completed its first six Panthers and MNH one further vehicle. By 28 February 1943, therefore, the Germans had delivered 22 Ausf D tanks to the two new Panther battalions. Thereafter, newly produced Panthers featured a fixed radius steering gear instead of the clutch-brake

Soviet soldiers clamber over an abandoned PzKpfw V Panther Ausf D on the Eastern Front. On average, only a quarter of the Panther Ausf D tanks deployed in the Panzer regiments in 1943 were operational at any given time. (AirSeaLand/Cody)

steering gear fitted in the first 22 Panthers. During March, Daimler-Benz, MAN and MNH delivered 58 Ausf D Panthers to the Army, while Henschel completed its first ten tanks, so that by the end of the month the Germans had 90 such tanks on strength. But as yet the Germans had not passed a single Ausf D tank as combat-ready since the early trials had identified 45 modifications that needed to be made before the tank could be used in battle.

At this time, the High Command believed that the Panther would make a decisive contribution to the strategic victory that the planned German summer 1943 offensive in the East was expected to achieve. During early April, however, the Army concluded that before this could happen it had to rebuild its completed Panthers to rectify the faults identified during the early field trials. The Germans, however, remained anxious that the modification work should not slow down the rate of completion of the part-assembled Panther tanks already on the production lines. Consequently, the four firms then producing Panthers did not take back the 90 vehicles already completed for modification work, but instead continued manufacturing Ausf D vehicles according to the original design, despite its known faults. Only after 160 incomplete tanks had been finished would the Germans send them to the DEMAG factory at Falkensee for post-production modification work. In the interim, the 90 tanks already delivered would remain with the Panzer-Abteilungen 51 and 52 for training purposes and would only be dispatched to Falkensee for modification once the subsequent 160 completed Panthers had been rebuilt at DEMAG. The rebuilding work undertaken by the latter firm during April and May included major modifications to the engine compartment and adjustment to the steering gears, suspension, final drives and transmission.

Although the German firms completed these remaining 160 Panthers essentially to the original design, they did at least make one modification to them. From April 1943 the factories outfitted new vehicles with thin Schürzen armoured side skirts to protect the relatively vulnerable tracks and hull sides from Soviet anti-tank rifles. By early May, frenzied German production had delivered the first batch of 250 Ausf D tanks to the proving grounds. In all subsequent construction, from vehicle 251 onwards, the assembly plants outfitted new Panthers with the 700bhp Maybach HL 230 P30 engine instead of the original HL 210. While this added power did not increase the overall speed of the Ausf D Panther, it did improve acceleration and cross-country performance; above all, it eased the excessive strain frequently imposed on HL 210-equipped tanks and thus went some way to improving the mechanical reliability of the tank.

Despite the extensive DEMAG rebuild programme, further field trials undertaken during May with the first 250 Panthers continued to reveal serious problems. Consequently, from June new HL 230-engined tanks underwent further modification, while existing vehicles were modified at Grafenwöhr. One of these alterations involved strengthening the tank's over-strained road wheels by fitting additional rivets between the existing 16 rim bolts. In addition, these vehicles underwent further alterations to their transmissions. Meanwhile, back at the factories, some of the new HL 230-engined

Here, in the mountains of Italy, a Panther turret has been independently mounted on a pillbox to form an improvised strongpoint. Such fittings became common during the last two years of the war. (AirSeaLand/Cody)

tanks completed during this month emerged without the characteristic set of three smoke-grenade launchers on each side of the turret, although Henschel-manufactured tanks still had them into June. The factories discontinued this feature because field trials had shown that surprise attacks by enemy small-arms fire often inadvertently triggered the smoke grenades when the vehicle still had its hatches open, and the smoke soon incapacitated the crew.

By 31 May, the Army had received 250 HL 210-engined and 118 HL 230-engined Ausf D tanks. However, many Panthers remained non-operational either because of the faults identified above or because they were being rebuilt and thus could not be deployed at the front for the imminent German summer offensive. Indeed, it was not until further modification work had been completed in late June that the Germans managed to redeploy 200 Panthers to the Soviet Union for their now much-delayed *Zitadelle* offensive.

ZITADELLE DEBUT

The Panther made its operational debut on 5 July 1943 during *Zitadelle*, in which the High Command expected the 200 Panthers to contribute decisively to the stunning victory it expected to secure. The Panther units employed in the operation – the Panzer-Abteilungen 51 and 52 – each fielded four companies of 22 Panthers, plus a further eight Ausf D tanks, to make a total unit strength 96 Panthers each. The two battalions came under the control of Major Meinrad von Lauchert's improvised brigade staff, itself equipped with eight Panthers, which fought alongside the Panzergrenadier Division Großdeutschland as part of the southern prong of the attack.

PzKpfw V Panthers make a halt during operations. Note the very smooth sloped front hull of the tank, with no significant 'shot traps' for enemy anti-tank shells. (AirSeaLand/Cody)

Major problems, however, dogged the contribution made by the Panthers even before the offensive began. Because the two Panther-equipped tank battalions were deployed in the East just a few days before *Zitadelle* commenced, the units had little time for acclimatization training in situ. Moreover, 16 tanks broke down on the short journey between disembarking from their transportation trains and reaching the front. Things went little better once the offensive began. In the face of fanatical Soviet resistance, large numbers of Panthers fell by the wayside. By 7 July, the third day of the offensive, just 40 of the 184 Panthers that started *Zitadelle* were still operational, while by 10 July only 10 of them remained in front-line service. Of the remaining 174 Panthers that had started the operation, 23 had been lost due to 'brewing up' after enemy hits on their relatively vulnerable side armour, while two had burned after engine fires before combat had even been joined. Another 44 Panthers were being repaired after mechanical failure and a further 56 because of damage caused by enemy fire or anti-tank mines. German workshops had already repaired a further 40 Panthers with minor damage or mechanical problems, but these were still on the way to rejoin the brigade. The remaining nine tanks, which had been abandoned on the battlefield after sustaining damage, had still to be recovered.

The much-vaunted debut of the Panther had proven to be a debacle. Admittedly the Germans could discern a few glimmers of hope from this serious setback. Post-combat reports from the fighting experienced at Kursk confirmed the anticipated combat power of the 7.5cm Panther gun; this weapon had accounted for many T-34 tanks, often at ranges of 1,500m or more. In addition, the Panther's two machine guns

Das Reich Division Panthers push forward in a line on the Eastern Front during fighting around the Kursk salient in 1944. These tanks do not have the optional machine gun fitted to the commander's cupola. (AirSeaLand/Cody)

had proven to be very reliable, with a very low incidence of jamming. However, most of the other aspects of the Panther mentioned in post-combat reports proved unfavourable. Troops observed, for example, that the Panther's turret grenade launchers soon became inoperative due to enemy small-arms fire, that its engine regularly broke down, that its over-stressed transmission often failed and that its road wheels sometimes fractured. In addition, crews complained about fuel pump leaks that often led to dangerous fires starting inside the tank, the dangerous build-up of gun exhaust gases inside the turret and the problems caused when driving rain entered the turret through the mantlet binocular periscope. Further modifications were needed, the Germans concluded, before the Panther realized the potential it clearly possessed to be a potent tank on the future battlefield.

Meanwhile, back in Germany, even as *Zitadelle* unfolded, the factories introduced further production simplifications designed to raise production rates. The new Ausf D Panthers that rolled off the production lines that month no longer had the circular communications hatch fitted to the left-hand side of the turret and had only one headlamp (on the left) instead of two. From late July, in response to the lessons gathered at Kursk, some newly completed Ausf D tanks featured more resilient road wheels fitted with 24 rim bolts instead of 16. In addition, these vehicles sported an extra ring mounted on the commander's cupola onto which an anti-aircraft machine gun could be fitted.

Yet at this time Panther production still remained hurried and poorly organized; consequently, some of the 115 Panthers produced during August did not incorporate these modifications because of over-hasty production or shortages of parts at the

A LATE AUSF D PANTHER OF 13. PANZER-DIVISION

In three-tone camouflage; Eastern Front, Autumn 1943.

Six features distinguish this vehicle as a late Ausf D. First, the tank has only one headlamp, on the left. Second, it lacks the circular communications hatch fitted to the left-hand side of turret. Third, its road wheels have 24 rim bolts instead of 16. Fourth, it has an additional ring mounted on the commander's cupola onto which an anti-aircraft machine gun could be fitted. Fifth, the vehicle has a wide rain guard mounted over the TZF 12 binocular gun sight on the turret mantlet to keep out driving rain. Finally, the tank has improved tracks with chevron cleats for enhanced traction in the muddy conditions prevalent on the Eastern Front during autumn. It is interesting to note first that the tank lacks Schürzen side skirts, and second, given the absence of a rippled finish to the vehicle's exterior, that the tank had not been coated with Zimmerit anti-magnetic mine paste, which during this period was increasingly being applied in the field.

(Jim Laurier © Osprey Publishing)

factories. Most of the 115 new Ausf D Panthers delivered in August – some 96 vehicles – arrived in the East at the end of the month to completely re-equip the Panzer-Abteilung 51, which in the aftermath of *Zitadelle* had given up its few remaining tanks to reinforce the remnants of the Panzer-Abteilung 52. Between them these battalions had suffered 58 Panthers lost by the end of *Zitadelle*, excluding another 50 in short-term repair.

Yet far worse was to transpire. In the desperate defensive battles the Germans fought to resist the Soviet counter-offensives that erupted over the following six weeks, these battalions lost a further 98 Panthers; consequently, fewer than 44 of the original Ausf D tanks dispatched to Kursk remained operational by early September.

During September 1943, the lessons learned from the disappointing debut of the Panther at Kursk led to further modifications to the last Ausf D tanks of the original 850-unit production run. Many of the last 37 Ausf D Panthers produced in September, for example, featured Zimmerit anti-magnetic mine paste, a substance that hindered Soviet infantry from placing magnetic hollow-charge devices onto the tanks' surfaces. In addition, the late Ausf D tanks had two new features – a rain guard mounted over

the gun sight on the turret mantlet to keep out driving rain, and improved tracks that sported chevron cleats for enhanced traction.

As these last Ausf D tanks emerged, the Panther production firms completed their development work on a successor vehicle, the Ausf A Panther, which was a slightly modified Ausf D chassis with an improved turret design. By September the first Ausf A tanks were going into service alongside the 600 or so remaining Ausf D tanks.

RIGHT In Belgium in 1944, a PzKpfw V Panther lies overturned in a river below a bridge. Bridge crossings were dangerous moments for heavy tanks like the Panther, and required precision driving. (AirSeaLand/Cody)

BELOW A unit of PzKpfw V Panthers is transported by rail up to the front line just prior to the launch of the German Ardennes offensive in late 1944. (AirSeaLand/Cody)

Although production of the Ausf D stopped in September 1943 after the 850th vehicle had been completed as per the contract, these tanks continued to serve at the front – alongside their successor Ausf A and G tanks – right up until the end of the war. Obviously, the number of Ausf D Panthers in service continually declined as losses ate into the numbers remaining, and so by 1945 only a handful of Ausf D Panthers remained. During autumn 1943, three new Panther units that fielded significant numbers of Ausf D tanks served in the East, including the II./SS-Panzer-Regiment 2 of the Das Reich Division. During September 1943, SS-NCO Ernst Barkmann joined the 4. Kompanie, II./SS-Panzer-Regiment 2. The Das Reich Division had recently been re-equipped with Panther Ausf D tanks, and in bitter defensive battles fought around the Ukraine that autumn, Barkmann's Ausf D tank performed sterling service before eventually being knocked out.

Subsequently, in early 1944, the SS Das Reich Division redeployed to Bordeaux in southern France for refitting with new Ausf A and G Panthers after incurring heavy losses during recent bitter battles in the East. During this process, Barkmann – now commander of the 4. Kompanie – received a new Ausf A command tank, vehicle number 424.

The discussion so far has centred on standard Ausf D combat tanks, but it should be noted that throughout the nine months of the Ausf D Panther production run, German firms made about 10 per cent of them into command tanks, or Befchls Panthers. These vehicles mainly served as commander's and adjutant's vehicles at company, battalion and even regimental levels. The Command Panther was simply a slightly modified standard Panther with ammunition stowage reduced from 79 to 64 rounds to make space for the powerful communications equipment and associated systems they carried. MAN alone completed 63 of these vehicles between January and August 1943.

COMMAND PANTHERS

Ausf D, A and G Command Panthers came in two similar but distinct forms, although both versions shared many common features, such as an additional generator set, the absence of the co-axial turret machine gun and the addition of three tubes fitted onto the hull sides in which spare antennae rods were housed. The standard SdKfz 267 Command Panther, irrespective of whether it was an Ausf D, A or G, featured the standard battle tank communications device, the Fu 5 10-watt transmitter and ultra-short wavelength receiver. Unlike on the combat tank, however, this device here worked through a 2m-long rod antenna usually mounted on the right turret rear, adjacent to the commander's cupola, in addition to the standard rod antennae mounted on the left hull decking behind the turret. In normal tactical conditions, operators could expect to obtain a range of 8km with this device.

In addition, the SdKfz 267 tank also mounted the powerful Fu 8 long-range device. This 30-watt transmitter and medium wavelength receiver operated on the frequency band 0.83–3.0MHz, and worked through a distinctive 1.4m star antenna normally mounted on the hull roof at the rear of the vehicle. The Fu 8 could communicate up to a maximum range of 65km, sufficient to secure effective communications with regimental and divisional staffs in almost every conceivable tactical situation. In total, throughout the war, the Germans delivered 350 SdKfz 267 Command Panthers, including roughly 75 Ausf D and 200 Ausf A versions. It should be also remembered that front-line troops could convert standard Panthers to command versions in the field with a dedicated conversion kit if their command vehicles had been destroyed and no replacement was forthcoming.

The SdKfz 267 Command Panther proved highly effective; by retaining the standard Panther gun and armour, it could engage the enemy directly while simultaneously controlling the actions of the unit it commanded. Moreover, by looking like the standard Panther tank its battlefield survivability improved, as striving to knock out enemy command tanks had always been a preferred tactic of armoured warfare.

The much less common SdKfz 268 'Flivo' Befehls Panther command variant was a dedicated air-ground liaison vehicle used for arranging tactical air support for Panther units. Rather than using the Fu 8, this vehicle mounted the Fu 7 device in addition to the standard Fu 5. The Fu 7 was a 20-watt transmitter and ultrashort wavelength receiver that operated on the frequency band 42.1–47.8MHz through a 1.4m rod antenna normally mounted on the rear hull roof. In theory, the two (or possibly three) rod antennae of the SdKfz 268 easily distinguished this vehicle from standard Panther combat tanks (with only one rod antenna) and the SdKfz 267 Command Panther with one star and either one or two rod antennae. However, pictorial evidence reveals that the SdKfz 267 and 268 command vehicles often featured non-standard positioning of their aerials, making definite identification problematic. The 'Flivo' Command Panther remained a very rare vehicle, with only 40 being completed by the end of the war.

The Bergepanther was an armoured recovery vehicle, built upon the Panther chassis. Note here how the rear spade is braced in the earth for stability during a winching operation. (AirSeaLand/Cody)

Indeed, given the increasingly adverse strategic situation under which the Luftwaffe laboured during 1944–45, it remains unclear whether many such vehicles actually fulfilled their intended air-ground liaison role, as German tactical air support by this time was extremely limited at best. Moreover, as both the Command Panther variants carried two mounting devices onto which the Fu 7 or Fu 8 could each be fitted, it seems highly likely that the Germans refitted some SdKfz 268 'Flivo' vehicles as much-needed standard command tanks by simply replacing the Fu 7 device with the Fu 8 set.

PANTHER II

During the summer of 1942, even as MAN began manufacturing its two Versuchs Panther pre-production tanks, the High Command had already grown concerned that the level of protection the new tank possessed might prove insufficient for the combat conditions likely to emerge on the Eastern Front in the immediate future. The initial German response was to investigate the feasibility of adding 20mm-thick bolt-on armoured plates to strengthen the vehicle's protection, as had been done previously with the Panzer III and IV tanks. However, as previously noted, MAN soon discovered that such work presented extraordinary technical problems that effectively precluded up-armouring the existing Ausf D design in this manner.

This setback forced the Germans in December 1942 to begin thinking of a new Panther version – the 47-tonne Panther II – that had thicker homogenous armoured plates. The Panther II was to have 100–150mm-thick turret and hull frontal armour instead of the 80–100mm thickness on the Ausf D. In addition, its side armour was to have 60mm-thick plates in place of the 40mm plates carried by the Ausf D.

Controversy still exists today as to the precise details of the Panther II project, in part because there remains ambiguity in the extant German documentation. Tom Jentz has argued that in December 1942 the Panther II design remained identical to that of the Ausf D except for the thickness of the armour. Walther Spielberger, in contrast, believes that from its very inception the Germans intended the Panther II to

PzKpfw V Panthers on the Eastern Front, carrying infantry with them. Improvements in production began to have an effect on the availability rate of the tanks deployed on the Eastern Front, going from 37 per cent in February to 50 per cent in April and 78 per cent by the end of May 1944. (AirSeaLand/Cody)

Mighty-looking PzKpfw V Panthers of the Waffen-SS Das Reich Division take a break behind the front in June 1944. It was always recommended that tanks park under the cover of trees and buildings, to shield themselves from air observation or attack. (AirSeaLand/Cody)

incorporate significant features that would distinguish it markedly from the Ausf D. Jentz argues that it was only during mid-February 1943 that the Germans altered the initial Panther II design to make it more than just an up-armoured Ausf D. For now, the High Command decided that the new tank would incorporate many features of the PzKfw VI Ausf B King Tiger heavy tank then being designed by Henschel, as well as have a completely new turret design. Spielberger, however, believes that commonality with the King Tiger was a key inspiration behind the Panther II design from its inception in late 1942.

Irrespective of these debates, both scholars agree that by spring 1943 the Panther II design incorporated features of the King Tiger, including the 700bhp Maybach HL 230 engine and resilient steel-tyred, rubber-cushioned, large road wheels. While the King Tiger would mount nine pairs of these road wheels, the Panther II would have seven pairs of identical wheels. The original Panther, in contrast, had eight pairs of non-steel-tyred road wheels. Even the 60cm-thick tracks of the Panther II would act as the narrow (transportation) tracks for the King Tiger. Incorporation of these features raised the weight of the Panther II to 51 tonnes.

During February 1943, the High Command contracted DEMAG to commence development work on the Panther II, with 18 then slated to enter service in September 1943, and simultaneously informed the existing Panther manufacturing firms that they would continue producing standard Panther tanks only until late 1944, and then switch over to construction of the Panther II. The health of the Panther II project, however, declined significantly during summer 1943, and in June plans to develop the tank were temporarily halted in favour of continuation of the Ausf D and Ausf A production runs. One explanation for this was that the Germans had discovered that by adding Schürzen side skirts to the Ausf D, the risk posed to the vehicle's 40mm hull side armour was significantly reduced; this development undermined a major justification for developing the Panther II. Consequently, during July 1943, the High Command contracted MAN to produce just two prototype Panther II vehicles.

With the impetus for the Panther II project dwindling, and given the many other pressing production demands MAN then faced, development work on the two prototype Panther II tanks languished. Indeed, by the end of the war, MAN had only completed one Versuchs Panther II chassis, but without a turret. The American Army captured this vehicle in the last weeks of the war, fitted it with a recently completed Panther Ausf G turret and shipped it off to America, where it remains today on public display. The turret the Germans earmarked for the Panther II never got beyond the design stage, and today controversy still exists over the precise form it would have taken. Initially the Germans planned to mount in the Panther II the same 7.5cm KwK 42 L/70 gun mounted on the standard Panther tank. Spielberger argues that the Germans intended to mount this gun in the Narrow Turret (*Schmalturm*) then being developed for the new Ausf F Panther tank. Jentz, however, argues that the Germans intended to mount a slightly different turret in the Panther II – the Narrow Gun Mantlet Turret. Whatever their precise designs, both turrets sought to reduce the size of the turret front and mantlet to help increase vehicle survivability.

To further complicate the matter, during February 1945 the Germans began work to rearm a modified version of the Narrow Turret with the 8.8cm KwK 43 L/71 gun of the King Tiger. From this Spielberger contends that if the Germans intended to mount the Narrow Turret in the Panther II, it follows that from spring 1945 they planned that the Panther II would mount the 8.8cm-gunned Narrow Turret and not its original 7.5cm-gunned version. Other plans that the Germans developed later in 1945, however, suggest that they simply intended to mount the 8.8cm-equipped Narrow Turret on any available Ausf G Panther chassis, to form (in effect) an up-gunned version of the Ausf F Panther.

Clearly, in the chaos that increasingly engulfed the Reich in the last months of the war, the Germans unveiled all sorts of often contradictory plans concerning future tank development. Given that German firms never completed a single Panther II tank, it seems unlikely that these controversies over what turret and main gun the vehicle would have mounted will ever be definitely solved.

PANTHER AUSF A

The second basic Panther design – the Ausf A – simply comprised the Ausf D chassis fitted with a redesigned turret. As far back as 18 February 1943, the High Command had decided that once the initial contract of 850 Ausf D tanks had been completed, subsequent Panthers would have an improved turret design. Although externally the Panther Ausf D and A turrets looked similar, several features distinguished them: most notably, the latter featured a new, up-armoured, hemispherical cast commander's cupola as opposed to the drum-shaped cupola of the Ausf D. The redesigned cupola had seven periscopes protected by armoured cowlings that improved the commander's field of vision, as well as an integral ring for affixing an anti-aircraft machine gun. Another externally visible difference between the two turrets was that on the Ausf A turret a squared-off joint fitted the turret front plate to the side plates, whereas on the Ausf D this joint was dove-tailed.

Two heavily camouflaged PzKpfw V Panthers at Kursk in June/July 1943. German Panzers were often sited in dug-in positions, acting virtually as static anti-tank gun emplacements. (AirSeaLand/Cody)

In addition to external differences, the Ausf A turret had a redesigned interior that featured a new variable-speed hydraulic turret traversing system instead of the single-speed one fitted in the Ausf D. This mechanism produced a turret rotation time of between 15 and 93 seconds, depending on the speed of the engine and the traverse speed ratio selected. In addition, the redesigned turret also had a new bore evacuator that cleared powder gases out of the gun more efficiently than its predecessor.

MNH delivered the first three Ausf A Panthers in August 1943, and during the following month Daimler-Benz and MAN commenced manufacture of this design after terminating Ausf D production at the 850th vehicle. Then in September, DEMAG replaced Henschel as the fourth firm involved in Panther production. Between them, these firms produced 149 Ausf A tanks during September 1943, and subsequently, during the period from December 1943 to March 1944, their deliveries averaged 270 tanks per month. In total, these four firms produced 2,200 Ausf A tanks in a year-long production run that ended in July 1944, when the last 11 Ausf A vehicles were completed. MNH produced the most vehicles, 830, with Daimler-Benz and MAN constructing 675 and 645 respectively; DEMAG, however, delivered just 50 Ausf A Panthers.

Troops of the 6. Panzerarmee march past a PzKpfw V Panther in the Ardennes in December 1944. The clearing of the weather in the later part of the Ardennes campaign meant that German tanks increasingly became prey to Allied fighter-bombers. (AirSeaLand/Cody)

VIEW OF WHITEWASHED EARLY PANTHER AUSF A; EASTERN FRONT, WINTER 1943–44

This plate depicts an early Ausf A Panther deployed on the Eastern Front during winter 1943–44. The Ausf A tank was essentially an Ausf D chassis mounted with a new turret. The most obvious new feature, in comparison with the Ausf D, is the new cast commander's cupola on the left rear of the turret. This cupola has an entirely new hemispherical shape and has seven armoured periscopes to enhance the commander's field of vision. A more subtle distinction between this Ausf A and its predecessor can be seen where the side turret plate interlocks with the turret front plate just behind the mantlet; on this tank, this joint is square-cut, whereas in Ausf D tanks the joint was dovetailed.

(Jim Laurier © Osprey Publishing)

Adding possibly another 1.5 tonnes to the tank's weight, soldiers of the SS-Panzer-Division Hitlerjugend cluster thickly around the hull and turret of a PzKpfw V Panther. Naturally, infantry catching a ride had to be aware that if the tank was suddenly engaged they needed to leap off before the turret began turning in response. (AirSeaLand/Cody)

A PzKpfw V Panther moves through a devastated French town in Normandy in 1944. The distinctive silhouette of the Panther, evident here, would attract a lot of Allied firepower. (AirSeaLand/Cody)

The factories delivered about 200 of the tanks as Ausf A Command Panthers with the same communication devices as fitted on the Ausf D Command variants. Finally, between October 1943 and February 1944, the Germans dispatched 300 new Ausf A tanks to the Königsborn factory for engine rebuilds after reports continued to arrive from the front line indicating a high incidence of mechanical failures. The modification work necessitated by these continuing problems meant that during winter 1943–44 the Army's receipt of combat-ready Ausf A tanks fell behind schedule, even though the number of vehicles rolling off the assembly lines was on target.

As with its predecessor, the Ausf A tank underwent a series of modifications during its year-long production run, the main ones of which are discussed in chronological sequence below. Many of these modifications were intended to simplify and therefore speed up the production process, while others represented responses to post-combat reports received from front-line units. First, from September 1943 onwards new Ausf A tanks increasingly emerged from the factories with their road wheels strengthened with 24 rim bolts instead of the 16-bolt wheels usually seen on the Ausf D. Simultaneously, factories began to coat newly completed tanks with Zimmerit anti-magnetic mine paste. Workers applied this thick, cement-like paste, which prevented the enemy fixing magnetic charges to the tank, in a rippled fashion that left a distinctive appearance on vehicles. That same month the assembly plants also incorporated modifications to the Maybach HL 230 engine after troops continued to report problems with blown head gaskets and faulty bearings. From January 1944, in an effort to address these continuing mechanical problems, new Panthers featured further modified engines that incorporated an eighth crank shaft. From December 1943, new Ausf A tanks also began to appear with an externally obvious modification – the machine gun port in the glacis plate was replaced with a Kugelblende 50 ball-mounted weapon that enjoyed a greater field of fire. This mount included a *Kugelzielfernrohr* (KZF) 2 sight for the radio operator, which meant that the operator's periscope sight on the hull roof could be dispensed with. The vehicles also had their binocular TZF 12 telescopic gun sight in the turret mantlet replaced with the monocular TZF 12a sight. From that same month, new Panthers also appeared with hull roof armoured plates that had straight sides instead of ones that interlocked with the hull side plates. Not all of the subcomponent pre-assembly firms adopted this modification, however, so the final assembly firms continued to deliver tanks with interlocked plates, alongside ones with straight plates, right up to the end of the war.

During December 1943, some new Panthers appeared with the pistol ports in the turret sides removed because they were to be replaced with a *Nahverteidigungswaffe* (close defence weapon) mounted on the right rear of the turret roof. Because of production delays, the close defence weapon – which fired grenades, smoke charges and flares – only appeared on Ausf A Panthers in March 1944, and so for three months newly produced Panthers lacked any close defence capability. Then from January 1944, new Ausf A Panthers appeared with two cooling pipes added to the left exhaust pipe to help air flow to cool the engine. During June–July 1944, the last eight weeks of Ausf A production, new Panthers emerged with three sockets fitted onto the turret roof. These allowed troops to mount a 2-tonne jib boom on the tank so that the engine could be removed or a new one off-loaded from a nearby vehicle into the tank.

The first Ausf A Panthers arrived on the Eastern Front in September 1943 with the II./Panzer-Regiment 23, when a handful of these new tanks joined a recently rebuilt battalion dominated by Ausf D vehicles. Then in October, the II./Panzer-Regiment 2 arrived in the East with 71 Panthers – most of them Ausf A vehicles – as part of the 13. Panzer-Division.

Because of the strategic danger posed by unfolding Soviet offensives, the Germans were forced to commit the battalion piecemeal as each company arrived to shore up the hard-pressed front-line defences. After several weeks of this bloody introduction to combat, the Ausf A crews began to file reports on the tank's performance in these series of bitter tactical engagements. The cupola proved an immediate success, with its enhanced field of vision being welcomed by vehicle commanders. In addition, crews reported that the Ausf A turret was superior to that of its predecessor. On the other hand, frontline units continued to report the high incidence of mechanical failures.

A PzKpfw V Panther in Normandy, where its combat effect was limited by its availability. Panther production never reached the intended goal of 600 per month, peaking in July 1944 at 379 tanks. (AirSeaLand/Cody)

Significant numbers of Ausf A Panthers, however, only began to reach the German front during winter 1943–44. The Germans dispatched some of the new tanks to front-line units as replacements, while many went straight to the Reich's tank training schools as part of a major re-equipment programme for Germany's Panzer divisions. In turn, each Panzer division's PzKpfw III-equipped tank battalion returned to Germany, where it received new Ausf A Panthers, undertook crew retraining and then returned to its parent formation at the front. Officially, these potent Panther-equipped tank battalions fielded 76 Panther tanks – each of its four companies deployed 17 standard tanks, while five standard and three Command Panthers served in the battalion's staff company.

During December 1943, the 1. Panzer-Division was the first formation to re-equip its PzKpfw III battalion with Panthers and return to the front. In the following months further armoured divisions rapidly followed suit, most notably the 2. and 5. SS-Panzer-Divisionen Das Reich and Wiking. Consequently, by 31 January 1944 – at which date total Ausf A production had reached 1,183 vehicles – 888 Ausf A Panthers had already reached the Eastern Front. Of these approximately 340 represented replacements for existing Panther-equipped units at the front, while the remaining 550 tanks formed six new Panther-equipped battalions that previously had fielded the now obsolete Panzer III tank.

1) Panther Ausf A as Panzerbefehlswagen, Panzer-Regiment 4; Anzio, Italy, 1944. This Panzerbefehlswagen was assembled by MAN in October/November 1943 and was one of the 76 Panthers brought to Italy by the I. Panzer-Regiment 4 in February 1944.

2) Panther Ausf G Mit Fg 1250; October 1944. This Panther Ausf G was built in October 1944 with all the modifications necessary for mounting night-fighting equipment: infra-red sights and illumination devices. The FG 1250, consisting of an infra-red sight and searchlight, was mounted in the commander's cupola and slaved to the main gun.

(Mike Badrocke © Osprey Publishing)

Although the Panther was certainly a huge vehicle compared to many others in the German arsenal, it still had convincing mobility and cross-country performance. (AirSeaLand/Cody)

By February 1944, therefore, most Panther-equipped battalions at the front overwhelmingly fielded Ausf A tanks, although a few old Ausf D variants continued to see service throughout 1944. After March 1944, however, Germany's Panther battalions began to receive deliveries of the new Ausf G variant; subsequently, as attrition gradually reduced the number of Ausf A tanks still available during 1944–45, the Ausf G became by far the most numerous Panther fielded by front-line German units.

Despite the arrival of the improved Ausf G, however, significant numbers of Ausf A Panthers continued to provide sterling service throughout the rest of the war. This fact is attested to, for example, by the famous case of SS-NCO Ernst Barkmann. During September 1943, Barkmann joined the 4. Kompanie, II./SS-Panzer-Regiment 2, which had recently been re-equipped with 24 Panther Ausf D tanks. In early 1944, Barkmann's parent formation – the SS Das Reich Division – was redeployed to southern France for refitting with new Ausf A and G Panthers after incurring heavy losses in the East. In the days following the 6 June Allied landings in Normandy, the division moved north and joined the German defensive line in the vicinity of St Lô.

On 8 July 1944, Barkmann's 4. Kompanie spearheaded a German counter-attack, during which his Ausf A command tank – vehicle 424 – knocked out its first American Sherman tank. In the bitter defensive battles that raged from 9 to 12 July, Barkmann's potent 7.5cm cannon destroyed a further five Sherman tanks before a hit by an Allied anti-tank gun forced his tank into the divisional workshops for repairs. On 27 July, Barkmann's tank found itself cut off from the rest of the division by the rapid advances achieved by the American *Cobra* offensive. During that day, Barkmann's by now damaged Panther nonetheless managed to knock out nine Shermans in a famous break-out attempt now known as the battle of Barkmann's Corner, and the next day he successfully rejoined his parent formation near Coutances.

In the bitter defensive stands that raged over the next two days, Barkmann accounted for another 15 Allied tanks before having to abandon his burning tank on 30 July. His crew nevertheless managed to escape on foot to fight another day. Re-equipped with a new Ausf G tank, Barkmann would go on to add further 'kills' to his personal tally during the mid-December 1944 German Ardennes counter-offensive.

Although destruction or abandonment was the fate of most remaining Ausf A tanks during winter 1944–45, it remains clear that small numbers of Ausf A Panthers that somehow had managed to survive over a year of front-line service continued to offer fierce resistance to the Allied advance right up to the very last days of the war.

PANTHER AUSF G

During May 1943, the Germans decided to postpone the intended start date for Panther II production and hence continue manufacturing the standard Panther design. Consequently, the High Command asked MAN to develop a new Panther variant – the Ausf G – that incorporated some of the features intended for the Panther II. The Ausf G Panther mounted the Ausf A turret on a modified chassis that lacked the downward wedge of the hull sides at the vehicle's rear. In profile, therefore, this new *entzwickelte* ('straightened') chassis featured a straight hull side bottom edge that tapered gently downwards towards the rear of the vehicle. In addition to this obvious modification, the Ausf G incorporated internal changes that resulted in its hull side plates being sloped at 29° instead of 40°. To maintain the level of protection possessed by the Ausf A tank, the designers increased the thickness of these plates from 40mm to 50mm, which added 0.3 tonnes to the vehicle. The designers, however, did not want the Ausf G to be heavier than the 44.8-tonne Ausf A, and so to compensate they decreased the thickness of the lower hull front plates to 50mm and that of the forward belly armour to 25mm.

A Waffen-SS Panther, possibly in France, moves forward, carefully negotiating infantry fighting positions. The Panther represented a significant shift in tank design philosophy, fostered in large measure by Germany's changing military fortunes. (AirSeaLand/Cody)

The increased space created by these modifications allowed the Ausf G to carry 82 main armament rounds instead of the 79 carried in previous Panthers. Other visible changes incorporated into the Ausf G included the removal of the driver's visor in the glacis plate in favour of a rotating periscope and a redesign of the driver's and radio operator's hatches on the front hull decking. Alterations to the rear of the vehicle included a new layout for the rear hull deck and modified twin exhaust pipes. Despite these modifications, however, the general performance of the Ausf G remained almost identical to that of its predecessor.

In early 1944, while Daimler-Benz and MNH continued producing the Ausf A, MAN switched to produce the new Ausf G version, the first examples of which appeared in March. During the next month MAN delivered 105 Ausf G tanks, while in May Daimler-Benz delivered its first examples of this new variant, having halted production of the Ausf A. Then in July 1944, MNH delivered its first Ausf G tanks, by which time production of the Ausf A had completely ended. German firms constructed a total of 2,943 Ausf G Panthers during a run that lasted 14 months from March 1944 to April 1945, with MAN producing 1,143 tanks, Daimler-Benz 1,004 and MNH 806 vehicles. Ausf G production peaked in July 1944 at 368 vehicles, but thereafter the impact of Allied strategic bombing held monthly delivery rates down to 275–350 for the rest of 1944. The Daimler-Benz factory in Berlin-Marienfelde suffered heavy damage from Allied bombing on 23–24 August, and that at MAN during October– and November. During 1945, as part of a wider collapse of the German war economy, Ausf G deliveries fell sharply to just 128 tanks completed during February, 66 in March and 49 during April, after which the advancing Allies overran the Panther factories.

In October 1944, after the factories had delivered 1,620 Ausf G tanks, the Germans announced plans to produce a further 2,650 (to make a total of 4,270 vehicles) before its successor – the Ausf F Panther – entered service after May 1945. Sustained Allied aerial attacks, however, held down Ausf G production to about 1,300 vehicles – less than half the earmarked total – and prevented a completed Ausf F tank from ever reaching the battlefield. In late April 1945, the German Army received the last Panther tank ever delivered, when the Daimler-Benz factory in Berlin rushed a completed Ausf G to the troops defending the capital. According to Jentz, the Germans delivered a total of 5,943 Panther tanks – including 350 command variants – during a 28-month production run from January 1943 to April 1945. This total included 850 Ausf D Panthers, 2,200 Ausf A vehicles and 2,943 Ausf G tanks. Spielberger's study, on the other hand, states that the Germans completed 6,042 Panthers, of which MAN completed 2,042, Daimler-Benz 1,982, MNH 1,838, Henschel 130 and DEMAG just 50.

As with previous Panther models, the Germans regularly introduced modifications to the Ausf G during its production run. From May 1944 onwards, new tanks featured welded guards to protect the base of the exhaust pipes at the hull rear. Next, from June, new Panthers were fitted with circular sheet-metal covers around the exhaust pipes to conceal the glow given off at night by hot exhausts. That same month, new examples of this variant also appeared with three sockets welded to the turret roof, to which troops could fit a jib boom so that the vehicle's engine could be removed for repairs. Subsequently, from August 1944, newly completed Panthers had a rain guard mounted over the driver's periscope, as driving rain entering the turret had caused problems for the crew. During that summer, German post-combat reports had also suggested that when the Panther's turret was in certain positions, the driver's and radio operator's

A PzKpfw V Panther Ausf G of the SS-Panzer-Regiment 12 is inspected by British and Canadian troops near Authie, Normandy, on 8 July 1944. The tank had apparently been knocked out by a PIAT, likely targeting weaker side or rear armour. (AirSeaLand/Cody)

PZKPFW V PANTHER TURRET

1. Rotating turret basket floor
2. Gunner's seat
3. Gunner's fire controls
4. Gunner's periscopic sight
5. Commander's vision cupola
6. 75mm gun
7. Co-axial machine gun
8. Loader's periscopic sight
9. Loader's seat

(Jim Laurier © Osprey Publishing)

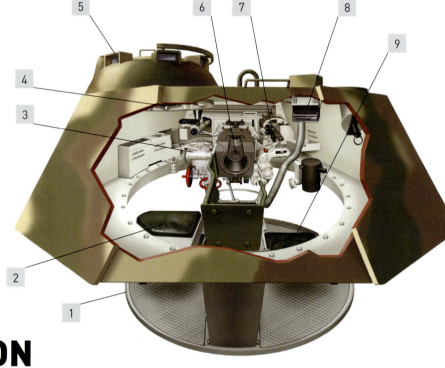

PZKPFW V AMMUNITION

1. Sprgr 42 (HE)
2. Pzgr 39/42 (AP)

(Jim Laurier © Osprey Publishing)

hatches could become obstructed, thus preventing the rapid escape of the crew in an emergency. From August, therefore, Ausf G tanks had redesigned driver's and radio operator's hatches; during an emergency the crew could simply detach both hatches and slide them aside to escape.

Commencing that same month, many new Ausf G tanks also featured a sheet-metal guard welded to the front of the turret roof to prevent debris becoming lodged in the gap between the top of the mantlet and the turret front. During September 1944, the factories ceased coating completed Ausf G vehicles with Zimmerit anti-magnetic mine paste because of rumours that, when hit, the coating caused vehicle

fires. Next, from October, the manufacturers began to deliver finished Panthers in their original red oxide primer, with just a few patches of olive green, red-brown and dark yellow camouflage added. That same month, the Germans added an elongated rain guard for the gun sight visor on the mantlet, as heavy rain was still found to cause problems when entering the sight. That autumn, the assembly factories also outfitted small numbers of Ausf G Panthers with infra-red night-fighting equipment. Next, from September 1944 onwards, the factories fitted some Panthers with a 'chin' along the bottom of the gun mantlet that prevented incoming rounds being deflected down into the hull roof.

During this period, a few Panthers also appeared that featured the more resilient steel-tyred road wheels used in the King Tiger and earmarked for the Panther II. Moreover, during the last weeks of the war, MAN produced a few Ausf G tanks that had a solitary pair of steel-tyred road wheels at the rear station alongside seven pairs of ordinary rubber-tyred wheels, either to compensate for particularly heavy wear on this station or simply because there was a shortage of available rubber-tyred wheels. Finally, the last modification incorporated into the Ausf G before production ended in April 1945 was a new exhaust muffler that reduced the problem of the glow sometimes generated by tank exhausts at night.

Two British soldiers from the Durham Light Infantry, 49th (West Riding) Division run past a knocked-out PzKpfw V Panther during Operation *Epsom* in late June 1944. (AirSeaLand/ Cody)

GERMAN TANK ACES

The concept of 'tank aces' was not particularly prevalent in World War II, even in the Wehrmacht. It was most common in the Waffen-SS, which was far more attuned to the propaganda imperatives of the Nazi state. It was especially common regarding the Tiger battalions, which enjoyed an envelope of invulnerability for one year, from summer 1943 to summer 1944, until the Allies finally fielded tanks, such as the T-34/85 and Sherman Firefly, that could defeat them. In Heer Panzer units, the concept was not widespread, and military awards focused on mission performance, not an arbitrary metric like tank kills. Panther aces were far less common in German propaganda than Tiger aces, as the Panther was far more vulnerable and had a much more troubled existence in its first year of service than did the Tiger. Tank kill claims during World War II on all sides should be taken with a grain of salt; the German Eastern Front intelligence service, Fremde Heere Ost, regularly cut claims in half to more accurately assess enemy losses. This was not so much to account for deliberate inflation as to limit double counting when multiple tanks engaged a single enemy tank without knowledge of the others' actions or when a tank was 'knocked out' again and again as other units moved through an area.

The best known of the Panther aces of the Battle of the Bulge was Ernst Barkmann, who was a platoon leader in 4./SS-Panzer-Regiment 2 in the Ardennes. Barkmann joined the SS in 1936 and took part in the Polish and French campaigns in the infantry. He was seriously wounded during the Russian campaign in summer 1941. After serving as an instructor while convalescing, he joined the new Waffen-SS Panzer force in early 1943, serving as a gunner on the PzKpfw III tank of Alfred Hargesheimer. Following the battle of Kursk, Barkmann became a tank commander on one of the new Panther Ausf D tanks and earned both classes of the Iron Cross during the fighting in Russia in late 1943. Barkmann was commander of a Panther Ausf A tank when the 2. SS-Panzer-Division Das Reich was deployed to Normandy. He came to prominence on 27 July 1944 when he ambushed an American column near Le Lorey, claiming nine US Shermans and other vehicles, for which he was awarded the Knight's Cross.

During the Ardennes campaign, Barkmann took part in one of the most famous tank encounters of the battle, a wild nighttime melee against elements the 7th Armored Division retreating into Manhay on Christmas Eve. In his Panther Ausf G, Barkmann wandered into unsuspecting American columns, blasting a number of vehicles of the 40th Tank Battalion and 48th Armored Infantry Battalion. Barkmann was wounded on Christmas Day but returned to the 2nd SS-Panzer Division in early 1945, taking part in the final campaigns in Hungary against the Red Army. By the war's end, Barkmann claimed over 80 tanks to his credit.

Another tank ace was Panther commander of SS-Panzer-Regiment 2, Fritz Langanke. Volunteering at 18, Langanke first served in the Germania Regiment as an infantryman in 1937 and transferred as a radio operator in an armoured car in 1938. He was awarded the Iron Cross 2nd Class in December 1940 and the 1st Class in December 1941. His first combat in tanks took place in 1942: he served as a tank commander on the Eastern Front in a reconnaissance battalion until late 1943. Langanke was credited with one Russian tank kill. During a divisional reorganization, he became an ordnance officer in the I./SS-Panzer-Regiment 2 until D-Day, and during the fighting in Normandy he served as a Panther commander and subsequently platoon commander with 2./SS-Panzer-Regiment 2, credited with 18 Allied tank kills during the Normandy fighting. He earned the Knight's Cross for his role in leading a breakout from the Roncey pocket of several dozen troops and a few tanks on the night of 28 July 1944.

The considerable attention paid to German tank aces in recent years obscures the fact that they were an exception to the rule and that most of the anonymous young German tankers in late 1944 were thrown into combat with poor training.

Three French schoolboys study a destroyed Panther in the Falaise Pocket, France, 22 August 1944. The hooks along the side of the turret could be used to mount Schürzen armour plate or hang supplies, equipment or camouflage. (AirSeaLand/Cody)

AUSF G IN ACTION

During winter 1944–45, the Ausf G Panther became a key asset with which the increasingly hard-pressed German Army fought its last series of defensive battles. As with all the Panther models, German tank units of this period fielded Ausf D, A and G Panthers without distinction. However, after summer 1944, Ausf G tanks dominated Panther-equipped units as high attrition rates made Ausf D vehicles exceedingly rare and Ausf A tanks increasingly uncommon.

In such defensive actions, the potent 7.5cm gun of the Ausf G provided sterling service. The desperate rearguards enacted by the Panther battalion of the 5. SS-Panzer-Division Wiking, for example, helped slow down the headlong advance of the Soviet *Bagration* offensive in White Russia during July–August 1944. During this same period, on the Western Front, the fanatical defensive stands enacted by the 57 Ausf G Panthers fielded by the teenage Nazis of the 12. SS-Panzer-Division Hitlerjugend did much to slow down the Western Allied advance from the D-Day bridgeheads deep into Normandy. Indeed, right until the very last weeks of the war, whether it was the defence of the surrounded Ruhr industrial zone or of the Seelöwe Heights in front of Berlin, Ausf G Panthers continued to dominate the determined rearguard stands made by an Army now in its last moments of survival.

But the Army's employment of the Ausf G was not restricted to defensive actions; indeed, a key battle in which Panthers played a crucial role was rather a surprise counter-offensive – the Battle of the Bulge, the German mid-December 1944 Ardennes campaign. This operation aptly demonstrates the strengths and weaknesses of the Ausf G Panther.

Back in September 1944, after the advancing Western Allies had stalled short of Germany's borders, Hitler decided to launch a surprise counter-attack in the Ardennes that aimed to seize the vital port of Antwerp. On 16 December, 399 Panthers and 551 other AFVs of Heeresgruppe B initiated this counter-blow, spearheaded in the north by SS Oberst-Gruppenführer 'Sepp' Dietrich's 6. Panzerarmee. The Germans chose to attack in the hilly, wooded Ardennes because its unsuitability for armoured operations meant that the Americans had defended this sector only weakly. Though Hitler insisted that his forces advance 153km to seize Antwerp and thus cut off Montgomery's forces from the Americans to his south, his spearhead commanders recognized that their forces remained too weak – especially logistically – to secure this ambitious objective.

On 16 December, Dietrich's forces broke through the American defences and thrust west toward the River Meuse bridges south of Liége, spearheaded by SS Standartenführer Joachim Peiper's battle group, part of 1. SS-Panzer-Division Leibstandarte Adolf Hitler (LSSAH). SS Major Werner von Pötschke's tank battalion – which included two companies each of 17 Ausf G Panthers, plus two SdKfz 267 Command Panthers in the headquarters group – headed Peiper's force.

Through the early hours of 17 December, Peiper's spearhead Panthers moved cautiously along a series of narrow muddy Belgian roads towards Honsfeld. To maintain surprise, the Panthers advanced without lights, being guided along the narrow roads by Panzergrenadiers walking alongside them with white cloths tied to their rifles. In this way, Peiper's Panthers caught the American garrison of Honsfeld by surprise and overran them. Despite this success, however, the drawback of relying on the Panther's potent firepower in such terrain became obvious; on many occasions the cumbersome tanks had to manoeuvre back and forth for several minutes so that they could make it round the tight corners of these narrow winding roads. Nevertheless, Peiper's Panthers continued to push west along poor roads until at midday they took a short cut past Thirimont to the N23 road along a narrow muddy track. Not surprisingly, the lead Panther soon became bogged down as the muddy track passed over waterlogged ground; Peiper's other tanks had no choice but to reverse carefully up the track and then take the longer route through Baugnez.

A PzKpfw V Panther on display at the Aberdeen Proving Ground Museum in Maryland, United States. A serious problem in the Panther was the final drive, which had a nominal life expectancy of 1,500km, but which in practice was sometimes as low as 150km. (AirSeaLand/Cody)

Despite this delay, Peiper's forces reached Ligneuville early that afternoon, where, just as a command Panther passed the Hôtel des Ardennes, a concealed Sherman knocked it out with a hit to its flank that made the vehicle burn fiercely. Nonetheless, Peiper's lead Panthers kept advancing, and during the following morning the potent firepower they delivered helped his Panzergrenadiers fight their way across the River Amblève at Stavelot.

Having eventually negotiated the sharp bends in the narrow lanes adjacent to Stavelot's market square, Peiper's spearhead Panthers dashed west along better roads toward Trois Ponts; here they intended to secure a bridgehead south of the Amblève and west of the River Salm that would facilitate his planned thrust west. As Peiper's lead Panther emerged from under the railway viaduct north of Trois Ponts, however, a brave American 57mm anti-tank gun team fired from close range and disabled the Panther, blocking the German advance, while American engineers blew the Amblève and Salm river bridges.

These setbacks forced Peiper – who lacked bridging equipment – to race that afternoon along the poor road north of the Amblève toward Stoumont and thence beyond to the Meuse bridges. Then, during the next morning, he launched his Panthers and Panzergrenadiers in a series of frontal attacks against the American positions that blocked the road west.

A PzKpfw V Panther seen in the winter of 1944–45. Later models featured large sheet metal guards fitted around each exhaust pipe. It was not uncommon for a passing infantryman to rest his hand unthinkingly on a superheated exhaust and lose most of the skin off his hand. (AirSeaLand/Cody)

PANTHER GUN SIGHT VIEW

A view of Sherman tanks through a TZF 12a set at 2.5 power. The enemy tank is 900m away.

(Jim Laurier © Osprey Publishing)

The view through the same gun sight but set at 5 power shows a much clearer view of the enemy tanks.

The Panther Ausf G tank's 7.5cm KwK 42 gun was aimed through a TZF 12a monocular telescope in place of the binocular TZF 12 used in the Panther Ausf D. The telescope operated at two magnifications, 2.5× and 5×, with the lower magnification being used for general observation and the higher magnification for precision aiming. The TZF 12a telescopic sight had an engraved reticle consisting of an aiming triangle in the centre with smaller triangles on either side. The gunner placed the target at the apex of the centre triangle. This reticle provided a limited stadiametric ranging capability in the same way as that described for the Leitz TZF 5b in the previous chapter. For example, a Sherman tank was about 2.7m wide, so if the front view of the tank filled the centre triangle, it was about 670m away. The small graduations around the periphery of the reticle were to help adjust the weapon, depending on the weapon and type of ammunition being used. The gunner would dial in either the machine-gun or main gun graduations, and set the range of the ammunition type at the apex of the upper triangle, seen here set at 900m for the Pzgr 39/42 armour-piercing projectile. This would adjust the telescope relative to the gun to provide for the modest change in elevation needed to compensate for the drop of the projectile at varying ranges.

The presence of US P-47 fighter pilots alongside these US infantry likely indicates that an air strike was responsible for the destruction of this vehicle; note the large hole in the engine compartment armour. (AirSeaLand/Cody)

In bitter fighting that lasted all day, his Panthers destroyed 13 American AFVs and overran several enemy positions. In the process, however, American tank, anti-tank and bazooka fire knocked out five Ausf G tanks. Three of these fell in close succession at Stoumont station, their burning hulls forming an effective block to any advance further west by Peiper's forces. Indeed, by dawn on the next day, 20 December, powerful American reinforcements had already virtually surrounded Peiper's isolated battle group.

During 22–23 December, Peiper's encircled force – now virtually out of fuel and ammunition – fell back to make a last stand at La Gleize until a relief column arrived. His tank crews dug in and camouflaged their remaining 21 Panthers to form a defensive hedgehog around the village. All day on 24 December, as massed Allied artillery pounded Peiper's positions and his Panthers used up their ammunition, the Germans waited in vain for the arrival of rescue forces. With no sign of relief, Peiper disobeyed his orders to stand and fight; he disabled his remaining AFVs and during the night of Christmas Eve his remaining 800 unwounded soldiers left La Gleize on foot for the German lines.

PANZERBEOBACHTUNGSWAGEN PANTHER, 1943

The Artillerie requested an armoured observation vehicle with the characteristics of a battle tank that could replace the lightly armoured Beobachtungswagen based on the semi-track chassis. Initially, a series of Panzerbeobachtungswagen were created using rebuilt PzKpfw IIIs, but the Artillerie wanted a larger vehicle based on the new Panther chassis. Design work was completed and a *Versuchsturm* (experimental turret) was mounted on a Panther chassis to undergo tests. Due to the high demand for Panthers for the Panzertruppe, the Artillerie were not allowed to order series production for the Panzerbeobachtungswagen Panther.

(Mike Badrocke © Osprey Publishing)

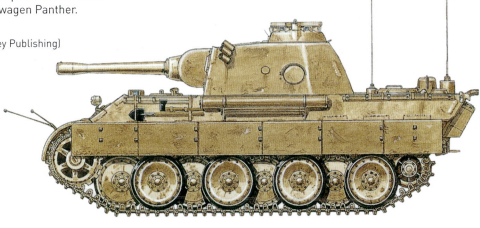

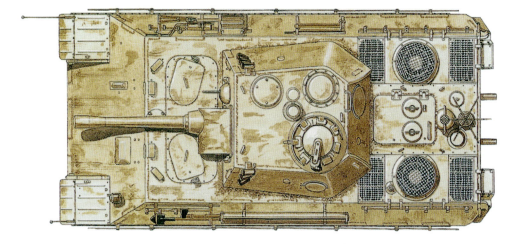

Only just over 400 of the Jagdpanther (Hunting Panther) SdKfz 173 tank-destroyers were produced during the war years. The Panther's turret was replaced with a fixed, open superstructure mounting the 8.8cm PaK 43 cannon. Other Panther variants included the Bergepanther armoured recovery vehicle, the Panzerbeobachtungs-wagen Panther (armoured artillery observation vehicle) and various self-propelled artillery designs. (AirSeaLand/Cody)

Although Peiper's force, with the help of the potent firepower generated by his Panthers, had got further than any other formation in Dietrich's command, even his battle group had not reached the Meuse River bridges, let alone got across them, to realize Hitler's ambitious expectations.

As a postscript to the role played by Ausf G tanks in the Ardennes, a unique Panther mission should be mentioned. The Germans attempted to compensate for their lack of combat power by employing surprise and confusion as a force multiplier. On 16 December, Dietrich committed SS Obersturmbannführer Otto Skorzeny's Panzer-Brigade 150 to a covert operation. The brigade fielded ten modified 'Ersatz' Panthers that had been cleverly disguised to resemble American M10 tank destroyers. Backed by these vehicles, Skorzeny's commandos – some dressed as American military police – infiltrated the American lines to misdirect Allied traffic and spread confusion. Although initially the commandos did create disruption, the Panthers were not employed in their intended covert role. Subsequently, the Germans committed Skorzeny's modified Panthers to conventional ground operations, during which they all soon succumbed to Allied fire.

PANTHER MODEL F

The Ausf F was the final combat version of the Panther that the Germans intended to introduce during the war, although in reality German factories did not manage to finish a complete Ausf F tank before the war ended. This variant married the newly developed Narrow Turret (*Schmalturm*) with its modified 7.5cm L/70 gun to an altered Ausf G chassis. The latter featured thicker frontal hull roof armour (25–40mm instead of 16–40mm), improved armour casting on the glacis plate surrounding the

Kugelblende 50 machine-gun ball mount and modified guides for the sliding driver's and radio operator's hatches. The Germans decided to develop a new turret to replace that of the Ausf A and G tanks because combat experience had shown that this design sometimes deflected incoming rounds down onto the thin hull roof armour.

In addition, the Germans had concluded that the front of the current Panther turret presented too large a target to the enemy. During winter 1943–44, German firms developed two prototype narrow-fronted and better-armoured Panther turrets – the Narrow Gun Mantlet Turret (which Jentz asserts was to be mounted on the Panther II) and the Rheinmetall Narrow Mantlet Turret. As an outgrowth of these designs, during 1944 Daimler-Benz designed a new Narrow Turret that the Germans intended to install on a modified Ausf G Panther chassis to create the Ausf F variant. The Narrow Turret mounted a slightly modified gun, the 7.5cm KwK 42/1 L/70, together with a co-axial MG 42 (instead of the MG 34 included on previous Panther designs). The turret had a narrow conical gun mantlet and a narrow turret front, as well as 40–150mm-thick armour instead of the 16–100mm plates on the Ausf G turret.

German firms produced several Experimental Narrow Panther Turrets (*Versuchs-Schmalturm*) during mid-1944, and then in August mounted one of them on a standard Ausf G chassis for test purposes. Next, in late October, the High Command issued a production schedule for the Panther F: Daimler-Benz was to produce the first 50 tanks during February 1945, and by May – when Ausf G construction was to have ended – Krupp, MAN, MNH and Ni-Werk were to join Ausf F production. But the combination of Allied air strikes and ground advances, plus the administrative chaos engulfing the tottering Nazi Reich, delayed manufacture of the Ausf F. Consequently, when the Soviets overran the Daimler-Benz factory at Berlin-Marienfelde in late April 1945, they discovered four well-advanced Ausf F chassis, plus several completed Narrow Turrets. Indeed, during late April, Daimler-Benz did fit several Ausf G Panther turrets to completed Ausf F chassis and delivered these tanks to the troops then

This PzKpfw V Panther Ausf G was captured in Luxembourg in February 1945, having simply run out of fuel, a common issue for tank units during the last months of the war. (AirSeaLand/Cody)

desperately defending Berlin. Clearly, while the Germans did not manage to finish a single Ausf F Panther prior to the end of hostilities on 8 May 1945, they remained literally only a few days away from achieving this goal when the Soviets overran the Marienfelde factory. And so, with this event ended the story of Germany's Panther medium tank.

THE PANTHER CREW

The Panther had five crewmen. The Panther tank commander (*Panzerführer*) was a lieutenant (*Leutnant*) and was stationed in the left rear of the turret below an armoured cupola, with all-around vision via a set of seven periscopic sights. A seat was provided for while riding inside the turret; when riding outside the cupola, the commander stood on a small footrest, hinged on the empty-round bin. German tank commanders were regularly provided with a set of binoculars for long-range target search. The cupola had a simple frame mount for attaching an MG 34 light machine gun for anti-aircraft defence, but the German tactics did not place as much emphasis on machine guns for use against ground targets as did the US Army. The Panther commander instructed his crew via an intercom system (*Fusprech*). In contrast to US and British practice, the radio was positioned in the hull next to the bow gunner, who operated the transceiver at the instructions of the commander.

A Panther tank commander of the SS-Panzer-Regiment 12, 12. SS-Panzer-Division, scans the surrounding scenery. Note the armoured periscope by the side of his waist. (AirSeaLand/Cody)

Sitting in front of the commander was the gunner (*Richtschütze*), who was usually an NCO or senior enlisted man (*Unteroffizier, Obergefreiter*). The gunner sat in a cramped, claustrophobic position with the main gun against his right shoulder. A British motion study of the Panther concluded that 'little consideration has been given in the design of these vehicles for the comfort of the gunner, and most of the crew's controls are so positioned as to be operated only with discomfort and fatigue'. The gunner's main instrument was a TZF 12a monocular telescopic sight. This did not have a brow pad, so it was not especially safe for the gunner to keep his eye to the sight during travel, and his head was so close to the gun assembly that he had to move his right earphone out of the way when sighting.

The gunner did not have a periscopic sight for general observation during travel as did the Sherman. As a result, he depended on the commander for targeting instructions. This was not a significant problem when the Panther was static and looking for targets, but it slowed the firing cycle to about 20–30 seconds when the Panther had to engage targets while on the move. Upon receiving the commander's instructions, the gunner first searched for the target using the 2.5× power magnification, then switched to 5× magnification for the engagement. The gunner flipped the reticle to the proper ammunition type depending on the commander's instructions and used the commander's range estimate to make the necessary elevation adjustment. In the case of Panthers with experienced gunners, the commander would usually leave the range estimate to the gunner. The gunner had two foot-operated controls for the hydraulic turret traverse and a backup wheel operated by his right hand in the event that the tank's engine was shut off. Gun elevation was by means of a wheel at the gunner's left hand. The gun trigger was located on the elevating wheel and discharged the gun electrically. When the gun fired, it ejected the spent casing back against a deflector plate that dropped it into a bin below. The bin automatically opened and shut to prevent fumes from filling the turret; a hose sucked fumes out of the turret. A British study concluded that, 'The gun arrangement in this vehicle is bad; the gun controls are badly positioned relative to the gunner's seat, [and] the power traverse and elevating control are unsatisfactory to use.'

The loader (*Ladeschütze*) stood in the right side of the turret during combat operations or sat on a small foldout seat attached to the empty-round bin. The position was relatively spacious compared to the left side of the turret, but the space between the turret floor and roof was cramped, so most loaders had to crouch when servicing the main gun. The loader had a small episcope that covered the forward right quadrant of the tank, but he had no roof hatch, only a rear turret escape hatch. The ammunition stowage was adequate; when the gun was aimed straight ahead, the loader had access to two sponson racks and a rear rack for a total of 27 rounds. All other rounds were inaccessible to the gunner and would have to be passed to him by other crewmen or the turret traversed to provide access.

This PzKpfw V Panther was knocked out near Autrey in France, the vehicle obviously having suffered a major fire. Observe how the tank has been lightly 'dug in', with earth piled against its front hull for additional protection. (AirSeaLand/Cody)

The driver (*Fahrer*) sat in the left front of the hull. Beginning in October 1944, the driver had a second seat added. The basic one was for operating the Panther in combat conditions with the hatch closed, and the new one was in an elevated location for road travel with the hatch open, the driver riding with his shoulders outside the hatch for better visibility. The driving controls could be adapted for the closed and travel positions and consisted of steering levers on either side of the driver's legs, a gear lever and a handbrake. After the commander and gunner, the driver was the most important and senior member of the crew since German practice was to encourage driver initiative in moving and positioning the tank, based on the commander's general instructions. When in closed combat position, the driver had a traversable periscope. This had been

A PzKpfw V Panther unit pauses in a village. On the front right (as viewed) we see the driver, while on the left is the radioman, who also operated the bow machine gun. (AirSeaLand/Cody)

adopted on the Ausf G in place of an opening armoured hatch in front of the driver, which compromised the armour integrity of the glacis plate. British evaluations of this sight considered it inadequate.

The final member of the crew was the radio operator (*Funker*), who sat in the right front corner of the hull opposite the driver. His main role was to operate the tank's Fu 5 SE 10U radio transceiver, which was located to his left. The Fu 5 was an AM radio with two receivers, one with preset frequencies and the other to dial up channels. In addition to operating the radio, he also manned the bow machine gun, an MG 34 in a ball mount sighted through a KZF 2 cranked sight. Besides the machine gun sight, he also had an episcope which covered the right front quadrant of the tank. The position was not well configured as the episcope orientation prevented the gunner from using it to locate targets for the machine gun, and the machine-gun sight had a very narrow field of view.

THE PANTHER ASSESSED

A tank's overall effectiveness is determined by the combination of five factors. The first is the vehicle's lethality – the penetrative capabilities of its main armament, its accuracy (determined chiefly by the quality of its optical equipment) and the number of rounds carried. The second factor is the tank's battlefield survivability – the degree of protection afforded by its armour. The third is the vehicle's mobility – its ability to move and manoeuvre at speed across various types of terrain, including the ability to cross bridges without them collapsing under its weight, as well as its ability to obtain a reasonable operational range from the fuel carried. The fourth is the tank's mechanical reliability, particularly that of its engine, transmission and suspension. The last factor is the financial and resource costs involved in producing the tank and then maintaining it in an operational state on the battlefield. When these criteria are considered, it is clear that the Panther was one of the best tanks of World War II.

Undoubtedly, its most impressive aspect was its lethality. The 7.5cm KwK 42 L/70 gun was a superb weapon, as attested to by the numerous 'kills' obtained in combat at even long range.

The gun carried three main types of ammunition – the Pzgr 39/42 armour piercing ballistic-capped (APBC) round, the rare Pzgr 40/42 tungsten AP shell and the Sprgr high explosive round. Firing the Pzgr 39/42 and 40/42 rounds at the normal combat range of 1,000m, the Panther could penetrate 111mm and 149mm-thick armour sloped at 30°, enough to deal with virtually all enemy tanks. In addition, the Panther's excellent TZF 12 or 12a telescopic sight permitted accurate

A knocked-out Panther Ausf G in Belgium, January 1945. The Panther's side armour in particular remained vulnerable to a wide range of weapons (AirSeaLand/Cody)

AN EARLY PANTHER AUSF G

In three-tone camouflage, early summer 1944

Key

1. Tow cable shackles
2. Steering brakes
3. Mudguard
4. Brake link
5. Sloping hull glacis armour plate
6. Barrel of 7.92mm MG 34 hull machine gun
7. Housing for Kugelblende 50 machine-gun ball-mount
8. Stock and trigger for MG 34 hull machine gun
9. Radio operator's armoured periscope
10. Radio operator's hatch
11. Gun barrel travel lock
12. Co-axial 7.92mm MG 34 machine gun (obscured by base of gun barrel)
13. Turret roof
14. Gun mantlet
15. Semi-circular rain guard protecting gun-sight mantlet aperture
16. Main armament compensator
17. Gun cradle
18. TZF 12a monocular telescopic gun sight
19. Sighting vane
20. Mounting ring for anti-aircraft machine gun
21. Armoured periscope on commander's cupola
22. Hatch in commander's cupola
23. Rod antenna
24. Commander's cupola
25. Turret traversing gear
26. Elevator handwheel
27. Commander's headset
28. Armour-piercing ammunition for 7.5cm gun
29. Cylindrical external casing for main armament cleaning kit
30. Engine ventilation grilles
31. Spare track sections
32. Sloping lower rear hull sides (trademark of Ausf G Panther)
33. Road wheel rim-bolts
34. Maybach engine
35. Gunner's seat
36. Interleaved road wheels

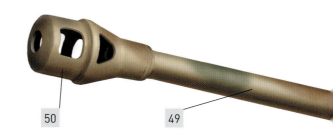

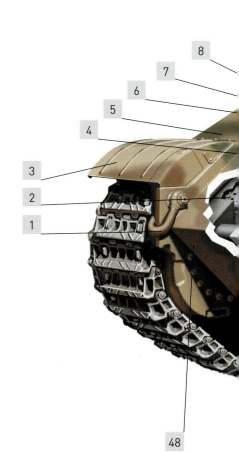

37. Co-axial machine gun firing pedal

38. Compressor

39. Hydraulic traversing unit

40. Front sprocket wheel

41. Track

42. Headlight

43. Driver's instrument panel

44. Final drive

45. Radio racks

46. AK 2-700 gearbox

47. Track brake cooling duct

48. Lower hull front armour plate

49. 7.5cm KwK 42 L/70 main armament

50. Double baffle muzzle brake

(Jim Laurier © Osprey Publishing)

Allied bombing had a huge effect on German tank production. Here US troops inspect Panther turrets inside a devastated factory. (AirSeaLand/Cody)

targeting even at long range. This enabled the L/70 gun to achieve an impressive 97 per cent probability of hitting a target first time at 1,000m with the Pzgr 39/42 under normal combat conditions; indeed, even at the long range of 2,500m, the Panther still obtained a 29 per cent first-hit probability with this round.

The other chief strength of the Panther was its survivability, which rested mainly on its thick, well-sloped frontal armour. The Soviet T-34/85, for example, could only penetrate the Panther frontally at a range of 500m, whereas the 75mm-gunned Sherman M3A2 could not do so even at point-blank range. However, by 1944–45, new threats had emerged – notably the Soviet IS (Josef Stalin) and the American Pershing heavy tanks, plus the 17-pdr anti-tank gun – that proved capable of penetrating the Panther frontally at 1,500m. The side and rear armour of the Panther, however, remained much more vulnerable, with most Allied tanks being able to penetrate these plates at ranges of 1,500m or more. Significantly, with the exception of the IS and Pershing tanks, throughout its operational career, the Panther always proved capable of knocking out opposing tanks at ranges at which the latter were incapable of penetrating the Panther.

The combination of potent firepower and impressive survivability might have made the Panther the most effective tank of the war. However, it was less impressive in terms of mobility, reliability and cost; consequently, some scholars believe that the solid all-round performance of the Soviet T-34/85 tank gave it the edge over the Panther as the most effective tank of the war. For in terms of mobility, the Panther's performance was only reasonable. This 44.8-tonne tank had an unimpressive ground pressure, remained relatively underpowered at 15.6bhp/tonne (with the 700bhp engine) and had an unimpressive cross-country range of only 100km. The problems the bulky Panther experienced in confined terrain were aptly demonstrated, as we have seen, by the difficulties Peiper's tanks experienced in the Ardennes.

In addition, the Panther was dogged by mechanical reliability problems throughout its career, even though by the time of the Ausf G these weaknesses had been ironed out to a significant degree. Last, it should also be remembered that the Panther was a complex and sophisticated vehicle that proved both expensive and time-consuming to produce – each tank took 2,000 man-hours to complete – as well as to maintain in the field. The combination of these three factors served to undermine somewhat the superb lethality and impressive survivability delivered by the Panther. Nevertheless, it remains clear that the Panther medium tank was one of the most effective of the entire war, and its employment at the front undoubtedly enabled the German Army to resist overwhelming Allied pressure for significantly longer than would otherwise have been possible. Given this effectiveness, it remains surprising that after the end of the war, no more than two dozen captured Panthers saw service in other armies (such as the Bulgarian and French forces). Consequently, it would be fair to say that the impressive operational history of the Panther tank ended in the ruins of Hitler's supposed 1,000-year Nazi Reich in May 1945.

The remnants of war. German PzKpfw V Panthers and PzKpfw IVs lie as so much scrap metal in a French scrapyard during the late stages, or immediate aftermath, of the German surrender in Europe. (AirSeaLand/Cody)

CHAPTER 5

TIGER I HEAVY TANK

A Tiger I on the Orel front in August 1943, moving past a burning Russian house. Despite the smoke, the commander's hatch cover is open – it usually was, except in the most intensive combat situations with top-down threats. (AirSeaLand/Cody)

Probably the most famous tank of World War II, the Tiger I was, ironically, quickly designed utilizing components that had been partially tested in previous heavy Panzers. The chassis had been invented primarily for the 30- and 36-tonne class of heavy Panzer in the DW series from Henschel & Sohn GmbH, Kassel. The gun and turret were designed by F. Krupp AG, Essen, for the 45-ton Panzer conceived by Dr Ing h.c. F. Porsche KG, Stuttgart.

While limited development of heavy Panzer designs had commenced in 1937, the first serious efforts resulted from a meeting with Hitler on 26 May 1941. Design of the Tiger I was thus not initiated as a response to the T-34 and KV tanks encountered following the German invasion of Russia on 22 June 1941. Instead, the main concerns addressed during this meeting were the problems of successfully combating British tanks and anti-tank guns. However, after the appearance of the T-34 and KV, the design and production of an effective heavy Panzer was pursued with increased urgency. Among the key circumstances that helped to create the Tiger I were: problems with the automotive design for the Porsche-Tiger; Krupp's ability to maintain a monopoly on tank guns; inadequate supplies of tungsten for AP rounds; the report by Porsche that the higher-performance 8.8cm Flak gun invented by Rheinmetall couldn't be mounted in the existing turret design; and the ease with which the previously designed VK 36.01 *Fahrgestell* (fully tracked, 36-tonne class, 1st model, chassis) could be modified to accommodate the larger turret already designed by Krupp for the VK 45.01 (P).

In autumn 1940, Prof Dr Ferdinand Porsche was commissioned to develop a 45-tonne tank, later designated VK 45. 01 (P) – seen here. Later it was decided to mount an 8.8cm gun. Nibelungenwerk in Austria was awarded the assembly contract. (AirSeaLand/Cody)

DESIGN AND DEVELOPMENT

Since the Heereswaffenamt was hesitant in yielding to Hitler's demands for development of heavy Panzers, in the autumn of 1940 Dr Porsche was commissioned to develop independently a 45-tonne Panzerkampfwagen. To support this effort, on 12 November 1940 Nibelungenwerk was awarded an order by Wa Prüf 6 (the design office for Panzers in the Heereswaffenamt) to assemble the *Versuchsserie* (trial production series) of the PzKpfw VI (Porsche).

Porsche had started development without clearly establishing which gun would be used as the main armament. To prevent another firm from breaking into Krupp's virtual monopoly on tank guns, in February 1941 Dr Müller of Krupp sought a teaming agreement with Porsche, proposing that an 8.8cm KwK L/56 (840m/sec initial muzzle velocity, with complete rounds 931mm long) be used in the new heavy Panzer. This gun was based on the same gun tube and ammunition as the proven 8.8cm Flak 18 L/56.

In an internal meeting on 2 April 1941, Krupp discussed the possibilities of two alternative guns. Conceptual designs for a 10.5cm KwK L/47 (840m/sec initial muzzle velocity, with complete rounds 1,100mm long) and an upgraded 8.8cm KwK L/56 (940m/sec initial muzzle velocity, complete rounds still 931mm long, but with larger-diameter shell cases) were to be completed by 18 April 1941. By 25 April 1941, the 8.8cm KwK L/56 had been selected, as related in a priced proposal to Nibelungenwerk for: six turrets, 80mm frontal and 60mm side armour, turret ring diameter of 1,900mm, complete with 8.8cm KwK L/56, each at 110,000 Reichsmarks; three armoured hulls fabricated in accordance with Porsche design, each at 75,000 Reichsmarks, initial delivery of the first hull planned for November 1941; and a full-scale wooden model of the turret for 5,000 Reichsmarks.

Krupp's proposal was accepted by Nibelungenwerk, who placed an urgent order on 13 May 1941. The wooden model of the turret was completed by Krupp for delivery to Nibelungenwerk by 20 May 1941. The most important meeting, one which greatly influenced the future development of the heavy Panzers, took place with Hitler on 26 May 1941. After reviewing the current status and plans for the development of Panzers and anti-tank weapons, Hitler decided that the development of both of the heavy Panzers from Dr Porsche and Henschel was to be accelerated so that six of each would be available in the summer of 1942. It was considered necessary to make the frontal armour 100mm thick – 60mm was sufficient for the sides of the Panzers. An 8.8cm KwK was to be retained for the Porsche design, but its effectiveness was to be upgraded to that achievable by the 8.8cm Flak 41 designed by Rheinmetall. The effectiveness of the 8.8cm KwK and the AP round were to be increased so that 100mm-thick armour plate could still be penetrated at a range of about 1,500m.

Another view of the VK 45. 01 (P). Porsche had used the nickname 'Leopard' for the previous VK 30.01 (P) design, and adopted the name Tiger for the new design. (AirSeaLand/Cody)

In response to Hitler's decisions, Porsche KG was commissioned by Wa Prüf 6 on 21 June 1941 to determine if it was possible to mount the 8.8cm Flak 41 instead of the 8.8cm KwK L/56 in the turret already designed for the VK 45.01 (P). Porsche responded by telegram on 10 September 1941 that only the 8.8cm KwK L/56 could be considered for the VK 45.01 (P). Therefore, the decision was made to complete only the first 100 VK 45.01 (P) with the turret originally designed by Krupp for the 8.8cm KwK L/56, instead of the more effective tank gun based on the 8.8cm Flak 41 as ordered by Hitler.

Krupp received a contract to fabricate the armoured components for 100 hulls and turrets for the VK 45.01 (P) and to assemble the turrets in operational condition and ship them for mounting on the *Fahrgestell* (chassis) assembled at Nibelungenwerk. The first eight turrets had lower sides and a flat roof with a raised centre section to allow the gun to be depressed through a larger arc. The rest of the 92 turrets had the higher sides and slanted roof typical of the Tiger I.

The new hull design for the VK 45.01 (P) had 100mm-thick armour plates on the front, 80mm on the sides and rear, 25mm the deck and 20mm the belly. Porsche chose to install a petrol/electric drive train. Power was provided by two ten-cylinder, air-cooled, 15-litre, Porsche Typ 101/1 engines (rated at 320hp at 2,400rpm), each coupled to a matching electric generator. The electricity generated was used to drive two electric motors, one for each track, and steering was controlled by regulating the electric power supplied to each motor. The complete drive train was designed to propel the tank at up to 35km/h. A longitudinal torsion bar suspension was upgraded to support the additional weight. The combat loaded weight of 59 tonnes was distributed over three pairs of steel-tyred, rubber-cushioned road wheels per side travelling on unlubricated 640mm-wide tracks with a track of 130mm. The official Wa Prüf 6 designation from 5 March 1942 was PzKpfw VI (VK 45.01 P) (Ausf P). The Inspekteur der Panzertruppen (In6) designation, specified for use in training and maintenance manuals and in organization tables, was PzKpfw VIP (8.8cm) (SdKfz 181) Ausf P. Suggested names were 'Tiger (P)', 'Tiger P1' or 'Porsche Tiger'.

From 5 January 1942, the monthly production goals were established as ten in May, ten in June, 12 in July, 14 in August and 15 in September, with further production continuing at the rate of 15 per month. The first VK 45.01 (P) was completed in April 1942 in time for a demonstration on Hitler's birthday. The second, completed in June, was sent to Kummersdorf for gun firing and other tests. Problems with the engine and suspension delayed further production, and in September 1942, Nibelungenwerk reported that assembly of the Tiger (P) had stopped because engines and suspension parts had not arrived. At this time five Tiger (P)s were undergoing trials at the troop training grounds at Dollersheim.

Between 26 and 31 October 1942, a Tiger-Kommission met to determine which model, the Tiger (H) or Tiger (P), would be chosen for further series production. During the subsequent comparative trials, the Henschel Tiger proved to be superior and was therefore selected. In the status report for October 1942, Nibelungenwerk reported that Tiger (P) production had been discontinued. A total of ten Tiger (P)s – Fgst Nr (*Fahrgestellnummer* – chassis number) 150001 through to 150010 – had been assembled by Nibelungenwerk before the end of October 1942. From the original order for 100 VK 45.01 (P), 90 turrets were converted for mounting on the Tiger I; 90 hulls were converted for the Ferdinand Panzerjäger; three hulls were converted for Bergefahrzeuge (recovery vehicles); three chassis were completed with Ramm-Tiger superstructures; four complete PzKpfw VI VK 45.01 (P) with *Turmnummer* – turret number 150004, 150005, 150013 and 150014 were retained for further tests and trials.

Before October 1942, Porsche had designed a Typ 102, which was virtually the same Panzer as the Typ 101, but with a Voith hydraulic drive in place of the electric drive. On 17 February 1943, Dr Porsche reported that a Tiger P1 with hydraulic drive was being completed at Nibelungenwerk.

A Tiger I bedecked with a Nazi flag, theatre unknown. The protrusion just to the left of the gun manlet, on the turret itself, is a trunnion, used as an anchor point when lifting off the turret. (AirSeaLand/Cody)

The Henschel model

On 28 May 1941, Wa Prüf 6 placed an order with Henschel to design a new chassis suitable for carrying a turret with an 8.8cm KwK. This Panzer was to have a new feature known as *Vorpanzer*, consisting of a frontal armoured shield to protect the tracks and drive sprockets. This order was based on the meeting with Hitler on 26 May 1941, where the current design status of the heavy tanks had been discussed and directives for future actions established. Before the meeting, Henschel had not contemplated mounting an 8.8cm gun turret on their VK 36.01 chassis, but had closely followed specifications and orders originating from Wa Prüf 6. At the same time, another order to alter the VK 36.01 was also given a high priority and tough deadlines. Therefore, Henschel did not immediately pursue the option for an 8.8cm gun turret. Instead, they concentrated on the high-priority order to modify the VK 36.01 chassis to carry a turret with the tapered-bore Waffe 0725.

During the meeting on 26 May 1941, a major design breakthrough was achieved as a result of the decision to install deep fording equipment. Freed from the weight restrictions imposed by bridges, the designers could specify heavier armament and armour protection which drastically increased the weight of the vehicle. Previously, Wa Prüf 6 had never aggressively pursued the design of Panzers above the 30-ton class due to the perceived tactical handicap associated with Panzers dependent on the location

A captured PzKpfw VI Ausf E Tiger I. Note the very large heat shields over the exhausts in the centre rear of the vehicle, flanked by engine fans. (AirSeaLand/ Cody)

and existence of heavy bridges. Another justification for exceeding the 30-ton weight class was that the warfare would be conducted in the hinterlands of Europe, where suitable weight-bearing bridges did not exist. However, the designers still had to meet the restrictive specifications governing the maximum dimensions for rail transportation.

The decisions that specifically created the VK 45.01 (H) have been preserved in a letter written on 27 September 1941 by Oberst Fichtner, head of Wa Prüf 6. In response to a further directive from Hitler, tapered-bore weapons were not to be used in production series Panzers. With limited modifications, the turret with the 8.8cm KwK L/56 designed by Krupp for Dr Porsche had to be adopted for the PzKpfw Typ Henschel. No other options could have met the demanded schedule. Henschel was left with no other choice but to create a design for a Panzer in the 45-tonne class by modifying the VK 36.01 chassis. Thus, the VK 45.01 (H) was not created by following the standard practice of controlled design projects that were defined by careful implementation of a systematic series of conceptual and design stages. Instead the Henschel model came into being as a rush job, quickly assembled from a mixture of components available from previous heavy Panzer designs. From the Henschel DW chassis series came the Maybach Olvar 40 12 16 *Schaltgetriebe* (transmission) and Henschel L600C *Lenkgetriebe* (steering gears), as well as the entire suspension and running gear including; *Seitenvorgelege* (final drives); *Triebrad* (drive wheel with sprocket); *Laufrad* (road wheels); *Drehstäbe* (torsion bars); *Stossdampfer* (shock absorbers); *Leitrad* (idler wheel); and Kgs 63/ 520/ 130 *Verladekette* (rail transport track). The only new, major components inside the VK 45.01 (H) chassis were the Maybach HL 210 powerplant, fuel tanks, cooling system and deep fording provisions.

From the Porsche VK 45.01 (P) came the turret designed by Krupp, mounting the 8.8cm KwK L/56, and the Henschel turret design remained fundamentally the same as the original Porsche turret. Minor modifications implemented to create the VK 45.01 (H) turret design included a different turret travel lock, traverse drive motor (hydraulic replacing electric) and drive for the azimuth indicator.

The turret was designed in a horseshoe shape, with the open end covered by the 100mm-thick gun mantlet. The armour thickness was 80mm for the turret walls, with 25mm for the turret roof. Access to the turret was provided through a hatch in the cupola and a hatch directly over the loader's position. An exhaust fan was mounted behind the loader's hatch on the turret roof.

A top rear view of a PzKpfw VI Ausf E Tiger I, clearly showing the pipework leading out to the Feifel air filters. (AirSeaLand/Cody)

Adequate vision devices provided all-round viewing for the crew in the turret. The gunner had a binocular TZF 96 sighting telescope with 2.5× magnification and a vision block to his left, the loader a vision block to the right front and a pistol port to the right rear, and the commander had all-round vision blocks in the cupola and a pistol port to the left rear. Secondary armament was provided by an MG 34 mounted co-axially to the right of the main gun, while a second MG 34 could be mounted on the cupola ring for anti-aircraft defence.

On 25 July 1941, Krupp was given an order from Wa Prüf 6 to complete a full-scale wooden model of the VK 45.01 turret (Porsche) for the Henschel chassis and delivered it on 18 November 1941. On 23 January 1942, Wa Prüf 6 presented Krupp with an order to complete three operational VK 45.01 turrets for the *Versuchsserie*. Krupp's annual report stated that it had volunteered to produce the armoured components and assemble finished turrets for the three Henschel *Versuchsserie* Panzers in order to prevent the appearance of showing favouritism toward Porsche.

The first VK 45.01 (H) turret with 8.8cm KwK 36 Nr l and TZF 96 Nr 3 was assembled by Krupp and sent to Henschel on 11 April 1942. The turret was mounted on the Henschel VK 45.01 (H) Versuchsfahrgestell Nr. VI and was inspected on 15 April 1942.

Hull design

The new chassis for the VK 45.01 (H) was created by altering the hull design for the VK 36.01. The superstructure sides were extended out over the tracks to create panniers, limited in their width due to restrictions for rail transport. These extensions were used to house the radiators, which were relocated on both sides so that the centre engine compartment could be sealed leak-tight for deep fording. There was a large, hinged rectangular hatch over the engine compartment. Unlike previous designs where the superstructure was bolted to the hull along a flange, in this case it was welded to the hull. Access for maintenance of the engine, cooling system and fuel system was provided by unbolting the sections of the rear deck.

The armour consisted of the driver's front plate which was 100mm at 9°, front nose plate 100mm at 25°, superstructure side plates 80mm at 0°, hull side plates 60mm at 0° vertical, tail plate 80mm at 9°, deck plates 25mm at 90° horizontal and belly plate 25mm horizontal.

A total of 92 rounds of ammunition was carried for the main gun, of which 64 rounds were stored horizontally in covered bins in the panniers along the superstructure sides. Another 16 were located in closed bins along the hull sides, six in a closed bin under the turret floor and six in a closed bin beside the driver.

The driver had a visor mounted in the front plate, which for more protection could be closed, and he could use the twin driver's periscopes. A fixed periscope in the driver's hatch provided him with a view toward the left front. The radio operator had a

Kugelzielfernrohr (sighting telescope) 2 to aim the ball-mounted MG 34 and a fixed periscope in the hatch above his head.

The drive train consisted of a high-performance Maybach HL 210 P45, 12-cylinder engine delivering 650hp at 3,000rpm, through an eight-speed Maybach Olvar 40 12 16 transmission onto the Henschel L 600 C double radius steering gear and final drives, designed to provide a maximum speed of 45.4km/h. Maintaining a transverse torsion bar suspension, the combat weight of 57 tonnes was distributed over eight sets of *geschachtelte* (interleaved) 800mm diameter rubber-tyred road wheels per side. The unlubricated 725mm wide *Gelandeketten* (cross-country tracks) provided an acceptable ground pressure (when the tracks sank to 20 cm) of 0.735kg/cm².

Main armament

In the meeting with Hitler on 26 May 1941, it was decided to give preference to a smaller calibre (such as 60mm or 75mm instead of 88mm) gun for the new heavy Panzers, if the same penetration ability (100mm at a range of about 1,500m) could be achieved. A smaller-calibre gun had inherent advantages; the size of the rounds allowed a larger number to be stowed and the turret would weigh less. The calibre that was chosen had to be suitable for defeating tanks, emplacements and bunkers. From the previous designs, the 8.8cm KwK required a turret ring diameter of 1,850mm, compared to 1,650mm for the tapered bore 7.5cm Waffe 0725. This resulted in an increased weight of 2.2 tonnes for a turret with 80mm frontal and 60mm side armour.

A front view of a PzKpfw VI Tiger I captured by the British in North Africa in April 1943 and subsequently put through a series of evaluation trials. (AirSeaLand/Cody)

OFFICIAL DESIGNATIONS

During the development of the Tiger I, this heavy Panzer was referred to by Wa Prüf 6 and the design firms under various names, including PzKpfw 4501 (Typ Porsche und Henschel), PzKpfw VI Ausf H1 (VK 45.01) and PzKpfw VI (VK 45.01/H) Ausf H1 (Tiger). From 1941 up to March 1942, the design and procurement project had been known as the *Tigerprogram*, but it wasn't until early 1942 that the Panzer itself was identified by the name 'Tiger'. The designation applied by the Inspekteur der Panzertruppen (In 6) was originally PzKpfw VI H (8.8cm) (SdKfz 182) Ausf H1 (Tiger). This name remained in use until 5 March 1943, when it was officially changed to PzKpfw Tiger (8.8cm L/56) (SdKfz 181) Ausf E. The short 'Tiger H1' name had by this time been changed to the now familiar 'Tiger I', first used on 15 October 1942, but the designations PzKpfw VI, Tiger, and PzKpfw Ausf E, and combinations thereof, remained in common usage by the units and operational staffs until the end of the war.

In accordance with Hitler's directive, on 17 July 1941, Wa Prüf 6 gave Rheinmetall an order to design a turret with a gun which could penetrate 140mm of armour at a range of 1,000m, without expressly requiring that an 8.8cm calibre gun be used. Rheinmetall's solution was a 7.5cm KwK L/60 with a normal cylindrical gun tube based on the design of its 7.5cm PaK 44 L/46 demanded by Hitler. The 7.5cm gun barely met the specification, so Rheinmetall extended the barrel length to L/70 (which became famous as the 7.5cm KwK 42 L/70 mounted in the Panther) and delivered a full-scale wooden model of the turret. By 5 March 1942, it had been established that, starting with the 101st Tiger (H), the 7.5cm KwK L/70 would be mounted in the Rheinmetall turret and the tank designated the PzKpfw VI H (7.5cm L/70) Ausf H2. On 15 July 1942, however, the decision was taken to continue production of the Ausf H1 with the 8.8cm KwK L/56. As a result, the order for the Ausf H2 equipped with the 7.5cm gun was cancelled.

Command variants

The command version of the Tiger I was initially designated as the PzKpfw VI H (8.8cm) (SdKfz 182) (also PzBefWg), and after March 1943 as the PzBefWg Tiger (SdKfz 267 und 268) Ausf E. Due to the large space needed to mount the additional radio sets, the ammunition stowage was reduced to 66 main gun rounds and 3,300 machine-gun rounds; the co-axially mounted machine gun, the vision block in the

right turret side and the turret periscope were not mounted. The holes left behind by the removal of this equipment were all sealed with armour plugs.

The SdKfz 267 was outfitted with a FuG 8 (30-watt transmitter with medium wavelength receiver, operated in the frequency band 0.83–3 MHz) and a FuG 5 (10-watt transmitter with ultra-short wavelength receiver, operated in the frequency band 27.2–33.4 MHz). The 267 can be identified by an *Antennenfuss* Nr 1 (antenna base, 104mm base diameter) mounted on an insulator protected by a large armoured cylinder fitted on the right rear deck. A *Sternantenne* D (star antenna) for the FuG 8 was fitted to this base. A 2m-high *Stabantenne* (rod antenna) for the FuG 5 was mounted on the turret roof on the right side of the commander's cupola. The SdKfz 268 was outfitted with a FuG 7 (20-watt transmitter and ultrashort wavelength receiver, operated in the frequency band 42.1–47.8 MHz) and a FuG 5. The 268 can be identified by the 1.4m *Stabantenne* for the FuG 7 mounted on the left side of the rear deck, with a 2m *Stabantenne* for the FuG 5 mounted on the turret roof.

A PzKpfw VI Ausf A Tiger I. Note how three smoke grenade dischargers are fitted to each side of the turret; these were positioned to create a pattern of smoke when fired simultaneously. (AirSeaLand/Cody)

PRODUCTION HISTORY

An initial order for three *Versuchsserie Fahrgestelle* was followed by an order for 100 production series VK 45.01 (H). Following cancellation of the Ausf H2 in July 1942, the order for the Henschel variant was increased to 300. Following cancellation of the Porsche variant, Reichsdienstsleiter Saur decided that to prevent wastage, the turrets previously fabricated for the Tiger P1 would be utilized for the Tiger H1. Krupp sent the first four of these turrets to Wegmann by 27 November 1942, and out of the total of 90, Wegmann was ordered to assemble 50 and Krupp 40. Krupp completed assembly of the last of their turrets by June 1943. Except for the three turrets for the Versuchsserie and the 40 converted turrets completed by Krupp, Wegmann assembled and delivered completely operational turrets for mounting on completed chassis at Henschel.

Additional orders were placed for the Tiger I by extensions to the contracts. These additional Tiger Is were ordered only as an interim solution to meet the monthly production goals until the Tiger II could be produced in large numbers. These extensions increased the total order for the VK 45.01 (H) from 390 to 1,346, running in an unbroken series from Fgst Nr 250001 to 251346.

Like the VK 45.01 (P), the first *Versuchsserie* PzKpfw VI H 'V1' was also demonstrated on Hitler's birthday in 1942. The first production series VK 45.01 (H) (Fgst Nr 250001) was completed and sent to Kummersdorf on 17 May 1942 for testing. Delays in production were encountered due to problems with the brakes and steering gear, both of which needed minor modifications. The monthly production goal was continuously increased in an attempt to supply as many Tigers as possible to the front, and the production run continued through August 1944, tapering off at the end as Tiger II production took over.

PRODUCTION MODIFICATIONS

As with all series of German Panzers, modifications were frequently introduced during production runs. These modifications were prompted by a desire for improved automotive performance, increased firepower, additional protection, simplification of design for easier manufacturing or in response to shortages.

Numerous changes associated with replacing seals and gaskets, changing bolt sizes and improving interior drive train components were of significant value in improving mechanical reliability. In some cases, it took several months to have a new modification incorporated on all new production Tigers, largely due to 'first in, last out' tendencies. This resulted from stockpiles of older parts being covered or buried by deliveries of newer parts which were therefore used first. The

OPPOSITE Tigers from schwere Panzer-Abteilung 503 move forward in column on the Eastern Front. The Tiger availability rate was better in the West than on the Eastern Front, probably due to the proximity of the main assembly plant at Kassel. (AirSeaLand/Cody)

A Tiger I in the Leningrad area of the Eastern Front. The Tiger I was armed with the 8.8cm KwK 36 L/56 gun that shared the ammunition types of the various 8.8cm anti-aircraft guns. (AirSeaLand/Cody)

modifications are listed in the order in which the changes occurred. The highlighted month is the first in which the modification was present on Tiger Is leaving the factory. When exact dates or Fgst Nr are known for the start of a new modification, they have been listed. In the other cases, all that is certain is that the change first occurred on Tiger Is completed at the factory sometime during the specified month.

April 1942

The first Versuchsfahrzeug 'V1' was the only Tiger I completed with *Vorpanzer*. Using hydraulic lifters mounted at both ends, the *Vorpanzer* could be raised to provide extra protection in front of the superstructure or lowered to protect the hull front and the tracks.

May 1942

Tigers with Fgst Nr 250001–250020 had type Kgs 63/725/120 *Geländeketten* (tracks for cross-country travel) specifically designed so that tracks on the right side were a mirror image of those on the left side. In the place of the discarded *Vorpanzer*, track mud guards fabricated from bent sheet metal were attached at the front on both sides.

August 1942

Nebelwurfgeräte (each consisting of three smoke candle dischargers) were mounted on each side of the turret. Toggle bolts on both sides of the hull machine-gun mount were used to secure a cover to seal the opening during deep fording. These bolts were no longer installed after June 1943.

September 1942

Removable mud guards (consisting of four sections on each side) were bolted along the hull sides to cover the exposed ends of the wider cross-country track. Fasteners were attached on the left superstructure side to hold the long 15mm-thick cable used for track replacement. A box for the track adjusting and replacement tools was mounted on the left hull rear. This was discontinued after November 1943.

TIGER I SPECIFICATIONS

Crew: 5
Overall length: 8.4m
Width: 3.7m
Height: 3.0m
Weight (combat loaded): 56.9 tonnes
Main gun: 8.8cm KwK 36
Main-gun ammunition: 92 rounds
Secondary armament: Two 7.92mm (hull, co-axial)
Engine: Maybach HL 210P45, V-12 gasoline engine
Transmission: Maybach Olvar OG 401216A with eight forward, four reverse gears
Fuel capacity: 570 litres
Road speed: 38km/h
Road range: 140km

(Jim Laurier © Osprey Publishing)

3.7m

3.0m

8.4m

October 1942

Starting with Fgst Nr 250021, type Kgs 63/725/ 120 *Geländeketten* of the same design were mounted on both sides of the Tiger, with the right side track mounted in reverse to the track on the left. This caused the Tiger I to pull slightly to the side.

November 1942

For Tigers sent to 'tropical climates' (Tunisia, Sicily, Italy and Heeresgruppe Süd and Mitte in Russia), Feifel air filters were mounted on the upper corners of the hull rear. After August 1943, these were no longer installed at the factory. Improved, hinged mud guards for the tracks were mounted at the front and rear to cover the track extending beyond the hull.

December 1942

Starting with Turm Nr 46, an escape hatch replaced the MP Klappe (machine-pistol port) on the right rear turret wall. Originally the sides of this escape hatch were bevelled to conform to the curve of the turret side, but after June 1943, escape hatches were installed consisting of flat 80mm-thick discs. Starting with Turm Nr 50, an adjustable commander's seat was installed, and with Turm Nr 56, a large stowage bin was mounted on the turret rear. This stowage bin was retrofitted onto all of the Tigers with schwere Panzer-Abteilung 501 destined for Tunisia, but not onto those with schwere Panzer-Abteilung 503 until the summer of 1943. For additional protection, the armour thickness at the sides of the gun mantlet and in the area of the gun sight aperture was increased.

Five *S-Minenwerfer* were mounted on the deck of the Tiger, one at each of the four corners, and one in the middle along the left side. On Panzerbefehlswagen only four were mounted, the one on the left side being omitted.

January 1943

Due both to glowing exhaust mufflers and exhaust flames that could be observed at long range at night, a heat guard and deflector were installed. The driver's periscopes were no longer mounted and the associated apertures in the driver's front plate were welded closed.

March 1943

Starting with Turm Nr 179, a sheet metal shield was installed to protect the commander from back-blast and flames from the main gun breech. Starting with Turm Nr 184, a fixed periscope for the loader was installed in the turret roof. Spare track links were

mounted on brackets on the turret sides. The location on the turret side was selected because there was insufficient space to store the spare track on any other surface.

April 1943

The internal seals and gears of the final drives were improved and the design for the drive sprocket hub was altered.

May 1943

Starting with Fgst Nr 250251, the Maybach HL 230 P45 engine with two air filters was installed in place of the Maybach HL 210 P45. This modification included a change to the fan drives for the cooling system and a second hole in the alignment plate for the *Schwungkraftanlasser* (crank starter) to line up the shaft with the new engine.

A PzKpfw VI Ausf A Tiger I of the I. SS-Panzer-Corps. The extent of the Zimmerit anti-magnetic mine paste covering is evident in this photograph. (AirSeaLand/ Cody)

June 1943

Starting with Turm Nr 286, the *Nebelwurfgeräte* (smoke candle dischargers) were no longer mounted on the right and left turret sides for the same reason as for the Panther. During a reported action in February 1943, small-arms fire had set off the smoke candles which had temporarily incapacitated the crew members. Starting with Fgst Nr 250301, the forward shock absorbers were fastened using mounting bolts with a large external head because the previous conical head design had vibrated loose.

July 1943

Starting with Turm Nr 391, the turret was extensively redesigned. A *Prismenspiegelkuppel* (commander's cupola with periscopes) with a swivel hatch was installed. To protect the periscope, armoured guards were welded over the protruding periscope heads and a partial ring was welded to the top of the periscope guards to serve as a track for the improved *Fliegerbeschussgeräte* (anti-aircraft machine-gun mount). The exhaust fan on the turret roof was moved forward to improve fume extraction. The MP Klappe on the left turret rear was replaced by an MP Stopfen (pistol-port plug). Internally, a fireproof

A close-up of the track and overlapping *Gummigefederten Stahllaufrollen* (steel road wheels with internal rubber cushioning) on a PzKpfw VI Ausf E Tiger I. (AirSeaLand/Cody)

cloth, hanging in front of the commander, replaced the sheet metal guard; a new design turret traverse lock that engaged with the teeth of the turret race was introduced; and an improved spring counter balance connected with a chain was installed for the 8.8cm main gun. The fasteners for the long 15mm-thick cable used for track replacement were redesigned and located in new positions along the left superstructure side. A single headlight was mounted on the top left corner of the superstructure. Previously two lights had been mounted, one at each forward corner.

August 1943

In order to simplify production, Henschel and Wegmann were ordered to immediately cease installation of deep fording components. These included many seals, covers and plugs as well as the four-part telescoping air intake pipe. To ensure that the Tiger I could ford streams up to a depth of 1.5m, gaskets were still to be installed where components penetrated the hull.

September 1943

Starting with Fgst Nr 250501, the *Motortrennwand* (firewall) was redesigned to allow easier access to the engine compartment and relocation of components. A C-Clamp for use with towing cables was mounted on the hull rear to the left of the left exhaust guard. Zimmerit was applied at the factory to all upright surfaces that could be reached by a man standing on the ground. The surface was rippled to increase the distance to the steel surface without increasing the weight of the coating.

November 1943

Starting with Fgst Nr 250625, an improved fan driven by the main drive shaft was installed at the firewall, which, with associated ducts, was designed to remove fumes created by the gears and brakes. The *S-Minenwerfer* on the deck and the track tool box on the left hull rear were dropped. Starting with Fgst Nr 250635 (and continuing until Fgst Nr 250875 in February 1944), a *Heckzurrung* (rear travel lock) for the 8.8cm gun was mounted on the right rear corner of the hull. With the internal travel lock this protected the gun sight alignment on long marches or over rough terrain. The rear position was technically better since it held the gun near the end of the barrel, but had the disadvantage that a crew member needed to be exposed to bring the gun into action.

December 1943

The single headlight was moved to the centre of the driver's front plate. To increase traction on ice and packed snow, six chevrons were added to the face of each track link.

229

January 1944

Starting with Fgst Nr 250762, the *Lenzpumpe* (suction pump) and associated discharge pipe were no longer fitted. The *Lenzpumpe* had originally been installed to remove water from the hull that may have seeped past the seals during deep fording operations. From Fgst Nr 250772, the mount on the right hull rear was modified to hold a 20-tonne *Winde* (jack), replacing the lighter 15-tonne *Winde* that had been previously carried. The MP Stopfen were no longer installed on the left turret rear, being superfluous since close defence was provided by a *Nahverteidigungswaffe* (close defence weapon) mounted on the turret roof. This weapon could fire smoke cartridges, signal cartridges and grenades, but due to shortages, was not mounted on the Tiger I until March 1944. The hull side extension at the front on both sides was cut out to allow free movement of the shackle for towing and lifting the Tigers.

A PzKpfw VI Ausf E Tiger I is mounted on an Allied train after its capture near Reims, 29 September 1944, destined for an Allied salvage depot to the rear. (AirSeaLand/Cody)

A photograph of the Tiger I that belonged to famous SS tank commander Michael Wittmann, who died on 8 August 1944 when shells from British or Canadian anti-tank guns penetrated his vehicle, detonating the ammunition and blowing the turret off. (AirSeaLand/Cody)

February 1944

Gummigefederten Stahllaufrollen (steel road wheels with internal rubber cushioning), adopted from the Tiger II, were mounted starting with Fgst Nr 250822. These were chosen because of their ability to bear the weight of heavy armoured vehicles. They were based on those for the Russian KV series of heavy tanks, but were significantly altered with improved bearings and weight reduction. The rubber tyres had occasionally failed, especially those on the inside bearing the greatest weight. With steel tyres replacing rubber tyres, the number of road wheels per axle was decreased from three to two.

From Fgst Nr 250823, a *Kuhlwasserheizgerät* (motor coolant heater) was installed on the left side of the Maybach HL 230 Motor. An access port for a blow-torch was located on the tail plate below the armoured guard for the left muffler. When not in use, this port was covered by an oval-shaped armoured cover secured by two bolts. The heater was used in the winter for preheating the coolant prior to attempting to start the engine. A turret ring guard was welded to the deck beginning with Fgst Nr 250850. This prevented artillery shell fragments or anti-tank projectiles from jamming the turret.

Starting with Fgst Nr 250861, five electrical components were moved out of the engine compartment and mounted on a panel on the firewall in the fighting compartment.

March 1944

Hits by large-calibre (greater than 150mm) artillery shells on the turret had penetrated the 25mm-thick roof plate, so the turret roof armour was increased to 40mm. The loader's hatch originally designed for the Tiger II turret was installed in the thicker turret roof.

April 1944

The monocular TZF 9c (sighting telescope) replaced the previously used binocular TZF 9b. Until gun mantlets became available which had not been drilled for the binocular sight, the additional aperture was welded shut with an armoured plug. Beginning with Fgst Nr 251075, wooden decking was installed over the top of the upper fuel tanks to catch artillery shell splinters and bullet splash that came through the cooling air grates on the rear deck.

June 1944

To aid in maintenance, three sockets were welded to the turret roof to anchor the base of the 2-tonne *Kran* (jib boom). The boom could be used to lift the rear decking and motor from the vehicle on which it was mounted, or lift the turret, transmission and steering gears from an adjacent vehicle. This modification was authorized to be retrofitted by Tiger units.

October 1944

The units were authorized to increase the internal stowage of 8.8cm ammunition by 16 rounds. These were to be stored in two groups of four along each hull side. These additional rounds were secured in place by flat iron straps installed above the existing ammunition bins.

TIGER CREW LAYOUT

The Tiger tank commander (*Panzerführer*) was stationed in the left rear of the turret below an armoured cupola. Sitting in front of the tank commander was the gunner (*Richtschütze*), with the main gun against his right shoulder. In the initial versions of the Tiger I, the gunner's main instrument was a TZF 9b binocular telescopic sight, but as an economy measure, this was replaced by a TZF 9c monocular sight on the later models of the Tiger I. The gunner did not have a periscopic sight for general observation during travel. As a result, he depended on the tank commander for targeting instructions. This was not a significant problem when the Tiger was static and looking for targets, but it slowed the firing cycle to about 20–30 seconds when the Tiger had to engage targets while on the move. The loader (*Ladeschütze*) stood in the right side of the turret during combat operations, or sat on a small fold-out seat. The position was relatively spacious compared to the left side of the turret. The ammunition stowage was 92 rounds on the Tiger I and 72 rounds on the Tiger II. The 8.8cm ammunition was quite substantial, weighing 16kg for the KwK 36 on the Tiger I with a length of

TIGER I TURRET

1. Turret stowage bin
2. Gunner's turret stowage
3. Commander's vision cupola
4. Gunner's seat
5. Gunner's side vision port
6. Gunner's telescopic sight
7. 8.8cm gun breech
8. 8.8cm gun
9. Muzzle brake

10. Co-axial MG 34 machine gun
11. Loader's seat
12. Gunner's foot control pedal
13. Turret basket floor
14. Turret traverse motor
15. Spent casing buffer and gun safety guard
16. Commander's seat

(Jim Laurier © Osprey Publishing)

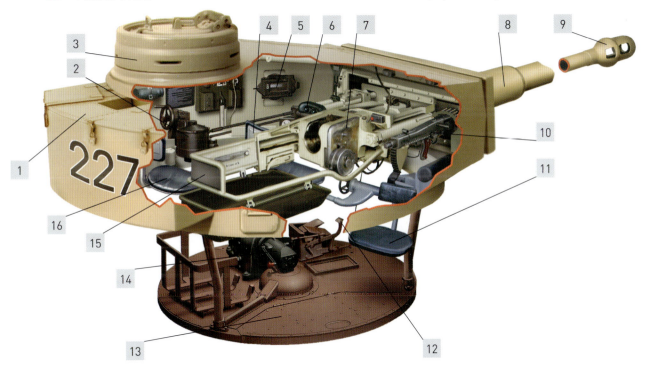

0.9m. The 8.8cm projectiles for the KwK 43 gun on the Tiger II were longer and heavier, weighing about 23kg. The driver (*Fahrer*) sat in the left front of the hull, and the radio was positioned in the hull next to the radio-operator (*Funker*), who sat in the right front corner of the hull opposite the driver. The radio-operator's main role was to operate the tank's Fu 5 SE 10U radio transceiver which was located to his left. All tanks in a Tiger company operated on a single, predetermined channel; according to doctrine, only the company commander (and platoon commanders in an emergency) was to

A British soldier takes cover next to a dead German Tiger I tank crewman in France near Tilly sur Seulles on 28 June 1944. (AirSeaLand/Cody)

send voice messages so that they would be clearly picked up by all tanks in the company. A Tiger crewman from schwere Panzerkompanie Hummel recalled that in reality 'everybody talks all the time, except the company commander, who can hardly get a word in edgewise'. Besides operating the radio, the radio-operator also manned the bow machine gun, an MG 34 in a ball mount.

FIREPOWER

The effectiveness of a tank's main gun depends on the penetration ability of the armour-piercing rounds, accuracy of the gun, characteristics of the gun sights and the ability to quickly acquire the target. Penetration statistics for armour plate expressed the thickness in mm that could be penetrated at an angle from the vertical of 30°.

OPPOSITE This PzKpfw VI Ausf E Tiger I appears to have improvised barbed wire on the sides of the vehicle, possibly to prevent enemy infantry approaching from the flanks to lay magnetic mines. (AirSeaLand/Cody)

The penetration of AP rounds fired from the 8.8cm KwK 36 L/56 shown in Table 1 was determined by tests conducted at firing ranges. Of the total ammunition load of 92 rounds, the recommended ratio was 50 per cent Pzgr 39 (AP, capped, ballistic capped with explosive filler and tracer) and 50 per cent Sprgr (HE shells). Occasionally, when available, a few rounds of Pzgr 40 (high-velocity, sub-calibre, tungsten core) were carried for use against the heaviest armoured Russian tanks and tank destroyers. The Pzgr 40, without an explosive filler charge, was not as lethal after penetration as the Pzgr 39.

TZF 9C TELESCOPIC SIGHT

The Tiger I's 8.8cm KwK 36 gun was aimed through a TZF 9c monocular telescope in place of the binocular TZF 9b used in the earlier versions of the tank. The telescope offered 2.5× magnification. The TZF 9c telescopic sight had an engraved reticle consisting of an aiming triangle in the centre with smaller triangles on either side. The gunner placed the target at the apex of the centre triangle.

(Jim Laurier © Osprey Publishing)

Inside the turret, a
close-up of the Tiger I's
main 8.8cm gun breech.
A spent casing buffer and
gun safety guard sat just
behind the breech.
(AirSeaLand/Cody)

A fourth type of round was the Gr 39 HL (HEAT) based on the hollow-charge principle. The Gr 39 HL was less accurate and much less destructive than the Pzgr 39, but could be carried in place of Sprgr, and used either to combat armour or as an effective HE round against soft targets.

The 8.8cm KwK 36 L/56 was a very accurate gun capable of first round hits at ranges exceeding 1,000m. The estimated accuracy is given as the probability of hitting a target 2m high and 2.5m wide, representing the front of an opposing tank. These tables are based on the assumption that the actual range to the target has been determined. Firing on the practice range was obviously more accurate than in combat conditions. This is reflected in the accuracy tables from an original manual on the 8.8cm KwK 36 L/56 as shown in Table 2. The sight for the Tiger I produced up to April 1944 was the articulated, binocular TZF 9b mounted parallel and on the same axis as the main gun. Each of the two sight tubes had a different sight reticle. The pattern in the left reticle consisted of seven triangles, separated by four mils. Placing the target on the point of a triangle allowed the gunner to aim without obstructing the view of the target. The distances between triangles were used to lead moving targets. The triangle height and separation distances in mils were also used as an aid in estimating the range to a target. The pattern in the right reticle also contained the seven triangles plus four adjustable range scales that allowed the gunner to register the exact range to the target. The range scale for the Pzgr 39 was graduated at 100m intervals out to a range of 3,000m, and the second range scale for the Sprgr was graduated out to a range of 5,000m.

Table 1: Armour Penetration

	Pzgr 39	Pzgr 40	Gr 39 HL
Shell weight	10.2kg	7.3kg	7.65kg
Initial velocity	773m/sec	930m/sec	600m/sec
Range			
100m	120mm	171mm	90mm
500m	110mm	156mm	90mm
1,000m	99mm	138mm	90mm
1,500m	91mm	123mm	90mm
2,000m	83mm	110mm	90mm

Table 2: Accuracy

Ammunition	Pzgr 39		Pzgr 40		Gr 39 HL	
Range	Practice %	Combat %	Practice %	Combat %	Practice %	Combat %
100m	100	100	100	100	100	100
500m	100	100	100	100	100	98
1,000m	200	93	99	80	94	62
1,500m	98	74	89	52	72	34
2,000m	87	50	71	31	52	20
2,500m	71	31	55	19		
3,000m	53	19				

With the replacement gun sight TZF 9c introduced in April 1944, the gunner could select two magnifications, 2.5× and 5×. The lower magnification provided a wider field of view for target identification, while the higher assisted in precise aiming at long ranges. Two adjustable range scales allowed the gunner to register the exact range to the target. The range scale was graduated in the same way as the 96 sight.

To traverse quickly onto a target, the Tiger I was outfitted with a hydraulic motor for the turret drive. The speed of traverse was dependent on the engine speed, the maximum being 360° in 60 seconds. The hydraulic traverse enabled coarse laying in order for the gunner to quickly acquire the selected target within the sight picture. The gunner's hand traverse and elevation wheels were used to make fine adjustment (laying the target onto the peak of the proper triangle in the sight reticle). If the power traverse failed, the turret could be traversed by hand. The gunner could be assisted by the commander using the auxiliary hand traverse.

Loading the 8.8cm ammunition though the top hatches was a long and exhausting job. The warhead of each shell alone weighed 6.8kg. (AirSeaLand/Cody)

MOBILITY

The capability of the Tiger I to negotiate obstacles and cross terrain was as good as or better than most German and Allied tanks, as shown by the performance characteristics listed in Table 3. The Tiger I initially experienced numerous automotive problems that required a continuous series of minor modifications to correct. These problems can be traced to three main causes: improperly sized brakes, leaking seals and gaskets, and an overtaxed drive train originally designed for a 40-tonne vehicle. Following modification of key automotive components, with experienced drivers taking required maintenance halts, the Tiger I could be maintained in a satisfactory operational condition.

The first production series Tiger Fgst Nr 250001 with Motor Nr 46052 was only run-in for 25km by Henschel before being sent to Kummersdorf for testing. During a test drive on 28 May 1942, with only 52km on the odometer, a blockage occurred in the steering gear. This Tiger quickly went through the original and two replacement engines (Motor Nr 46051 from 1 to 3 July, Motor Nr 46065 from 6 to 8 July), and was fitted with a fourth motor, Nr 46066, after 13 July. By 3 August 1942, this Tiger had covered a total of 1,046km; by 31 March 1943 5,623km; and by 31 July 1943 7,736km. These figures clearly demonstrate that once the Tiger had overcome its teething troubles, it could withstand a lot of purposefully administered abuse during test programmes.

Table 3: Performance

Maximum speed	45.4km/h
Maximum sustained road speed	20km/h
Average cross-country speed	15km/h
Radius of action, road	195km
Radius of action, cross-country	110km
Smallest turning radius	3.44m
Maximum turning radius	165m
Trench crossing	2.5m
Fording	1.6m
Step climbing	0.79m
Gradient climbing	35°
Ground clearance	0.47m
Ground pressure	0.735kg/cm²
Power to weight ratio	12.3 metric hp/ton with the Maybach HL 230 P45

BATTLEFIELD SURVIVABILITY

Along with the extremely effective main gun, a major asset of the Tiger I was the thick frontal armour. Even the side and rear armour protection was sufficient to eliminate any serious threat from the American 75mm or Russian 76mm tank guns at normal combat ranges. The tables extracted from a Wa Prüf 1 report dated 5 October 1944 catalogue the relative ability of the major opponents to penetrate the Tiger I and vice versa as shown in the Penetration Range Tables (Tables 4–6). The penetration ranges were determined based on the assumption that the tanks stood at a side angle of 30° to the incoming round. The data shows that the American Sherman with a 76mm M1 gun and the Russian T-34/85 both stood a chance at close range against the Tiger I. However, not a single Sherman that landed on the beaches at Normandy on 6 June 1944 had a 76mm gun. On 6 September 1944, only 250 out of 1,913 Shermans with the 12th Army Group had 76mm guns. Based on opposing ranges, without considering other factors, the Tiger I had only been outclassed by the Russian Josef Stalin heavy tank with the 122mm gun. The original report did not show the effectiveness of British tank guns against the Tiger I. The data presented in Penetration Range Table 7 was found in an STT secret document dated April 1944: it is obvious that the 17-pdr firing normal armour-piercing capped ballistic cap (APCBC) rounds could defeat

A PzKpfw VI Tiger I, on what appears to be the Eastern Front. On the mantlet, the tank has the single opening for the monocular sight that was introduced in April 1944. (AirSeaLand/Cody)

the frontal armour of the Tiger I at most combat ranges for tank vs tank actions in Europe. Although by 23 June 1944, only 109 Shermans with 17-pdrs had landed in France, along with six replacements, by the end of the war, on 5 May 1945, the British 21st Army Group possessed 1,235 Shermans with 17-pdrs, compared to 1,915 with 75mm M3 guns.

Table 4: Tiger I – Penetration Table: Cromwell, Churchill

		Tiger I vs Cromwell (8.8cm KwK)	Cromwell vs Tiger I (75mm M3)	Tiger I vs Churchill (8.8cm KwK)	Churchill vs Tiger I (75mm M3)
Front:	**Turret**	2,000m	0m	1,700m	0m
	Mantlet	2,700m	0m	1,400m	0m
	DFP	3,500m	0m	1,300m	0m
	Nose	2,500m	0m	1,100m	0m
Side:	**Turret**	3,400m	100m	1,700m	100m
	Super	3,500m +	100m	3,000m	100m
	Hull	3,500m	900m	3,000m	900m
Rear:	**Turret**	3,500m +	100m	2,600m	100m
	Hull	3,500m +	0m	3,500m +	0m
*DFP = Driver's Front Plate					

Table 5: Tiger I – Penetration Table: Sherman A2, Sherman A4

		Tiger I vs Sherman A2 (8.8cm KwK)	Sherman A2 vs Tiger I (75 mm M3)	Tiger I vs Sherman A4 (8.8cm KwK)	Sherman A4 vs Tiger I (76 mm M1A1)
Front:	Turret	1,800m	0m	1,800m	700m
	Mantlet	200m	0m	200m	100m
	DFP	0m	0m	0m	600m
	Nose	2,100m	0m	2,100m	400m
Side:	Turret	3,500m +	100m	3,500m +	1,800m
	Super	3,500m +	100m	3,500m +	1,800m
	Hull	3,500m	900m	3,500m +	3,200m
Rear:	Turret	3,500m +	100m	3,500m +	1,800m
	Hull	3,500m +	0m	3,500m +	1,700m

Table 6: Tiger I – Penetration Table: T-34/85, JS-122

		Tiger I vs T-34/85 (8.8cm KwK)	T-34/85 vs Tiger I (85mm S53)	Tiger I vs JS-122 (8.8cm KwK)	JS-122 vs Tiger I (122mm A19)
Front:	Turret	1,400m	500m	100m	1,500m
	Mantlet	400m	0m	100m	500m
	DFP	100m	300m	100m	1,300m
	Nose	100m	200m	300m	1,000m
Side:	Turret	2,200m	1,600m	1,000m	2,900m
	Super	2,100m	1,600m	1,000m	2,900m
	Hull	3,500m +	2,900m	1,500m	3,500m +
Rear:	Turret	3,200m	1,600m	100m	2,900m
	Hull	2,100m	1,500m	300m	2,700m

Table 7: Tiger I – Penetration Table: British Guns

		6-pdr APCBC	17-pdr APCBC
Front:	Turret	0yds	1,900yds
	DFP	0yds	1,900yds
	Nose	0yds	1,700yds
Side:	Turret	700yds	2,500yds +
	Super	700yds	2,500yds +
	Hull	1,000yds	2,500yds +
Rear:	Turret	700yds	2,500yds +
	Hull	600 ys	2,500yds +

OPERATIONAL HISTORY

Four Tigers with the 1. Kompanie/schwere Heeres Panzer-Abteilung 502 made their combat debut near Leningrad on 29 August 1942. The reputation of the Tiger was immediately distorted by false reports concerning the loss of Tigers involved in this first action. To counter some of the mythology, the short operational history that follows provides a concise history of each Tiger unit, as well as details on exactly when Tigers were delivered, including replacements. Although many veterans can provide stories of having to fend off Tigers continually, the following account reveals the actual numbers sent to each front.

The limited number available for action nevertheless left an overwhelming impression on their opponents. The original goal in creating Tiger units was not to construct complete battalions with 45 Tigers. As revealed during the famous meeting on 26 May 1941, the intention was to create units with 20 heavy Panzers to be used as spearheads for the Panzer divisions. This organizational concept was expanded by including light tanks within the unit. These light tanks were needed to perform numerous duties for which Tigers were not suited, including scouting, reconnaissance and messenger running, in addition to the escort role. Thus the first five independent battalions (501–505) and the first four companies organic to Panzer regiments (Großdeutschland and SS-1, 2 and 3) each had company organizations consisting of nine Tigers accompanied by ten PzKpfw III in accordance with K St N 1176d dated 15 August 1942, revised 15 December 1942. Only after the initial after-action reports

A damaged PzKpfw VI Tiger I is transported to the rear on a railcar after being captured by Soviet troops in 1944. (AirSeaLand/Cody)

The fate of this Tiger I in Normandy is unknown to the author. There does not appear to be any explosive effect around it, so it might have been toppled off the road following a breakdown or disability kill. (AirSeaLand/Cody)

were available was the decision made to outfit each company with 14 Tigers, as reflected in K St N 1176e dated 3 March 1943. Some unit commanders had argued that light tanks should still be retained in the organization to perform duties unsuitable for Tigers. By the end of June 1943, all of the units (with the exception of the 2./504) had been upgraded to the new organization with 14 Tigers per company.

SCHWERE HEERES PANZER-ABTEILUNG 501

Following the Allied landings in north-west Africa, Germany quickly sent troops to Tunisia to block access to Libya and deprive the Allies of bases within easy striking distance of Italy. One of these units was the schwere Heeres Panzer-Abteilung 501, which was one of the two Tiger units that had been promised to Rommel and prepared for tropical deployment. Originally, the 501st was to have been outfitted with the Porsche Tigers, but due to the delays and subsequent cancellation of Porsche-Tiger production, the 501st was issued normal Henschel Tigers in the Fgst Nr sequence 250011 to 250033.

TIGER I, SCHWERE HEERES PANZER-ABTEILUNG 501; NORMANDY, 1944

1. Maybach Olvar 40 12 16 gearbox
2. Maybach L600C steering gear
3. Zimmerit anti-magnetic paste
4. Bosch headlight
5. 7.92mm MG 34 hull machine gun
6. Spare glass blocks for driver's visor
7. Radio sets
8. MG 34 ammunition
9. Ammunition bags for machine gun
10. Co-axial 7.92mm MG 34
11. Loader's periscope
12. Loader's roof hatch
13. 8.8cm ammunition stowed in sponsons
14. Rear escape hatch
15. *Nahverteidigungswaffe* (close defence weapon)
16. Armoured roof (40 mm)
17. 8.8cm Kwk 36 L/56 gun
18. Small stowage bin
19. Recoil guard
20. Chain from spring to rear of gun recoil shield
21. Commander's cupola
22. Spring counterbalance
23. Commander's auxiliary hand traverse
24. Auxiliary traverse mechanism
25. Air inlet
26. Fire extinguisher
27. Radiator filler cap
28. Air outlet
29. Oil bath air filters
30. Heat shield
31. Cap for telescoping snorkel for deep fording
32. Maybach HL 230 P-45 V12 23-litre engine
33. Accessories box
34. Twin fans (left side)
35. Idler sprocket
36. Radiator (left side)
37. Fuel tank (left side)
38. Turret ring guard
39. Hydraulic traverse motor

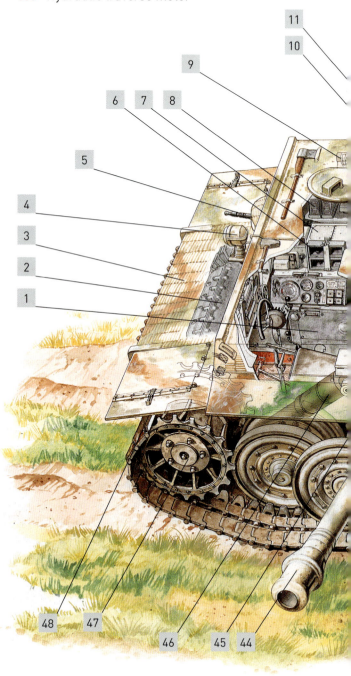

40. TZF 9c monocular sight
41. Gunner's hydraulic traverse pedals
42. Turret floor
43. Steel road wheels with internal rubber cushioning
44. Muzzle brake

45. Under-floor stowage bins
46. Shock absorber
47. Drive sprocket
48. 725mm-wide battle tracks

(Peter Sarson © Osprey Publishing)

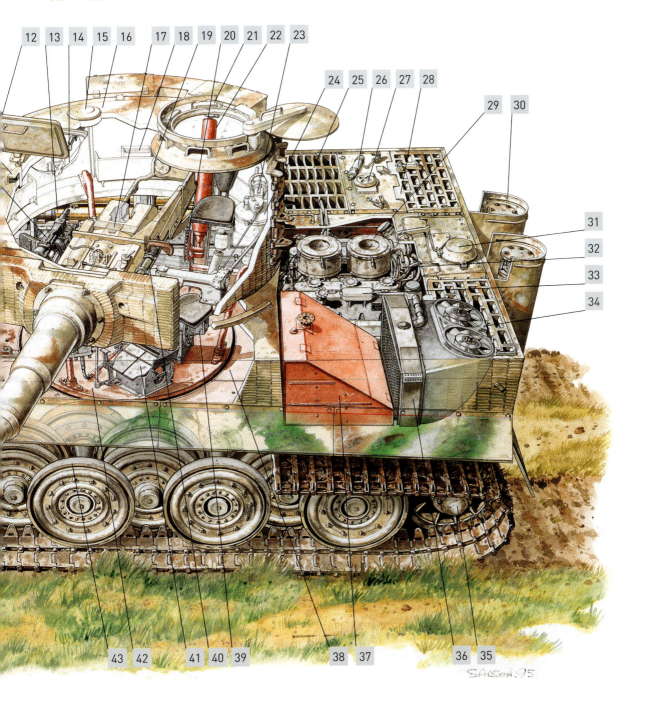

The 501st had been outfitted with 20 Tigers (two in September, eight in October and ten in November) and 25 PzKpfw III (7.5cm) Ausf N. All 20 Tigers safely made the crossing to Tunisia, the first three Tigers of 1. Kompanie being unloaded at Bizerta on 23 November 1942. The last two Tigers did not arrive until 24 January 1943, the second company having been diverted due to the occupation of southern France and therefore delayed in reaching Tunisia.

The 501st surrendered in Tunisia on 12 May 1943, but was re-formed from

A ditched Tiger I. No dedicated armoured-recovery vehicle was manufactured for either the Tiger I or the Tiger II. (AirSeaLand/Cody)

the surviving remnants in September and received 45 Tigers from the ordnance depot in October and November. Sent to the Eastern Front in November, the 501st did not receive any new production replacements until six Tigers were sent in June 1944. Decimated by the Russian summer offensive, the 501st was pulled out in early July 1944, re-formed again and issued with the Tiger II.

schwere Heeres Panzer-Abteilung 502

On 23 July 1942, Hitler had ordered that the first company of Tigers be formed quickly and sent to the front at Leningrad. The first unit to receive Henschel Tigers was the l. Kompanie of schwere Heeres Panzer-Abteilung 502, four arriving on 19 and 20 August. These Tigers, accompanied by four PzKpfw III (7.5cm) Ausf Ns, arrived at the front and went into combat on 29 August. Two of the four Tigers were still operational at the end of the day and the other two were recovered and repaired. On 21 September 1942, the Tigers and PzKpfw IIIs were sent into action again, with the loss of one Tiger and two PzKpfw IIIs. This action resulted in the first Tiger that was permanently lost. Having become hopelessly mired, the Tiger was subsequently filled with explosives and destroyed on 25 November 1942.

The hasty combat debut of the Tiger I had been a mistake. The boggy terrain on the Leningrad Front was hardly ideal for so heavy a tank. Heinz Guderian, Generalinspekteur der Panzertruppen (General Inspector of the Panzer Force), later blamed Hitler's impatience for the initial problems:

He was itching to try to try out the big tank. He therefore ordered that the Tigers be committed in a quite secondary operation, in a limited attack carried out in terrain that was utterly unsuitable, for in the swampy forest near Leningrad heavy tanks could only move in single file along the forest tracks, which, of course, was exactly where the enemy anti-tank guns were posted, waiting for them. The results were not only heavy, unnecessary casualties, but also the loss of secrecy and of the element of surprise for future operations.

It took three weeks to get the unit ready for combat again. During an attack near Tortolovo on 22 September, a PzKpfw III was knocked out and a Tiger I was hit and the engine failed; the crew abandoned the tank and set it on fire with a grenade to prevent its capture. The other three Tiger I tanks became bogged down in the marshy soil but were recovered.

The rest of the l. Kompanie of the 502nd arrived at the front on 25 September 1942 with five Tigers, nine PzKpfw IIIs (5cm KwK L/60) and five PzKpfw III (7.5cm) Ausf Ns. Renewed combat in January 1943 led to the first loss of a Tiger I to the Red Army. During fighting on 18 January, five Tiger I tanks were lost, including one that became stuck in a peat bog, two destroyed by their own crews and two more lost to Soviet anti-tank guns. The Red Army later recovered the bogged Tiger I and sent it to the Kubinka proving ground near Moscow for testing, soon followed by a second example. The 502nd's first nine Tigers were Fgst Nr 250002–250010, and seven new Tigers arrived at the front in February 1943 to replace losses. Ordered to upgrade to the current organization, the l. Kompanie received seven Tigers in June 1943 to fill their complement of 14 Tigers.

Having been outfitted in December with nine Tigers and ten PzKpfw III Ausf Ns, the 2. Kompanie was attached to the 503rd and left for the front on 29 December 1942. It arrived at the front on 5/6 January 1943 and first saw action on 7 January. On 10 February 1943, the 2. Kompanie of the 502nd was renamed 3. Kompanie/schwere Panzer-Abteilung 503 and became a permanent part of the 503rd.

On 1 April 1943, a new 2. Kompanie and a 3. Kompanie were formed for the

PzKpfw VI Tiger Is on the Eastern Front shelter beneath trees in late 1944. By this stage of the war, the Luftwaffe had virtually lost air superiority over the Eastern Front, and German tanks were regularly attacked by Red Air Force tank-killers such as the Ilyushin Il-2 Shturmovik. (AirSeaLand/ Cody)

1) Tiger I, l. Kompanie/schwere Heeres Panzer-Abteilung 502; near Leningrad, January 1943. Four Tigers of the 1./schwere Heeres Panzer-Abteilung 502 were sent to the front near Leningrad and were the first to see action when committed near Mga on 29 August 1942.

2) Tiger I, schwere Heeres Panzer-Abteilung 501; Tunisia, November 1942. The schwere Heeres Panzer-Abteilung 501 was one of the two Tiger units that had been promised to Rommel and prepared for tropical deployment. Originally outfitted with the Porsche-Tigers, the 501st was issued Henschel-Tigers due to the delays and cancellation of the Porsche-Tiger. The 501st was originally outfitted with 20 Tigers and 25 PzKpfw III (7.5cm) Ausf Ns, which were shipped to Tunisia between November 1942 and January 1943.

(Peter Sarson © Osprey Publishing)

502nd, and to fill these two companies and the Stab (headquarters) company, 31 Tigers were shipped from the ordnance depot between 19 and 26 May. The 1. Kompanie was joined at the front by the Stab, 1. and 2. Kompanien in early July 1943, bringing the unit strength up to 45 Tigers. They received 32 replacements in January and a further 20 in February 1944, bringing the strength of the 502nd to a total of 71 Tigers on 29 February, although only 24 were operational. The 502nd, renamed as the schwere Panzer-Abteilung 511 on 5 January 1945, continued the struggle on the Eastern Front until the end of the war.

In this interesting photograph, taken in France shortly after the Normandy landings of 6 June 1944, a Tiger I follows a captured British Daimler Dingo armoured car. Note how, with the endless threat of air attack, the tankers have camouflaged their vehicle heavily with foliage. (AirSeaLand/Cody)

schwere Heeres Panzer-Abteilung 503

The second unit promised to Rommel, the 503rd, was to receive Porsche Tigers, but the cancellation of production resulted in the 503rd being outfitted with 20 Henschel Tigers in November and December 1942 and 25 PzKpfw III Ausf Ns. Due to the successful Russian winter offensive, the 503rd was sent east, with the first elements arriving on 1 January 1943. The 503rd was upgraded and received 24 new Tigers in April 1943, completing their complement of 45 Tigers. Having lost only four Tigers during the Kursk offensive and a further four during the withdrawal, the unit received 12 replacements in August 1943. The 503rd was rested and outfitted with 45 new Tigers and re-entered combat on 21 January 1944. It received a further 35 new Tigers in February and March 1944 before being withdrawn from combat in late April that year. Transferred back to the West, the 503rd received a further 33 Tiger Is and 12 Tiger IIs and was sent to Normandy. The unit first saw action on 11 July 1944 and subsequently lost most of its Tiger Is in the withdrawal during August 1944. On 9 September 1944, the 503rd was ordered to rest and refit with the Tiger II.

schwere Heeres Panzer-Abteilung 504

The 504th was the second Tiger unit to be sent to Tunisia. It was issued 25 PzKpfw IIIs plus two Befehls-Tigers in January, and 18 Tigers in February 1943. The first three Tigers arrived in Tunisia on 12 March 1943, followed by five on 22/23 March, two on 1 April and the last of the 11 on 16 April. Only the Stab and l. Kompanie, with 11 Tigers and 19 PzKpfw IIIs, were transported to Tunisia, the 2. Kompanie being held on Sicily with the remaining nine Tigers and six PzKpfw IIIs. The elements in Tunisia surrendered on 12 May 1943.

On 13 April 1943, the OKH ordered that six Tigers were to be stationed on Sicily and that until transferred to Tunisia, the 2./schwere Heeres Panzer-Abteilung 504 was to be attached to Panzer-Abteilung 215, with a reinforced platoon of six Tigers being immediately shipped to Sicily.

Altogether 17 Tigers gathered on Sicily: the original nine from the 2. Kompanie of the 504th, two Tigers that had been issued as replacements for the 501st in February and the six Tigers issued in April 1943 for the 215th. Attached to Panzer-Division

This Tiger I appears to have been destroyed by its crew before being abandoned; the split muzzle was usually a sign of putting a grenade or demolition charge into the barrel, to wreck the gun. (AirSeaLand/Cody)

Hermann Göring, the 17 Tigers under the 2. Kompanie of the 504th attacked the American landing zone on 11 July 1943, but were neutralized by naval gunfire. Within the first three days, ten of the 17 were destroyed to prevent capture, and a further six Tigers were destroyed later for the same reason. The last Tiger was shipped back across the strait of Messina to Italy.

The 504th was rebuilt and received 45 Tigers in March 1944, remaining in training for an unprecedented three months, before it was decided to send the unit to the Eastern Front. However, the Allied successes in Italy in May 1944 caused Guderian to reverse this decision, and on 3 June 1944 he requested that the 504th be transferred to Italy, just three days before the Allied landings in Normandy. Heavily engaged in stemming the Allied drive in Italy, the 504th lost half its Tigers before the end of June. Remaining in Italy until the end of the war, the 504th received only 12 new replacement Tigers in July 1944 and the 15 left behind by the 508th in February 1945.

schwere Heeres Panzer-Abteilung 505

The 505th was the last independent battalion created with the old organization of 20 Tigers and 25 PzKpfw IIIs. Formed in February 1943, the 505th received several Tigers and the rest in March along with 25 PzKpfw IIIs. The unit was loaded on rail cars on 29/30 April and sent to Heeresgruppe Mitte on the Eastern Front, where it was ordered to upgrade to the new organization and received 11 Tigers that were shipped from the ordnance depot between 8 and 10 June 1943.

At the start of the Kursk offensive on 5 July 1943, the unit had 31 Tigers and was joined on 9 July by 3. Kompanie, which had formed in April and received Tigers in June. The 505th lost only four Tigers during the Kursk offensive, but lost a further six by the end of July. The first five replacement Tigers were shipped from the ordnance depot on 23 September 1943; 12 more were shipped in April 1944 (six on 8 April and six on 14 April) and another 12 on 18 May. Decimated during the Russian summer offensive, the 505th was ordered to return to Germany to refit with Tiger IIs on 11 July 1944.

schwere Heeres Panzer-Abteilung 506

Formed on 20 July 1943, the 506th was the first independent battalion to be created with an original complement of 45 Tigers, which it received in August 1943. It left by rail for the Eastern Front on 12 September and reached Heeresgruppe Süd on 19 and 20 September. The first 12 replacements were shipped on 29/30 January 1944, quickly followed by five more Tigers on 10 February. The 506th was completely refitted with 45 new Tigers, the last arriving at the unit on 8 April 1944. Their last six replacement Tigers were shipped on 22 July 1944, and on 15 August the 506th was ordered to refit with the Tiger II.

THE TIGER AT KURSK

Tiger strength was gradually built up in anticipation of Operation *Zitadelle*, the offensive to cut off the Kursk salient in July 1943. The bulk of these were in two Heer battalions, schwere Heeres Panzer-Abteilung 503 in the south and schwere Heeres Panzer-Abteilung 505 in the north, each with a nominal strength of 45 Tiger I tanks. Panzergrenadier Division Großdeutschland had a reinforced Tiger I company and the three SS-Panzer-Divisionen each had a Tiger I company, each with a nominal strength of 14 tanks. A total of 133 Tiger I tanks were available at the start of *Zitadelle*, but only 97 were ready on the first day due to lingering mechanical problems and difficulties moving such a heavy tank to the front without adequate tactical bridging. Tiger strength quickly fell due to combat attrition. Although very few Tiger I tanks were written off as total losses, many were disabled in the first days of fighting upon encountering minefields. In the case of one of the Tiger battalions, an entire company was disabled by mines in one day.

The Tiger I's thick armour offered it excellent protection except against the heaviest of Soviet anti-tank weapons. Most Tiger tanks withstood multiple hits against their frontal armour; the few penetrations that did occur were usually of the more vulnerable side and rear armour. At this stage of the war, Soviet T-34 and KV-1 tanks were armed with the 76mm gun which could not penetrate the Tiger frontally at normal combat ranges. The Tiger I was essentially invulnerable to most Soviet tank and anti-tank guns in frontal engagements. The only effective Tiger killers were the relatively rare 57mm anti-tank guns, or overmatching weapons such as heavy field guns or 85mm anti-aircraft guns used in a direct-fire mode. For example, a number of Tiger I tanks were knocked out when their commander cupolas were completely blown off by a direct field-gun hit. The Tiger I's 8.8cm gun proved to be a formidable weapon against the Soviet tanks: the two Heer Tiger battalions claimed 182 Soviet tanks up to 16 July, when the offensive was called off.

In spite of the Tiger's overwhelming advantage when facing Soviet tanks, its actual tactical impact was far more modest. The Tiger's one moment of glory during the Kursk fighting was on 5 July, when schwere Heeres Panzer-Abteilung 505 was able to penetrate the initial defensive belt of the Soviet 15th Rifle Division near Butyrki in the Heeresgruppe Mitte sector. However, the rapidity of this breakthrough was unanticipated, and follow-on Panzer divisions were not ready to exploit the success. In the Heeresgruppe Süd sector, schwere Heeres Panzer-Abteilung 503 proved far less effective. Against doctrine, it was split up into its three constituent companies and used piecemeal, with little tactical effect. Within the first three days of fighting, the combat effectiveness of the Tiger units had been diluted by poor tactical employment, the ubiquitous Soviet minefields and mechanical breakdowns. On average, only about 38 per cent of the Tiger force was operational on any given day, though the readiness rate varied considerably from day to day. Overall, the Heer and Waffen-SS Tiger units reported total losses of only 13 Tiger tanks by 16 July, but they had suffered temporary losses of 87 tanks and had only 52 ready for action.

The technical superiority of the Tiger I was almost meaningless in view of the small number of tanks available from day to day, especially when so thinly spread across such a large front.

Tiger I availability reached its nadir in the wake of the Kursk fighting, with only 18 per cent of the available tanks actually operational, gradually increasing to 31 per cent by the end of 1943. The Tiger I was most extensively used on the Eastern Front. Of the 1,238 Tiger I tanks lost in combat, 859 (69 per cent) were lost on the Eastern Front and only 187 in the West, mostly in Normandy.

PzKpfw VI Ausf H1 Tiger I. The planned H2 turret was designed by Rheinmetall-Borsig and was supposed to be mounted on the 101st Henschel Tiger chassis. This Tiger variant was cancelled in July 1942 when the decision was made to continue production of the Ausf H1 with the 8.8 cm KwK L/56. The deadly L/70 gun was mounted in the Panther. (AirSeaLand/Cody)

Tiger I, schwere Heeres Panzer-Abteilung 506; Russia, 1943. The schwere Heeres Panzer-Abteilung 506, formed in July 1943, was the first to adopt the new organization with a complement of 45 Tigers from the very beginning. Issued their 45 Tigers in August 1943, the 506th was sent to the Eastern Front in September.

(Peter Sarson © Osprey Publishing)

schwere Heeres Panzer-Abteilung 507

The 507th, formed on 23 September 1943, was equipped with 45 Tigers between 23 December 1943 and 25 February 1944. Transferred to the Eastern Front in March 1944, the 507th received seven replacement Tigers before the end of the month and a further 12 in April, eight in July, six in August, ten in November and one final Tiger in December 1944. Overstrength at 55, the 507th met the Russian winter offensive on 14 January 1945 and by 1 February had only seven Tigers left, none of which were operational. On 6 February, the 507th was ordered to return to Germany to refit with the Tiger II.

schwere Heeres Panzer-Abteilung 508

Issued with 45 Tigers in December 1943 and January 1944, the 508th was ordered to Italy to attack the Allied bridgehead at Anzio. Unloaded at a railhead 200km from the bridgehead, about 60 per cent of the Tigers suffered mechanical failures negotiating the narrow, sharply curved mountain roads. The 508th, along with other units outfitted with Panthers and Ferdinands, were repulsed mainly by the threat of naval gunfire. Five replacement Tigers were shipped from the ordnance depot on 23 March, followed by six on 25 April.

Following the losses to the Allied drive in May and early June, the 508th received a further 27 replacement Tigers that were shipped from the ordnance depot on 3 and 5 June 1944. On 4 February 1945, the 508th gave their remaining 15 Tigers to the 504th and returned to Germany for outfitting with the Tiger II.

Tiger I, schwere Heeres Panzer-Abteilung 508; Italy, 1943. This Tiger was one of eight shipped from the ordnance depot to Tigergruppe Meyer on 28 July 1943. As was the custom in this Tigergruppe, the Tigers were given names, in this case *v.Eschnapur* in white on the driver's front plate, apparently getting the idea from the then popular adventure film *Der Tiger von Eschnapur*.

(Peter Sarson © Osprey Publishing)

A Tiger I in Italy in 1944. The schwere Heeres Panzer-Abteilung 508 was outfitted with 45 Tigers in December 1943 and January 1944 and ordered to Italy to attack the Anzio bridgehead. (AirSeaLand/Cody)

schwere Heeres Panzer-Abteilung 509

Formed on 9 September 1943, the 509th was issued 45 Tigers, the last of which arrived on 30 September 1943. Ordered to the Eastern Front on 28 October, the first elements unloaded on 3 November. The first eight replacements were shipped to the unit on 2 and 5 February 1944, and a major reinforcement occurred between 20 May and 1 June, when the unit was sent 30 Tigers. The final 12 new Tiger Is were sent by 1 August 1944, and in September the 509th returned to Germany to refit with the Tiger II.

schwere Heeres Panzer-Abteilung 510

The last of the ten independent heavy tank battalions was formed on 6 June 1944, and received its 45 Tigers between 20 June and 7 July. Sent to the Eastern Front in late July, six replacements were shipped to the 510th on 3 August and the 510th remained on the Eastern Front to the end of the war, having never been issued a single Tiger II.

schwere Panzer-Abteilung (FKL) 301

Panzer-Abteilung 301 returned from the Eastern Front to rest and refit with Tigers to use as control vehicles for the BIV Sprengladungstrager (remotely controlled demolition vehicles), and was organized with a headquarters and three companies each with ten Tigers. Twenty-one Tigers were shipped from the ordnance depot between 25 August and 15 September 1944 and an additional ten were taken over from the schwere SS-Panzer-Abteilung 103. The 301st was first reported on the Western Front by the LXXXI. Armeekorps on 6 November 1944 as having 31 Tigers (27 operational) and 66 BIV (61 operational).

1) Tiger I, schwere Heeres Panzer-Abteilung 509; Russia, late 1943.
This Tiger I, tactical number '122', of the schwere Heeres Panzer-Abteilung 509 saw action in the area of Shitomir in late 1943.

(Peter Sarson © Osprey Publishing)

2) Tiger I, schwere Heeres Panzer-Abteilung 505; Russia, February 1944. The schwere Heeres Panzer Abteilung 505 had one of the most spectacular non-regulation markings. They painted their unit emblem, a knight on a charger, on both turret sides.

(Peter Sarson © Osprey Publishing)

During the evening of 26 February 1945, Tiger I Nr 201 of schwere Panzer-Abteilung (FKL) 301 moved down Köln-Aachener Strasse in Elsdorf, Germany, to confront the approaching tanks of Task Force Welborn of the 3rd Armored Division. Around 2100hrs, an M4 Sherman tank was set ablaze, either by a Panzerfaust or German artillery fire. This fire silhouetted the turret of Pershing T26E3 *Fireball* that was partially hidden by a street barrier. The Tiger fired three shots in rapid succession from a range of about 100m. The first shot penetrated through the co-axial machine-gun opening in the gun mantlet, killing the Pershing's gunner and loader. The second 8.8cm round hit the muzzle brake of *Fireball*, jamming the barrel and causing the 90mm round to detonate prematurely in the tube. The third 8.8cm round glanced off the upper corner of the mantlet of *Fireball*. Moments later, Tiger I Nr 201 became immobilized in the rubble of house No. 74 when it tried to reverse back down the street. The crew abandoned the Tiger I and it was recovered by US troops the following morning.

(Jim Laurier © Osprey Publishing)

Four Tigers were lost before the 301st was engaged in the Ardennes offensive, and at the beginning of the attack on 16 December 1944 the 301st reported 27 Tigers available, of which 12 were operational. It still had 27 Tigers, of which 21 were operational, on 30 December. The 301st remained on the Western Front until the end of the war.

schwere Panzer-Kompanie (FKL) 316

Panzer-Kompanie (FKL) 316 was issued ten Tiger Is in September 1943 (three shipped on September 30 and seven on October 8) and five Tiger IIs in March 1944, which they did not use in combat. Attached to the Panzer-Lehr-Division and engaged in Normandy, the 316th had six out of eight Tigers operational on 1 June, and three Tigers undergoing repair on 1 July. By 1 August 1944, the 316th was no longer with the Panzer-Lehr-Division.

13. Kompanie/Panzer-Regiment Großdeutschland

At Kharkov in 1943, a PzKpfw VI Tiger I of the famous Großdeutschland Division. (AirSeaLand/Cody)

A schwere Kompanie was formed for Panzer-Regiment Großdeutschland on 13 January 1943 and received a total of nine Tigers and ten PzKpfw IIIs. The company was sent to the Eastern Front in February 1943 and in May received six additional Tigers to upgrade it to the new organization. On 1 July 1943 the unit was renamed as the 9./Panzer-Regiment Großdeutschland, and at the start of the Kursk offensive on 5 July the company had 14 out of 15 Tigers operational. None of these Tigers were lost during the battle.

III. Abteilung/Panzer-Regiment Großdeutschland

An entire heavy tank battalion of three companies with 45 Tigers was created for Panzergrenadier Division Großdeutschland as the III. Abteilung/Panzer-Regiment Großdeutschland. Its first company (9. Kompanie) was provided by the old 13. Kompanie; the second and third companies (10. and 11. Kompanien) were the former 3. Kompanie schwere Heeres Panzer-Abteilung 501 and 3. Kompanie schwere Heeres Panzer-Abteilung 504 respectively. The Stab, 10. and 11. Kompanien joined the 9. Kompanie at the front on 14 August 1943, by which time they had received 31 Tigers.

The first six replacements arrived at the front on 26 August. Further replacements followed in 1944, with ten in February, six in March, six in April, 14 in May, six in June, 12 in July, six in October and a final four in December. The battalion remained on the Eastern Front, without being relieved or refitted, until the final surrender.

ABOVE This PzKpfw VI Ausf E Tiger I has been fitted with a snorkel device for deep wading, although the practicalities of attempting to do so with such a large vehicle are questionable. (AirSeaLand/ Cody)

261

schwere Panzer-Kompanie Hummel

The Allied drive out of Normandy decimated the units trapped in the 'Falaise Gap' and the remnants trying to cross the Seine. With open space all the way to Berlin, the schwere Panzer-Kompanie Einsatz Dunkirchen was hastily formed by the schwere Panzer Ersatz und Ausbildungs Abteilung 500 at the training grounds near Paderborn. This unit, with 14 Tigers, was sent west on 19 September to stop the British spearhead at Arnhem in Holland. It was renamed the next day as schwere Panzer-Kompanie Hummel, and continued to fight on the Western Front after it was incorporated into schwere Heeres Panzer-Abteilung 506 as the 4. Kompanie on 8 December 1944.

Training and research/development units had originally received a total of 49 Tiger Is for training and ten Tiger Is for testing. As Germany's position continued to deteriorate, additional units were thrown together and given these worn-out Tigers in a last-ditch effort. Amongst these units were: schwere Panzer-Kompanie Paderborn with 15 Tigers on 21 October 1944, Panzer-Kompanie Panther with three Tigers (30 January 1945), Ersatz Brigade Großdeutschland with two Tigers (31 January 1945) and Panzer-Abteilung 500 Paderborn with 17 Tigers (2 April 1945).

Tigers of the schwere SS-Panzer-Abteilung 101 move through Normandy in 1944. In tank 205 is the legendary Michael Wittman. (AirSeaLand/Cody)

TIGER I HEAVY TANK

Panzer-Abteilung Kummersdorf

Having received the last five Tiger Is to be issued on 23 February 1945, this unit joined the makeshift Panzer-Division Muncheberg in an attempt to halt the Russian advance. Absorbing remnants from other units, it reported having 13 Tigers, of which ten were operational on 15 April.

Tigergruppe Meyer

Before the loss of Sicily, eight Tigers were shipped from the ordnance depot on 28 July 1943, to outfit an independent unit destined for Italy. Known as Tigergruppe Meyer, this small unit, with its eight Tigers, was attached to Panzerjäger-Abteilung 46 between August and November 1943, and by 4 February 1944 was renamed Tigergruppe Schwebbach and attached to the LXXVI. Panzer-Korps to attack the bridgehead created by the Allied landing at Anzio. None of the Tigers remained operational on 12 February, but seven of the eight were available by 15 February for the planned attacks. On 11 March 1944, the surviving crews and Tigers of Tigergruppe Schwebbach were incorporated into schwere Panzer-Abteilung 508.

schwere Panzer-Kompanien (SS-Panzer-Regiment 1, 2 and 3)

Effective 15 November 1942, three schwere Panzer-Kompanien were established, one each for the SS-Panzer-Regiments l, 2 and 3. Each Kompanie was to have nine Tigers and ten PzKpfw IIIs, and 28 Tigers and 30 PzKpfw IIIs were issued in December 1942 and January 1943. Sent to the Eastern Front, all three companies took part in Manstein's counter-offensive to retake Kharkov in February–March 1943, in which they lost three Tigers.

An order dated 22 April 1943 authorized these three companies to be upgraded to 14 Tigers, and by this same order the three companies became an organic part of the schwere Panzer-Abteilung of the I. SS-Panzer-Korps. However, the three companies remained with their regiments at the front. In May 1943, 17 Tigers were shipped to the front, bringing the total to 13 with the 13./SS-Panzer-Regiment 1, 14 with the s. Kp./SS-Panzer-Regiment 2 and 15 with the 9./SS-Panzer-Regiment 3.

Of these 42 Tigers, 35 were operational at the start of the Kursk offensive on 5 July 1943, of which three were lost, one from each company. Five replacements arrived for the 13./SS-Panzer Regiment 1 on 25 July before it was ordered to Italy with SS-Panzer-Division LSSAH. Before leaving on 28 July, nine Tigers were transferred to s.Kp./SS-Panzer-Regiment 2 and eight Tigers to 9./SS-Panzer-Regiment 3. The s.Kp./SS-Panzer-Regiment 2 remained on the Eastern Front, receiving five Tigers in September 1943 and a further five in January 1944. Having lost their last Tiger, the unit was ordered to return to the West on 14 April 1944.

A Tiger I opens fire with its main gun during the epic armoured battle at Kursk in the summer of 1943. Tiger strength had been gradually built up specifically in anticipation of Operation *Zitadelle*. (AirSeaLand/Cody)

The 9./SS-Panzer-Regiment 3 also remained in the East and received five replacement Tigers in 20 September 1943. It was originally ordered to return to the West to refit as part of the parent schwere SS-Panzer-Abteilung 101, but the order was rescinded by Hitler and 9. Kompanie was then refitted with ten Tigers in May 1944. The final five replacement Tigers were shipped from the ordnance depot on 26 July.

schwere SS-Panzer-Abteilung 101

By an order of 19 July 1943, a schwere Panzer-Abteilung was formed for I. SS-Panzer-Korps. Two new heavy companies were to be created and 13. Kompanie of SS-Panzer Regiment 1 was to be incorporated as the third company.

Having been pulled out of Russia in response to the landings in Sicily in July 1943, SS-Panzer-Division LSSAH was refitted and sent to Italy in August 1943. Attached to the division were elements of the newly formed schwere SS-Panzer-Abteilung of the I. SS-Panzer-Korps with 27 Tigers that had been issued in July 1943. As a result of Italy's defection, LSSAH remained in northern Italy until mid-October. The unit was then transferred back to the Eastern Front, where it was renamed schwere SS-Panzer-Abteilung 101.

The 1. and 2. Kompanie went east with LSSAH, but the rest of the battalion remained behind at a training ground. Eleven Tigers were received in February 1944, and on 4 April the remnants of Panzer-Division LSSAH were ordered to return to the West to refit. In the interim, the rest of schwere SS-Panzer-Abteilung 101 had received 19 Tigers, ten being shipped on 29 October 1943, six on 11 January and two on 14 January 1944. The nineteenth Tiger was provided as a gift from the Japanese, who had purchased one originally shipped from the depot on 16 October 1943. After the return of the rest of the battalion from the Eastern Front, a further 26 Tigers were received during April 1944.

The lead elements of the 101st reached the front in Normandy on 12 June 1944, six days after the Allied landings. By the end of June, the l. Kompanie had lost 15 of its 45 Tigers and was pulled out in July to refit with the Tiger II. The 101st still had 25 Tigers, of which 21 were operational on 7 August, but these were all lost during that month's retreat, the remnants of the 101st being ordered back to the training grounds to rest and refit with the Tiger II on 9 September.

The Tiger I made its first combat outing in North Africa, where this vehicle was photographed. The earliest US encounter with Tiger Is was near Sidi Bou Zid in Tunisia. (AirSeaLand/Cody)

schwere SS-Panzer-Abteilung 102

Originally created in April 1943 as the schwere Panzer-Abteilung for the I. SS-Panzer-Korps, three Tiger companies were deployed at the front but the headquarters remained behind at the training grounds. On 1 June 1943, the I. SS-Panzer-Korps was renamed the II. SS-Panzer-Korps and the 13./SS-Panzer-Regiment 1 was lost to the schwere SS-Panzer-Abteilung for the new I. SS-Panzer-Korps. A new third Tiger company was created, and on 22 October 1943 the unit was renamed schwere SS-Panzer-Abteilung 102.

When the 9./SS-Panzer-Regiment 3 was ordered to remain with the 3.SS-Panzer-Division Totenkopf in the East, the 102nd was left with two new companies with no combat experience and the decimated remains of the schwere Kompanie of SS-Panzer-Regiment 2 Das Reich, which returned from the front in April. Six Tigers were shipped from the ordnance depot on 21 April 1944, followed by another 39 between 20 and 29 May.

Ordered to the front in Normandy, the first seven trains unloaded west of Paris on 27 June, but the threat of attacks from Allied fighter-bombers was sufficient to delay their arrival at the front until 7 July. On 20 July, the 102nd still had 42 Tigers, of which 17 were operational. No fewer than 30 operational Tigers were reported on 30 July and 21 on 8 August, but all these had been lost by 7 September and the unit was ordered to return to the training grounds to rest and refit with the Tiger II. The six Tigers that had been shipped as replacements on 22 August never reached the 102nd, but were handed over to schwere SS-Panzer-Abteilung 103.

schwere SS-Panzer-Abteilung 103

The schwere SS-Panzer-Abteilung 103 was originally formed on 1 July 1943 as the II.Abt./SS-Panzer-Regiment 11 and sent to Yugoslavia to fight as infantry. However, at the end of November, the battalion was converted to the schwere SS-Panzer-Abteilung 103. Isssued six Tigers in February 1944 for training, the 103rd was ordered to give them to another unit in March. Another six Tiger Is arrived at the training grounds on 26 May and four more in August. On 20 October, all ten Tiger Is were given to schwere SS-Panzer-Abteilung (FKL)301 and the 103rd was outfitted with the Tiger II before being ordered to the Eastern Front.

Hungary

On 22 July 1944, three Tiger Is left the ordnance depot by rail for delivery to the Hungarian Army. In addition, an unknown number of Tiger Is were acquired from the schwere Heeres Panzer-Abteilung 503 or 509 who had been assigned to train the Hungarian crews.

EVALUATION

The Tiger proved most effective in combat in the 1943 campaigns, when it was almost invulnerable to Allied tanks. By the summer of 1944 it began to face improved Allied guns, including the British 17-pdr, Soviet 85mm gun and US Army's 90mm gun. A German report from 1944 recognized the difference:

When Tigers first appeared on the battlefield, they were in every respect proof against enemy weapons. They quickly won for themselves the title of 'unbeatable' … But in the meantime, the enemy has not been asleep. Anti-tank guns, tanks, and mines have been developed that can hit the Tiger hard and even knock it out. Now, the Tiger, for a long time regarded as a 'Life insurance policy' is relegated simply to the ranks of a heavy tank … No longer can the Tiger prance around,

267

OPPOSITE TOP A technical manual photograph shows the side of the PzKpfw VI Tiger I. This tank features the original rubber-tyred road wheels, replaced from 1943 by all-steel versions. (AirSeaLand/Cody)

OPPOSITE BOTTOM A Soviet soldier stands atop a PzKpfw VI Tiger I. He is prising open the turret storage box, on which the tank's tactical number was usually stencilled. (AirSeaLand/Cody)

oblivious to the laws of tank tactics. They must obey these laws, just as every other German tank must.

Aside from its increasing vulnerability, the Tiger was arguably less well suited to the conditions in the West than in the East. Tiger tank tactics favoured long-range engagements due to the power of their 8.8cm guns. Typical engagement ranges in the East in 1943 were in the order of 1,700–2,000m due to the more open terrain. In the West in the autumn and winter of 1944, engagement ranges were typically much shorter due to congested terrain and the urban-industrial sprawl along the western German frontier. The Tiger battalions saw most of their combat against the First US Army in the industrialized areas of western Germany, such as the Roer region east of Aachen in November 1944 and the Ruhr region around Kassel in February–March 1945. The fighting in the Ardennes in December 1944–January 1945 took place in a less industrialized area, but the forested and hilly terrain also reduced engagement distances. The shorter engagement ranges reduced the Tiger's long-range advantages while at the same time increasing its vulnerability to flank shots against its thinner side armour. There were more abundant terrain features that permitted US tanks to manoeuvre for side shots.

Tiger tanks in the West also suffered from the nature of their deployment. They were usually committed as part of a separate tank battalion attached at corps level rather than being attached to a Panzer division. As often as not, the German corps commanders had few Panzer reserves at their disposal, and so the Tiger battalions were often broken up into companies and sent off on separate missions in the hopes of fulfilling impossible defensive demands. Instead of being used as a concentrated mass, they appeared on the battlefield in small groups where they were vulnerable to attrition when pitted against much more numerous US tanks and anti-tank weapons. Furthermore, the tendency to split up the battalions on separate missions only served to exacerbate the Tiger's low durability, since the scattered companies were more difficult to support with the battalion's very limited maintenance and recovery assets.

Of the Tiger I and Tiger II, the Tiger I was the more efficient design when operating in the West. Its 8.8cm gun, though less powerful than the longer weapon on the Tiger II, was still deadly enough to deal with virtually any Allied tank encountered in the West. Even if its armour was not as effective as in 1943, it was still a very tough opponent, especially in a head-on engagement.

CHAPTER 6

KING TIGER

A Tiger II with its gun raised to maximum elevation; it could be elevated to +15° or depressed to -8°. (AirSeaLand/Cody)

A PzKpfw Tiger Ausf B with the Porsche turret. Porsche's design requirement for a 1,900mm turret ring proved too small for the 8.8cm main armament. (AirSeaLand/Cody)

By 1942 heavy tank design had advanced considerably since the German manufacturing firm Henschel began development of a 30-tonne Durchbruchwagen (breakthrough vehicle) in 1937. While Germany had been on the strategic offensive between 1939 and 1942, lighter armoured vehicles such as the 23-tonne Panzer III (main) and 25-tonne Panzer IV (infantry support) had proved sufficient in the manoeuvre and exploitation roles. Combat on the Eastern Front, however, necessitated tanks and self-propelled guns of increasing size and firepower as the Germans and Soviets both attempted to maintain an edge in the arms race.

As Germany's military stance steadily transitioned to the defensive, the continued modification and modernization of existing armoured vehicle types would not be a sustainable, long-term solution. An entirely new vehicle design was needed. Henschel's 57-tonne Tiger I had proved an effective counter to the Soviet T-34 and the heavier KV-1 and British designs, but by mid-war its boxy design was already six years old. The German authorities knew they would eventually need a more modern replacement, and Henschel, and their rival Porsche, were subsequently tasked with its development.

DEVELOPMENT

On 26 May 1942, the German Ordnance Department's Waffenprüfamt 6 (Wa Prüf 6, Weapons Proving Office) determined that the replacement for the Tiger I should be able to achieve 40km/h, have a main armament capable of penetrating 100mm of rolled homogeneous armour (RHA) from 1,500m and possess front and side armour of 150mm and 80mm respectively. Under Wa Prüf 6's office head, Oberst Friedrich-Wilhelm Holzhäuer, and chief designer, Heinrich Ernst Kniepkamp, development soon got underway for what would become the heaviest operational tank of the war. Henschel expanded on their 45-tonne VK 45.01 (H), essentially a heavier version of the Panzer IV mounting the experimental 7.5cm/5cm Waffe 0725; this relied on the Gerlich Principle, where a skirted round was fired through a tapering barrel to increase velocity, distance and hitting power. To assist penetration, the projectile's tip comprised very hard, dense tungsten-carbide, but as this material was also used to create armour machining tools, limited stockpiles forced the cancellation of the weapon. Porsche's VK 45.02 (P) proposal was based on their previous attempt to secure the Tiger I contract. The vehicle's weak engine and suspension, high ground pressure and an over-engineered fuel/electrical drive train – which relied on copper and other materials that would be in short supply for wartime mass production – sealed its fate. Intended to incorporate Rheinmetall-Borsig's new 8.8cm Flak 41 L/74 anti-aircraft gun, it was found to require a breech/counterweight that was too long to fit into turrets designed to house the shorter main armament of the Tiger I. Although Ferdinand Porsche held Hitler's favour, his efforts to produce the Tiger II were cancelled on 3 November 1942 in favour of the competition's improved prototype.

A PzKpfw VI Ausf B Tiger II with a Porsche turret. Porsche's VK 45.02 (P) proposal was based on their previous attempt to secure the Tiger I contract. (AirSeaLand/Cody)

As part of this *Tigerprogram*, Henschel's updated VK 45.03 (H) possessed the long 8.8cm KwK 43 main gun coupled with sloped armour that resembled a bulked-up medium Mark V Panther. To simplify future maintenance and supply, the Tiger II also included transmission, track, engine cooling system and other components that were interchangeable with the proposed Panther replacement. Hitler's calls for thicker armour and improved manoeuvrability meant that work on the prototype was slower than anticipated as the vehicle's side panels had to be strengthened during production to compensate for the added weight.

LAYOUT

The Tiger II's interior and crew positions adhered to conventional German tank layout, with the forward compartment housing the driver and radio operator/bow machine gunner behind the glacis on the left and right, respectively. The driver had an adjustable seat, which could be raised to allow his head to protrude through his open hatch to improve visibility when driving in non-combat environments. Both crewmen had their own hatches and were separated by the vehicle's drive train and radio equipment.

The central fighting compartment comprised the turret, which, because of the vehicle's lengthy barrel, needed to be long and roomy to accept the breech's recoil and function as a counterweight. An attached platform/'basket' enabled the turret to rotate as a complete entity with its component parts and floor, which improved safety and operating efficiency. The gunner sat to the left, just ahead of the commander, with the loader to the breech's right. Because of the turret's size it limited the commander's downward visibility from the cupola when 'buttoned up'. As the Tiger II's transmission and drive wheels were at its front, a universal joint needed to be run under the turret basket to the rear-mounted engine, which increased the vehicle's height by 0.5m and added to its weight as more armour was needed to cover the difference.

PRODUCTION HISTORY

Following an initial order for three prototype chassis, an initial production series of 176 Tiger IIs was ordered in October 1942. Following cancellation of the Porsche Tigers in November 1942, the contract was quickly expanded by an additional 350. Later extensions to the contracts increased the total order to more than 1,500.

A horse takes centre stage in this photograph, rather than the Tiger II behind it. The open hatch on the turret belongs to the loader, while the commander stands in the cupola to the right. (AirSeaLand/Cody)

In accordance with the original production plans from October 1942, the first Tiger II was to be completed in September 1943. The number produced each month was to be expanded to reach a target of 50 per month in May 1944. This production schedule satisfied the Inspekteur der Panzertruppen, who wanted 100 Tiger IIs available for a spring offensive in 1944. Due to delays, the first prototype Fgst Nr V1 was accepted by the Waffenamt inspector in November 1943. Two further prototypes, Fgst Nr V2 and V3, and the first three production series Tiger IIs (Fgst Nr 280001–280003) were accepted in January 1944. The production run continued through to March 1945 for a total of three prototypes and 489 production series Tiger IIs produced by Henschel.

Production at Henschel was severely disrupted by a series of five bombing raids on 22, 27 and 28 September and 2 and 7 October 1944. A total of 2,906 tonnes of high explosive and 1,792 tonnes of incendiary bombs were dropped, with the Henschel plant the intended target. This destroyed 95 per cent of the total factory floor area. A further bombing raid on 15 December, again aimed at the factory, delayed recovery. In addition, heavy area bombing raids on Kassel and its vicinity, resulting in further disruptions to Tiger II production, occurred during the period of 22 and 23 October, and 30 December 1944 to 1 January 1945. The bombing campaign caused the loss in production of at least 657 Tiger IIs (940 planned versus 283 produced) during the period from September 1944 to March 1945. Henschel ceased all tank production by the end of March 1945.

PZKPFW TIGER II AUSF B 'HENSCHEL TURM'

1. Muzzle brake
2. 8.8cm KwK 43 L/71 gun
3. Driver's hatch
4. Loader's auxiliary traverse wheel
5. Gun mantlet
6. Gunner's turret traverse wheel
7. TZF 9b monocular sighting telescope
8. Main gun recuperator and recoil mechanism
9. Loader's periscope
10. *Nahverteidigungswaffe* 'S' mine projector
11. Loader's hatch
12. Ventilating fan
13. Racks of 8.8cm ammunition (steel-cased)
14. Commander's cupola
15. 2m antenna for FuG 5
16. Henschel turret
17. Rear escape hatch
18. Pistol port
19. Shield for ammunition stowage
20. Wooden rollers for loading
21. Brackets for hanging spare track
22. Commander's seat
23. Gunner's seat
24. Fan cover
25. Fuel tanks
26. Fuel tank switch-over lever
27. Seven rounds of ammunition
28. Armoured bulkhead
29. Fighting compartment heater
30. Water container
31. Swing arm
32. Gunner's shield
33. Torsion bars
34. Lower fuel tank
35. Turret traverse gear
36. Tool box
37. Gear box cover
38. Driver's seat (can be raised for head-out driving)

39. Handbrake
40. Emergency track steering lever
41. Clutch pedal
42. Foot brake
43. Track steering lever
44. L801 steering unit
45. Gear shift (eight forward, four reverse)
46. Power steering wheel
47. Olvar gearbox

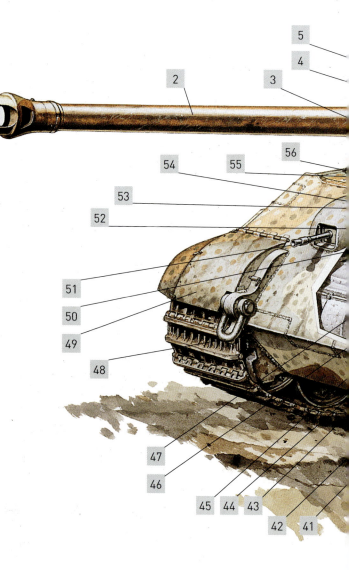

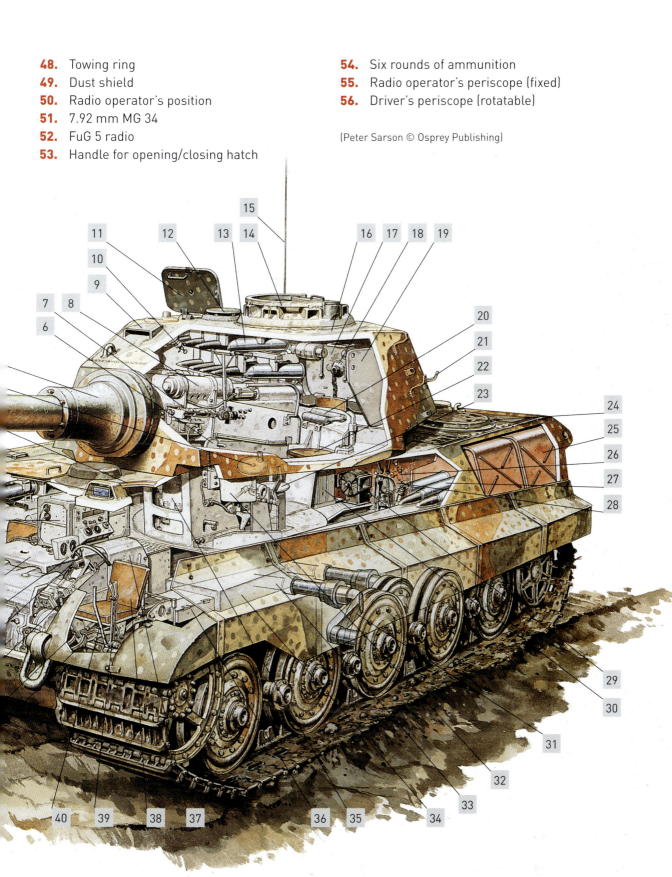

48. Towing ring
49. Dust shield
50. Radio operator's position
51. 7.92 mm MG 34
52. FuG 5 radio
53. Handle for opening/closing hatch

54. Six rounds of ammunition
55. Radio operator's periscope (fixed)
56. Driver's periscope (rotatable)

(Peter Sarson © Osprey Publishing)

MODIFICATIONS

As with all series of German Panzers, modifications to the Tiger IIs were frequently introduced during the production runs. Each of these modifications by itself did not substantially alter the appearance or tactical capability of the Tiger II. As with our analysis of the Tiger I, here we will summarize, in date order, the key modification to the vehicle.

January 1944

Curved front fenders with fixed form-fitting sideplates replaced the flat front fenders with hinged sideplates that were installed on the three prototypes, with the start of the production series from Fgst Nr 280001. The Zimmerit anti-magnetic coating was applied to the production series Tiger IIs starting with Fgst Nr 280001, but not to the three prototypes Vl, V2 and V3.

February 1944

To prevent hot exhaust gases from being sucked into the cooling system, the upright exhaust pipes with deflector were replaced by exhaust pipes bent to direct the exhaust away from the Tiger. The sheet metal heat shield that had surrounded the upright exhaust pipes was no longer mounted. This modification had already been tested on the three prototypes but was not present on several of the first production series Tiger IIs. Starting in February, a *Kuhlwasserheizgerät* (engine coolant heater) was installed on the left side of the Maybach HL 230 P30 engine. An access port for a blow-torch was located on the tail plate below the armoured guard for the left exhaust pipe. When not in use, the access port was covered by an oval-shaped armoured cover secured by two bolts. The *Kuhlwasserheizgerät* was used in the winter for preheating the coolant before an attempt was made to start the engine.

This photograph of a Tiger II nicely illustrates the curved upper profile of the turret, one of the key design elements that distinguished the vehicle from the Tiger I. (AirSeaLand/Cody)

May 1944

The original *Geländekette* (operational track) Gg 24/800/300 design for the Tiger II had double track links, consisting of the main link, a connecting link with three end connectors and two track pins. This design allowed the same track to be mounted on both the left and right side, without causing the vehicle to pull to one side. Each double link weighed 62.7kg and was driven by a sprocket with 18 teeth. This double link design was very loose, with little resistance to bending, and therefore little power was wasted in driving the tracks. However, this original track design was prone to climbing on to the sprocket and thereby being jammed or thrown. Due to the variations in the track pitch between links, the sprocket teeth wore unevenly, which was an indication of destructive stresses to the internal drive train components.

A new double-link *Geländekette*, having a cast connecting link without a guide horn, was installed by Henschel starting in May 1944. This new design was not as flexible as the old and resisted sideways motion. Only the main link was engaged by the nine-tooth drive sprocket. This new operational track was backfitted to Tiger IIs produced prior to May 1944.

The monocular TZF 9d (sighting telescope) replaced the previously used binocular TZF 96/1. An armour plug was welded in place to close the second sight aperture that had been cut into the face of the 'Porsche' turrets.

The original production version of the 8.8cm KwK 43 (L/71) consisted of a one-piece monobloc gun tube. Starting in May 1944, this was gradually replaced by a two-piece sectional monobloc gun tube that was easier to produce in quantity with no degradation in the performance. A lighter, smaller muzzle brake was fitted to the sectional monobloc guns.

In this view of the Tiger II the width of the tracks is evident – they measured 800mm wide, giving even such a heavy tank a generally practical ground pressure. (AirSeaLand/Cody)

June 1944

A Tiger II Ausf B captured by US troops in Belgium, 1944–45. In May 1944, a new type of track was introduced that minimized uneven wear and helped prevent it from climbing over the drive sprocket when in motion. (AirSeaLand/Cody)

The demand for deep fording equipment was not relaxed until mid-1944. The reason given for abandonment of total submersion was that it was thought that rivers would have to be waded until it was discovered that the standard 16-tonne engineer bridge could carry the Tiger II. The deep fording equipment was actually only installed in several Tiger IIs for experimental testing.

For most Tiger IIs built before and all built after June 1944, the hinged bell-shaped armoured cover was replaced by a wire mesh screen installed over the air intake hole that had been originally cut into the deck for the telescoping air intake pipe. By order dated 17 February 1943, from Wa Prüf 6, Krupp was only authorized to complete 50 of the 'Porsche' turrets, for which the curved armour plates had already been formed. Three additional turrets originally ordered for Porsche prototypes were also converted by Krupp for mounting on Henschel chassis from April–August 1944.

Turrets with the strengthened, sloping frontplate, without the bulge for the commander's cupola, were designed by Krupp and mounted on Tiger IIs, starting with Fgst Nr 280048 in June 1944.

Three Pilsen (cylindrical sockets) were welded to the turret roof to be used in securing the base of a 2-tonne *Kran* (jib boom). This *Kran* could be used to lift the decking and drive train components from the vehicle on which it was mounted, or to lift components from an adjacent vehicle. A general order from June 1944 authorized backfitting to Tiger IIs that had originally been produced without this modification.

July 1944

Starting in July 1944, hangers and fasteners to mount replacement double-track links were welded fore and aft on both turret sides. In November 1944, permission was given to the troops to backfit this modification for Tiger IIs with both turret types. This modification was first authorized on 8 May 1944 after extensive firing trials had been conducted to determine the effect extra track links had on the protection provided by the 80mm armour plate. The results were that on vertical and up to 10° sloped plates, the protection afforded against penetration by medium calibre anti-tank rounds was actually reduced. At 30° and greater sloped plates, the afforded protection increased. At angles between 10° and 30°, there was no change in the afforded protection.

These Tiger II hulls were recovered from the Tiger production plant at Kassel and were shipped back to the United States for tests at Aberdeen Proving Ground, Maryland. (AirSeaLand/Cody)

August 1944

The narrower (660mm wide) transport tracks were carried on the Ssyms-Wagen for rail transport of the Tiger IIs. To readily distinguish the transport tracks used for the Tiger II from those used for the Tiger I, two or three out of every ten links were to be painted red. This change was to have been completed within four to six weeks after issuing the general order on 3 August 1944. To comply with a general order dated 19 August 1944, all Tiger IIs were to be painted with a standardized camouflage pattern prior to being shipped from the Henschel factory. Every effort was to be made to deliver part of the August consignment of Tiger IIs with this new 'ambush' camouflage pattern. Patches of olive green (RAJ 6003) and red brown (RAL 8017) paint were sprayed over the dark yellow (RAL 7028) base coat. Prior to this, the Tiger IIs were all delivered with a base coat of dark yellow (RAL 7028) paint covering the red primer undercoat and Zimmerit, and each individual unit applied its own camouflage colours.

To simplify production, starting with Fgst Nr 280177, the inside of the Tiger II was no longer coated with *Elfenbein* (ivory) paint, but merely left with only the basic coat of red oxide primer that had been applied by the armour manufacturers.

September 1944

By an order dated 9 September 1944, the Zimmerit anti-magnetic coating was no longer to be applied at the factory to new production tanks. This was followed by an order dated 7 October 1944 directed at the troops not to apply Zimmerit to Panzers they received without this coating. These orders were based on rumours that the Zimmerit caught fire from shell hits, which could cause the loss of the tank even if the shells did not penetrate. Tests conducted in November, firing AP, HEAT and white phosphorus shells at two captured T-34s coated with Zimmerit, did not in any case result in setting a tank on fire. However, the orders to stop applying Zimmerit were never rescinded and all Tiger IIs delivered after mid-September 1944 did not receive a coating of Zimmerit.

By another order dated 9 October 1944, thinner paint was to be applied at the factory than had been previously used for painting the Tiger IIs that had been covered with Zimmerit. By an order dated 31 October 1944, Henschel was to cease covering

The rear turret of the Tiger II, liberally covered with Zimmerit anti-magnetic mine paste. The paste was applied to the vehicle in the factory and hardened with direct heat. (AirSeaLand/Cody)

A Tiger II on the streets of Budapest, Hungary, in 1944. It has a production turret (as evidenced by the two-piece barrel) and a Bosch headlight on the glacis. (AirSeaLand/Cody)

the external surface of the Tigers with a base coat of dark yellow (RAL 7028). Before leaving Henschel, the Tiger IIs were to be painted with a camouflage pattern using patches of dark yellow (RAL 7028), red brown (RAL 8017) and olive green (RAL 6003) applied directly to the basic red oxide primer. If dark yellow was not available, *Feldgrau* (field grey) could be used as a substitute, but only sparingly. Already prior to this order in September 1944, Tiger IIs had left the factory without the base coat of dark yellow, with large areas of red primer that hadn't been covered with paint. The areas that had been covered had a very thin coat of camouflage paint.

Starting with Tiger II, Fgst Nr 280255, completed on or about 15 September 1944, a circular plate was bolted over the opening in the rear deck originally intended for the telescoping air intake pipe to prevent shell splinters from penetrating the fuel tank mounted directly below this opening. This modification was authorized to be backfitted by the troops. In October 1944 the mounting brackets for the 20-tonne *Wagenwinde* (jack) were no longer welded on the rear, since *Wagenwinden* were no longer issued with the Tiger II.

December 1944

At the end of November 1944, the armour manufacturers (DHHV, Krupp and Skoda) were ordered to cover all armour components with a base coat of dark green (RAL 6003) paint prior to delivering the components to Henschel or Wegmann for use in assembly. Not waiting for the backlog of already delivered parts to be exhausted, on 20 December 1944 the Waffenamt ordered Henschel to immediately begin painting

KING TIGER TURRET

1. Recoil cylinder
2. Coaxial 7.92mm MG 34
3. Loader's forward vision port
4. Turret ventilator
5. Localized support port (smoke, flares, etc.)
6. Turret rotation handwheel
7. Loader's seat
8. Ammunition storage
9. Ammunition transfer support roller
10. Falling wedge breech
11. Commander's seat
12. Gunner's seat
13. Traverse and elevation handwheels
14. Commander's cupola
15. Ring mount for a 7.92mm MG (anti-aircraft)
16. TZF 9d telescope

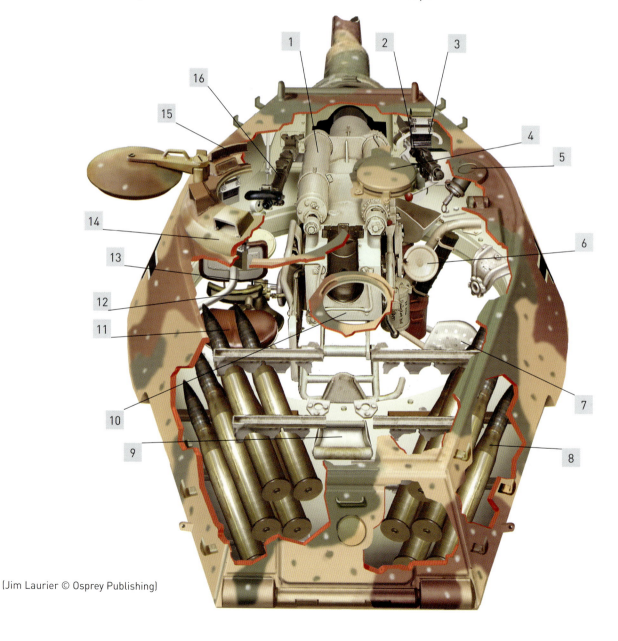

(Jim Laurier © Osprey Publishing)

the external surfaces of the Tiger II with a base coat of dark green (RAL 6003) paint. The camouflage pattern with sharp contours was to be applied using red brown (RAL 8017) and dark yellow (RAJ 7028) paint. The Waffenamt approved a modification for mounting plates over the air intake gratings on the rear deck to prevent entry of shell splinters or bullets from strafing aircraft. This modification was completed on one Tiger II belonging to the Waffenamt. From pictorial evidence, these plates were not installed by Henschel at the factory, and there is no evidence that the modification was attempted by the troops.

January 1945

In September 1944, the armour manufacturers were ordered to initiate a modification by welding an inverted U-shaped guard over the sight aperture. This guard was designed to prevent rain from fouling the gun sight. Extending well beyond the turret face, the guard also reduced the angle at which the gunner would be blinded when trying to aim in the direction of a rising or setting sun. Due to the backlog of turrets already delivered by the armour manufacturers, this modification did not routinely appear until after January 1945.

This view of a Tiger II shows the squat front profile of the tank. Dust shields normally seen over the tracks have either been removed or were not fitted. (AirSeaLand/Cody)

March 1945

A new single-link design for the wider operational tracks *Geländekette* Kgs 73/800/152 was accepted for production toward the end of November 1944. This new track, again driven by an 18-tooth sprocket, was available for Tiger IIs completed by Henschel in March 1945.

TIGER II AUSF B, POMERANIA, 1945

The specifications and illustrations are of a Tiger II Ausf B of 2. Kompanie, schwere Heeres Panzer-Abteilung 503, February 1945 (common to vehicles 269–72, 350–55 and 362–90).

General

Production run: November 1943–March 1945 (17 months)
Vehicles produced: 492 (inc three prototypes)
Combat weight: 69.8 tonnes (with 'series' turret)
Crew: five (commander, gunner, loader, driver, radio/bow machine-gun operator)

Dimensions

Length (hull/overall): 7.62m/10.29m
Width (without aprons/with aprons): 3.65m/3.75m
Height: 3.09m
Ground clearance: 0.5m

Armour (degrees from vertical)

Glacis (upper/lower): 150mm @ 50°/100mm @ 50°
Hull side (upper/lower): 80mm @ 25°/80mm @ 0°

Hull rear: 80mm @ 30°
Hull roof: 40mm @ 90°
Hull bottom (front/rear): 40mm/25mm @ 90°
Turret face: 180mm @ 10°
Turret mantlet: 150mm (Saukopf)
Turret side: 80mm @ 21°
Turret rear: 80mm @ 20°
Turret roof: 40mm @ 78°
Cupola side: 150mm @ 0°

Armament

Main gun: 8.8cm KwK 43 L/71 (22 turret/64 hull) (typically 50 per cent Pzgr 39/43 and 50 per cent Sprgr 43)
Sight: TZF 9d articulated monocular (2.5×/5×)
Secondary: 2 × 7.92mm MG 34 (co-axial; bow); additional 7.92mm MG (anti-aircraft) (5,850 rounds)
Main gun rate of fire: 5–8rpm
Turret rotation (360°): 10 sec @ 3,000 engine rpm; 19 sec @ 2,000 rpm; 77 sec by hand

3.09m

3.75m

(Jim Laurier © Osprey Publishing)

Communications

Internal: Bordsprechanlage B intercom

External: FuG 5 10-watt transmitter/USW receiver (wireless telegraphy and radio telephony stationary ranges were 6km and 4km, respectively; an FuG 2 (USW receiver only) was less common, and had a comparable range)

Motive power

Engine: Maybach HL 230 P30 12-cylinder (water-cooled) 23l (gasoline)

Power to weight: 600hp (sustained) @ 2,500rpm; 700hp (max) @ 3,000rpm (10hp/tonne)

Transmission: Maybach Olvar EG 40 12 16 B; eight forward, four reverse gears

Fuel capacity: 860 litres in seven tanks

Performance

Ground pressure (hard/soft): 1.03kg/cm^2/0.76kg/cm^2

Maximum speed (road/cross-country): 41.5km/h/20km/h

Operational range (road/cross-country): 170km/120km

Fuel consumption (road/cross-country): 5.1 litre/km/7.2 litre/km

Fording: 1.8m

Step climbing: 0.8m

Climbing: 35°

Trench crossing: 2.5m

10.29m

Factory modifications

The following modifications appeared on a Tiger II turret that was captured in the factory but had never been mounted on an operational tank. Other completed turrets that had not been mounted on Tiger IIs, which were also captured in the factory, did not have these three latest modifications. Three sets of hangers and fasteners were welded fore and aft on each turret side to each hold one spare *Geländekette* Kgs 73/800/ 152 track link. These replaced the two sets of hangers and fasteners designed for the earlier double-link track links. A ring for the clamped-on anti-aircraft machine-gun mount was no longer welded above the periscope guards on the commander's cupola. In its place, a double-arm variation was to be fastened to a mount welded in place at the base of the cupola. Five steel loops were welded to each turret side. These loops were to be used for holding tree branches carried for additional camouflage.

On 28 February 1945, the armour manufacturers were asked when turrets modified to mount *Entfernungsmesser* (rangefinders) would be produced. DHHV stated that they would strive to complete their first turret by 31 March and Krupp promised to start with their 601st turret planned for mid-July 1945. Therefore, the effort was initiated too late to complete any Tiger IIs with rangefinders before the factory in Kassel fell into the hands of Allied troops.

A knocked-out Tiger II, its right-hand track completely gone. The Tiger II incorporated a twin steel-rimmed, rubber-cushioned type of road wheel, which improved maintenance and cold-weather operation as ice and snow were less likely to impede rotation. (AirSeaLand/Cody)

US troops ride atop a captured Tiger II. Note that the bow machine gun has been completely removed when the tank was taken out of service. (AirSeaLand/Cody)

Henschel sent a change order to the armour manufacturers dated 12 December 1944, to enlarge the opening on the rear deck for improved access to the motor. The larger opening was to be covered by a three-piece hatch. Each separately hinged section had an air inlet cowling. The air intake gratings above the radiators were to be covered with a finer wire mesh screen. The armour manufacturers were allowed to complete rear decks to the previous design specifications until all parts were exhausted prior to switching to manufacturing rear decks of the new design. Based on a common two to six months' backlog of partially completed component parts, and the fact that enough armour components had already been delivered to complete all 489 Tiger IIs produced by Henschel, it is highly unlikely, but possible, that a few Tiger IIs were produced with the new rear deck with three hatches over the motor compartment.

FIREPOWER

For the Tiger II, Krupp and Rheinmetall-Borsig produced two prototypes of the new 8.8cm KwK 43 L/71 gun, with the former being an entirely new design and the latter simply a reworked Flak 41 L/74. As Krupp's version was shorter, possessed a muzzle brake and used shorter, more easily stored projectiles, it was deemed superior and accepted for production. (AirSeaLand/Cody)

For the Tiger II, Krupp and Rheinmetall-Borsig produced two prototypes of the new 8.8cm KwK 43 L/71 gun, with the former being an entirely new design and the latter simply a reworked FlaK 41 L/74. As Krupp's version was shorter, possessed a muzzle brake and used shorter, more easily stored projectiles it was deemed superior and accepted for production. As an internally mounted variation of the PaK 43 anti-tank gun it was initially developed with a monobloc barrel and mated to Porsche's 'pre-production' turret. Considerable stress from firing high-velocity rounds, however, necessitated a change to a two-piece weapon, which eased construction and the ability to change barrels. A falling wedge breech block ejected spent shell casings and remained open for another round, and because of the main gun's large size, a muzzle brake was installed both to vent unwanted propellant gases and to reduce recoil.

As with the Tiger I's gun, the penetrating ability of AP rounds fired from the 8.8cm KwK 43 L/71 was determined by tests conducted at firing ranges; the results are shown in Table 1. The total ammunition load was 86 rounds (80 for the Tiger II with 'Porsche' turrets), and the ammunition types and recommended ratios of AP types to HE types was largely the same as the Tiger I (see previous chapter). The 8.8cm KwK 43 L/71 offered similar accuracy to the KwK 36 L/56, with good possibilities of first-round hits at ranges exceeding 1,000m. Comparable accuracy charts to those shown in Chapter 5 are given in Table 2.

Table 1: Armour Penetration

	Pzgr 39/43	Pzgr 40/43	Gr 39/3 HL
Shell weight	10.2kg	7.3kg	7.65kg
Initial velocity	1,000m/sec	1,030m/sec	600m/sec
Range			
100m	202mm	238mm	90mm
500m	185mm	217mm	90mm
1,000m	165mm	193mm	90mm
1,500m	148mm	171mm	90mm
2,000m	132mm	153mm	90mm

Table 2: Accuracy

Ammunition	Pzgr 39/43		Pzgr 40/43	
Range	Practice %	Combat %	Practice %	Combat %
100m	100	100	100	100
500m	100	100	100	100
1,000m	100	85	100	89
1,500m	95	61	97	66
2,000m	85	43	89	47
2,500m	74	30	78	34
3,000m	61	23	66	25
3,500m	51	17	-	-
4,000m	42	13	-	-

The sight for most of the Tiger IIs that actually got into combat was the articulated, monocular TZF 9d mounted parallel and on the same axis as the main gun. The gunner could select two magnifications, 3× and 6×. The lower magnification provided a wider field of view for target identification. The higher magnification assisted in precise aiming at long ranges. Sight operation and graduations were the same as those described in Chapter 5.

The Tiger II was outfitted with a hydraulic motor for the turret drive. The speed at which the turret was traversed under power was dependent on the engine speed and selection of a low or high range by the gunner. With the high-range power traverse engaged and the engine turning over at 2,000rpm, the turret could be traversed through 360° in 19 seconds. At the maximum allowable engine speed of 3,000rpm, the turret could be traversed 360° in less than ten seconds.

Tiger II ammunition

The Pzgr Patr 39/43 (1), an APCBC/HE-T round, was the Tiger II's primary anti-tank round. Specifically designed to handle the high internal barrel pressures within the KwK 43 L/71 gun, the projectile possessed a tracer and a second driving band for added stability and accuracy over its PzGr 39-1 predecessor (which could still be used provided the main gun had fired fewer than 500 times). Its hard shell was capped by softer metal to minimize disintegration from high-velocity strikes, while the addition of a ballistic cap reduced drag. It also caused armour to crack and weaken before the shell made contact, and promoted better penetration, after which the shell's Amatol (60 per cent TNT/40 per cent ammonium nitrate) bursting charge would explode. The projectile could also be used by other 8.8cm guns as indicated by the text on the cartridge, which also gave the weight ('6,900kg'), the explosive charge ('GuRP-G1,5-(725/650-5,1/2)'), the manufacturer and manufacture date of the fuse ('dbg1943/1', where 'dbg' indicates Dynamit AG) and the manufacturing location and date of the round ('Jg20.1.43K').

The Sprgr Patr 43 (2), an HE round, was used against unarmoured vehicles, infantry and static defensive positions. The projectile had no tracer, and except for a second driving band it was the same as the older L/4.7 version. It relied on Amatol explosive, as per the Pzgr Patr 39/43, and the projectile could also be used by other 8.8cm guns as shown by the text on the cartridge. The text on the shell indicated where and when the fuse was manufactured ('14 Jg20.1.43'), the round's weight class ('III'), explosive charge ('R8') and the round's manufacturing location and date ('Jg18.1.43N'). The tip (firing pin and nose) and the piece extending into the round were the AZ 23/28 (*Aufschlagzünder* or 'impact fuse'), around which was the main explosive filling. This fuse type could be set for direct-action or delay; it was so sensitive that tank crews were warned against firing through trees or other obstructions just beyond the barrel for fear of premature detonation.

The Gr Patr 39/43 Hl (3) was a HEAT (high-explosive anti-tank) shell that relied on a shaped-charge to penetrate armoured vehicles. Again, the projectile could also be used by other 8.8cm guns as indicated by the text on the cartridge. The text on the shell indicated the kind of round ('Hl'), cyclonite/wax explosive ('91'), the fuse manufacturer and date ('Jg20.1.43'), the weight class ('III') and the round manufacturer and date ('Jg18.1.43N'). The round's tip comprised a small direct-action AZ 38 fuse, which on impact detonated a conventional hollow charge that was set back to allow the conical liner and explosive to properly form a high-velocity metal jet. The rear component was the detonator. As only about 7,000 shaped-charge Gr Patr 39/43 Hl rounds were produced, their use was uncommon, and the round's low velocity and degraded effectiveness from having to spin made it suspect with many crews.

The Pzgr Patr 40/43 (4), an HVAP/-T round, was to be used against the thickest enemy armour. The limited availability of tungsten after 1943 meant that the 'HK'

TIGER II GUN SIGHT

Here we see the view through a Tiger II's TZF 9d gun sight targeting a Red Army IS-2 as it and another are resupplied by a Lend-Lease supply truck. Believing themselves to be safely out of enemy range, the two halted IS-2s take on supplies and fuel before moving up for an attack. Soviet support personnel go about their business next to an American IHC M-5-6×4-318 supply truck. When the Soviets went over to the strategic offensive in 1943, foreign-provided Lend-Lease equipment and vehicles such as this one greatly assisted with logistics. The Tiger II's firing sequence proceeds similarly to that of the IS-2. With a projectile ready in the breech, and if the target is beyond some 500m, the gunner estimates the target's actual size and divides it by the number of mils it encompasses in the scope. The loader adjusts the tick marks on the TZF 9d monocular gun sight in accordance with both the selected ammunition and the range, the latter being agreed upon by the driver, gunner and commander. Once it is rotated so that the large black triangle at the scope's top points to the estimated range, the upper tip of the large central triangle atop the vertical line is located between the targeted IS-2's turret and hull.

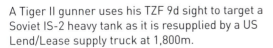

A Tiger II gunner uses his TZF 9d sight to target a Soviet IS-2 heavy tank as it is resupplied by a US Lend/Lease supply truck at 1,800m.

Fine-tuning his aim from 2.5× to 5× magnification, the gunner prepares to fire a Pzgr Patr 39/43 APCBC/HE-T round into the unsuspecting enemy vehicle's thinner side armour.

(Jim Laurier © Osprey Publishing)

(*Hartkernor*, 'hard core') Pzgr 40/43 armour-piercing composite rigid projectile was also produced with steel ('S' for *Stahlkern*) or iron ('W' for *Weicheisen*) core expedients. The all-black APCR (AKA high-velocity armour-piercing) acted as a kinetic penetrator and had a smaller explosive charge than the Pzgr Patr 39/43. Because of its lighter weight the shell was affected by wind resistance and decreased accuracy. Compared to the production of 1.98 million Pzgr Patr 39/43s and 2.48 million Sprgr Patr 43s, only about 5,800 Pzgr Patr 40/43s were made.

MOBILITY

A Tiger II chassis has here been converted into a locally produced mine-clearance vehicle. Panzer chassis appeared in a variety of ingenious industrial and commercial uses in the aftermath of the war. (AirSeaLand/Cody)

To avoid production delays and maximize vehicle hardware interchangeability, it was decided to use the HL 230 P (Panzermotor) 30 engine for the Tiger II. Built by Maybach, Auto Union (four automobile manufacturers, including Audi) and Daimler-Benz, it was being used in other heavy German armoured vehicles including the medium 45-tonne Panther and late-model Tiger I. Because of the Tiger II's additional weight, a transverse torsion-bar suspension system comprising nine load-carrying axles per side was incorporated. This provided independent wheel movement in the vertical, increased stiffness in turns, helped retain stability over rough terrain and allowed a theoretical maximum speed of 41.5km/h over hard, level surfaces, although a much lower pace was

recommended during general operation. As opposed to the Tiger I's interleaved road wheels, its successor incorporated a twin steel-rimmed, rubber-cushioned type, which improved maintenance and cold-weather operation as ice and snow were less likely to impede rotation. Changing gears was surprisingly easy for a front driving sprocket that provided power to the 'shoe' and 'connector link' style continuous tracks, which were tensioned by a rear idler and controlled via power steering.

Numerous statements have been made that the Tiger II was too heavy, too big, too slow, ungainly, unmanoeuvrable, etc. One is left with the impression that it was lucky to move at all. These banal generalities, stated as incontrovertible facts, are never substantiated by actual specifications, test reports or after-action accounts from the units that used the Tiger II. In spite of these frequently repeated remarks, the capability of the Tiger II to negotiate obstacles and cross terrain was equivalent to or better than most German and Allied tanks, as shown by the performance specifications in Table 3.

Table 3: Tiger II Performance

Maximum speed	41.5km/h
Maximum sustained speed	38km/h
Average cross-country speed	15–20km/h
Radius of action, road	170km
Radius of action, cross-country	120km
Smallest turning radius	2.08m
Maximum turning radius	114m
Trench crossing	2.5m
Fording	1.6m
Step climbing	0.85m
Gradient climbing	35°
Ground clearance	0.5m
Ground pressure	0.78kg/cm²
Power to weight ratio	10.7 metric hp/tonne

The Tiger II initially experienced numerous automotive problems which required a continuous series of minor modifications to correct. The main problems were leaking seals and gaskets and an overtaxed drive train. The problem of keeping a Tiger II in running condition was compounded by a shortage of skilled drivers, many of whom may have never experienced driving any vehicle prior to entering the service. In addition, they were provided only limited driver's training, and then usually on a different type of Panzer, and received their own Tiger II usually within a few days of being shipped by rail to the front. The first five production series Tiger IIs (Fgst Nr

PANZERWAFFE TACTICS

Panzerwaffe doctrine stressed offensive almost to the exclusion of defensive combat. Armoured regiments and battalions were doctrinally to employ one of three offensive actions. First, in a *Vorbut* (meeting engagement), an advance force, generally at least company-sized, was employed for taking an enemy by surprise so as to gain key terrain or a similar objective. Alternatively, *Sofortangriffe* (quick attacks), often conducted using the *Breitkeil* (broad wedge) formation (a reverse wedge with two platoons forward and the remaining platoon providing flank support as required), were used when supporting forces were not readily available and immediate action was needed. Finally, an *Angriff nach Vorbereitung* (deliberate attack) could be conducted as a complete unit against prepared defences.

As a result of the German Army's effective training and discipline, commanders were generally given a considerable degree of flexibility in carrying out tactical and small-unit operations. Given little more than the mission and the leader's intention, commanders could conduct an operation, while adjusting to battlefield situations as they occurred. This was perhaps best exemplified in the Panzerwaffe where timely intelligence, security, march discipline and communications were especially important elements in achieving victory on the battlefield.

When the Tiger I made its combat debut in November 1942, its battlefield tactics and the operations of heavy armour battalions were largely improvised by the crewmen based on their personal experiences. By the time the Tiger II was first fielded in early 1944, a more established doctrine had been developed to address specific battlefield eventualities in a unified manner. Officially, four-vehicle armour platoons were to deploy in either a *Linie* (line) (section leader/vehicle/platoon leader), a *Reihe* (row) (platoon leader/vehicle followed by section leader/vehicle), a *Doppelreihe* (double row) or a *Keil* (wedge), but in practice the terrain, the situation and the commander's experience meant these 'parade' formations were seldom used.

280001–280005) issued to the Panzer-Lehr-Division were in such poor automotive condition that they were destroyed to prevent capture without having been used in combat. The first unit sent to the Eastern Front outfitted with Tiger IIs, schwere Panzer-Abteilung 501, arrived at the front with only eight out of 45 operational, mainly due to the failure of the final drives. Schwere Panzer-Abteilung 505, which was

Tiger IIs gather en masse before their movement to Hungary. Tiger II deployments to Hungary mainly occurred between October 1944 and January 1945. (AirSeaLand/Cody)

issued its Tiger IIs in July and August 1944, reported that three factory-fresh Tiger IIs burnt out totally due to leaks in the engine compartment. Several other Tiger IIs had experienced smaller fires.

The 505th Battalion worked closely with Henschel technical representatives to correct many of the deficiencies before being sent to the Eastern Front. But with mature drivers, taking required maintenance halts and modification of key automotive components, the Tiger II could run with reasonable reliability. The statistics compiled from status reports for 15 March 1945 show that 59 per cent of the Tigers with front-line units were operational. This was about equal to the PzKpfw IV (62 per cent operational) and much better than the Panther (only 48 per cent).

BATTLEFIELD SURVIVABILITY

To resist penetration, tank armour needed to be hard to deflect or shatter an incoming round, but also flexible to diffuse its impact energy and retain structural integrity. Like other heavy, late-war armoured vehicles, the Tiger II relied on thickness to counter most anti-tank projectiles of the period. Its hull and turret comprised rolled homogeneous armour (RHA) made from cast ingots infused with chromium and molybdenum to increase deep internal hardening and stress resistance. By compacting and consolidating the metal's microscopic grains to a consistent size and orientation, the plate was strengthened and better able to defeat an incoming round. Homogeneous armour worked best when it was the same hardness throughout, as variations promoted stress concentration boundaries and weakened its ballistic resistance. With the vehicle's glacis and mantlet 150mm and 180mm thick respectively, achieving such consistency was not easy.

No less a figure than General Dwight D. Eisenhower, at this point (August 1944) supreme commander of the Allied Expeditionary Forces in Europe, inspects a Tiger II, blown clean over on its side. (AirSeaLand/Cody)

As the production process was consistently hampered by Allied bombing, the tempering process of heating the raw metal to 800°C, cooling it in water, reheating it at a lower temperature and cooling it again could not always be done to the accuracy required to produce the desired ductility of alloyed steel armour plate. As a result of this 'scale effect', a crystalline microstructure (collectively called bainite) could form internally, which increased hardness and the potential for cracking on impact. Subsequently, an impacting projectile's shockwave would be likely to produce an internal showering of sharp metal flakes known as spall. The Germans tended to use the Brinell scale to determine armour's hardness, which on the Tiger II's glacis and hull sides were BHN 220–265 (150mm) and 275–340 (80mm), respectively. With late-war stockpiles of molybdenum, nickel and manganese dwindling as the war progressed, vanadium was used as a grain-growth inhibitor to improve the RHA's toughness. As a smaller profile reduced the chance of being hit, the Tiger II's turret, probably the most exposed part during combat, was tapered in the front and backed up with 180mm of face armour and a dense, curved 'Saukopf' mantlet. This meant that when the barrel was pointed at an adversary, the turret would either defeat front-on shots owing to that area's great thickness or deflect those striking the sides owing to the great angle. A second benefit of using hard, thick armour was that high-speed incoming rounds often fell into a 'shatter gap', where they simply disintegrated upon striking the vehicle. Sloped armour also increased the plate's effective thickness.

Combined, these aspects translated into the vehicle's frontal armour being essentially impenetrable to existing Allied guns, while side plate armour proved adequate when fighting at the commonly long ranges afforded by the main gun. The penetration tables (Tables 4–6) extracted from a Wa Prüf 1 report dated 5 October 1944 relate the relative ability of the major opponents to penetrate the Tiger II and vice versa. The penetration ranges were determined based on the assumption that the target tank stood at a side angle of 30° to the incoming round. The Tiger II represented has the production series turret.

It is quite obvious that no Allied tankers made a living by attempting to engage Tiger IIs from the front. The original report did not show the effectiveness of British tank guns against the Tiger II. This was found in an RAC 3.d. secret document dated February 1945, as shown in Table 7. The front of the turret and lower hull of the Tiger II could theoretically be penetrated using the 17-pdr firing a special tungsten AP, super-velocity, discarding-sabot round. These rounds were not especially accurate, they did not have an explosive filler for blast effect after penetration and they ricocheted off steep angles like the lower hull front of the Tiger II. The author has been unable to find any photographs or other proof of the frontal armour of Tiger IIs being penetrated during combat.

Table 4: Tiger II – Penetration Table: Cromwell, Churchill

		Tiger II vs Cromwell (8.8cm KwK)	Cromwell vs Tiger II (75mm M3)	Tiger II vs Churchill (8.8cm KwK)	Churchill vs Tiger II (75mm M3)
Front:	Turret	3,500m +	0m	3,500m +	0m
	Mantlet	3,500m +	0m	3,500m +	0m
	Glacis	3,500m +	0m	3,500m	0m
	Nose	3,500m +	0m	3,400m	0m
Side:	Turret	3,500m +	0m	3,500m +	0m
	Super	3,500m +	0m	3,500m +	0m
	Hull	3,500m +	100m	3,500m +	100m
Rear:	Turret	3,500m +	0m	3,500m +	0m
	Hull	3,500m +	0m	3,500m +	0m

Table 5: Tiger II – Penetration Table: Sherman A2, Sherman A4

		Tiger II vs Sherman A2 (8.8cm KwK)	Sherman A2 vs Tiger II (75mm M3)	Tiger II vs Sherman A4 (8.8cm KwK)	Sherman A4 vs Tiger II (76mm M1A1)
Front:	Turret	3,500m +	0m	1,800m	0m
	Mantlet	2,600m	0m	2,600m	0m
	Glacis	2,000m	0m	2,000m	0m
	Nose	3,500m +	0m	3,500m +	0m
Side:	Turret	3,500m +	0m	3,500m +	1,100m
	Super	3,500m +	0m	3,500m +	900m
	Hull	3,500m +	100m	3,500m +	1,800m
Rear:	Turret	3,500m +	0m	3,500m +	400m
	Hull	3,500m +	0m	3,500m +	400m

Table 6: Tiger II – Penetration Table: T-34/85, JS-122

		Tiger II vs T-34/85 (8.8cm Kw.K)	T-34/85 vs Tiger II (85mm S53)	Tiger II vs JS-122 (8.8cm KwK)	JS-122 vs Tiger II (122mm A19)
Front:	Turret	3,500m +	0m	2,300m	0m
	Mantlet	2,800m	0m	1,800m	0m
	Glacis	2,600m	0m	2,100m	0m
	Nose	2,600m	0m	2,600m	0m
Side:	Turret	3,500m +	800m	3,400m	1,800m
	Super	3,500m +	500m	3,400m	1,400m
	Hull	3,500m +	1,600m	3,500m +	2,900m
Rear:	Turret	3,500m +	100m	1,800m	900m
	Hull	3,500m +	100m	2,500m	900m

Table 7: Tiger II – Penetration Table: British Guns

		6-pdr APCBC	6-pdr APSV (DS)	17-pdr APCBC	17-pdr APSV (DS)
Front:	Turret	0yds	0yds	0yds	1,100yds
	Glacis	0yds	0yds	0yds	0yds
	Nose	0yds	0yds	0yds	1,200yds
Side:	Turret	200yds	1,600yds	2,900yds	2,000yds +
	Super	0yds	1,400yds	2,600yds	2,000yds +
	Hull	1,000yds	2,000yds	3,000yds +	2,000yds +
Rear:	Turret	200yds	1,600yds	2,900yds	2,000yds +
	Hull	0yds	900yds	2,200yds	2,000yds +

OPERATIONAL HISTORY

Tiger IIs were to be issued only to the schwere Panzer-Abteilungen (heavy tank battalions) of either the Heer (Army) or SS. The only exceptions to this rule were those issued for research (Waffenamt), training (Ersatzheer) and the first five production series Tiger IIs to a unit subordinate to the Panzer-Lehr-Division. The standard organization called for 45 per battalion, three Panzerbefehlswagen Tigers with the headquarters and 14 Tigers in each of three companies. Each company was further subdivided, with two for the headquarters section and four for each of the three platoons.

Virtually the entire production run was devoted to filling units to their full complement before sending them to the front. Only in 1945 were units sent into action short of their fully authorized complement of Tiger IIs. Very rarely were replacements sent to units at the front. Replacements were only sent to three Abteilungen: the 506th, the SS 501st and Feldherrnhalle. A total of 194 Tiger IIs were issued to units that fought in the West, 274 for the East, 15 to the Waffenamt and 13 to the Ersatzheer.

The history of all the schwere Panzer-Abteilungen that were issued Tiger IIs includes the exact dates and the number of Tiger IIs that each received. The status reports reveal how successful the units were in maintaining operational Tiger IIs ready for combat and the rate at which losses occurred. The units are arranged in the order in which they were sent to the Western or Eastern Front.

A knocked-out Tiger II in France in 1944, there being indications of shell damage to the hull and the lower lip of the turret. (AirSeaLand/Cody)

OPPOSITE This Tiger II is missing sections of the armoured skirt that ran along the side of the vehicle, protecting the upper portion of the tracks. (AirSeaLand/Cody)

UNITS SENT TO THE WESTERN FRONT
Panzer-Kompanie (FKL) 316

The first unit to receive Tiger IIs for employment on the Western Front was the PzKp (FKL) 316 attached to the Panzer-Lehr-Division. This unit was issued the first five production Tiger IIs (Fgst Nr 280001–280005) which were sent to the unit on 14 March 1944. These five Tiger IIs were never employed in action and were destroyed to prevent capture.

schwere Heeres Panzer-Abteilung 503

The second unit sent to the West with Tiger IIs was schwere Heeres Panzer-Abteilung 503, which was ordered to return from the Eastern Front to rest and refit on 25 May 1944. Before the Allied landing at Normandy, the 503rd was selected for employment in the West due to its complement of Tiger IIs. This was not because there was a more urgent need for Tiger IIs in the West than the East; the Tiger IIs were still experiencing numerous automotive failures and were to be kept closer to the source of repair parts and factory personnel. These same automotive problems caused delays in production and resulted in the 503rd receiving only 12 Tiger IIs (Fgst Nr 280023–280035, shipped from the ordnance depot on 12 June) along with 33 Tiger Is to fill their authorized strength of 45 Tigers.

Outfitted at the training grounds in Ohrdruf, the 503rd was loaded on eight trains and transported to the Western Front starting on 27 June. The eight trains were all unloaded at Dreux, France, by 7 July, and proceeded to the front by road marches, first engaging in combat on 11 July.

The 3. Kompanie of the 503rd had been ordered to refit with a full complement of 14 Tiger IIs, which were shipped to the unit from the ordnance depot on 27 and 29 July. Five of the Tiger IIs were loaded and transported to the Western Front on 11 August. These were lost on the south side of the River Seine. Another seven Tiger IIs to the north of the Seine were lost in August and September 1944. Two of the Tiger IIs managed to survive and returned to the training grounds for further employment.

1. Kompanie/schwere SS-Panzer-Abteilung 101

Having lost 15 of their 45 Tiger Is in combat on the invasion front in Normandy before 5 July, the 1. Kompanie was pulled out of the front to refit. The unit received 14 Tiger IIs (Fgst Nr 280092–280112) that were shipped from the ordnance depot between 28 July and 1 August. Sent by train to the Western Front, these 14 Tiger IIs were quickly lost during the massive retreats in France in August and early September 1944.

Tiger II, schwere SS Panzer-Abteilung 501; Ardennes, December 1944. The Tiger II now on display at the Armour Proving Ground, Aberdeen, Maryland, was captured from the SS 501st. However, it was originally issued to the 509th and then handed over to the SS 501st to complete their establishment of 45 Tiger IIs for the Ardennes offensive.

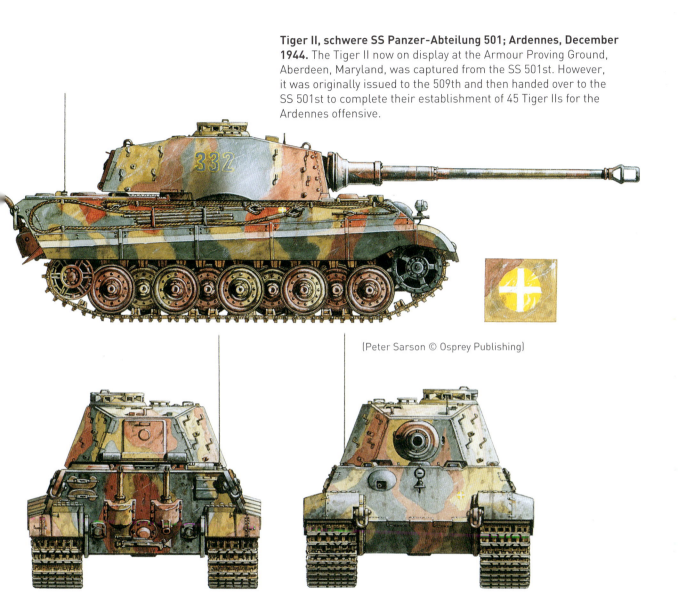

(Peter Sarson © Osprey Publishing)

schwere Heeres Panzer-Abteilung 506

The 506th was ordered on 15 August 1944 to return from the Eastern Front to reorganize and rebuild at Paderborn. Their 45 Tiger IIs were shipped from the ordnance depot between 20 August and 12 September. Loaded on trains on 22 September, the 506th was sent to Holland to help repulse the British spearhead at Arnhem. Reporting 33 tanks operational and ten in repair on 1 October, the 506th was reloaded on trains on 3 October and transferred to the front via Aachen.

German reserve troops pass a camouflaged Tiger II during the late months of the war. The Tiger II was at its best when used as a 'sniper', given open terrain and infantry support nearby. (AirSeaLand/Cody)

schwere SS-Panzer-Abteilung 501

The 101st (later renamed 501st) was ordered on 9 September 1944 to transfer to Sennelager to rest and refit. At first it was planned to outfit the battalion with two companies of Tiger IIs and one company of Jagdtigers. On 4 November, Hitler ordered that none of the Jagdtigers were to be issued to Tiger battalions. Therefore, the SS-Tiger-Abteilung was ordered to outfit the third company with Tiger Is. This order was later rescinded and the third company was also outfitted with Tiger IIs.

Due to the severe production problems, only six Tiger IIs had been sent to the SS-501st from the ordnance depot on 17 and 18 October. A further eight were shipped on 11 November, for a total of 14, sufficient to outfit one company. Finally, 20 were shipped between 26 November and 3 December. These 34 Tiger IIs were all that were available for issue from the ordnance depot before the SS 501st was loaded on trains and sent to the Western Front on 5 December.

This Tiger II belonged to the schwere SS-Panzer-Abteilung 501, which served on the Eastern Front and the Western Front, ending its days in the Ardennes. (AirSeaLand/Cody)

Previously, 11 Tiger IIs had been sent to the 509th from the ordnance depot between 28 September and 3 October. Due to the bombing campaign against Henschel, the SS 501st were short of 11 Tiger IIs. Therefore, the 11 Tiger IIs intended for the 509th were confiscated at the last minute and turned over to the SS 501st. The Tiger II (Fgst Nr 280243, completed at Henschel on 8 September 1944) now in the collection of the Aberdeen Ordnance Museum in Maryland was one of these 11. This explains the puzzle of why the tactical markings of the 509th were on a Tiger II captured in Belgium from the SS 501st.

1) Tiger II 'Porsche Turm', Panzer Ersatz und Ausbildungs Abteilung 500. The Panzer Ersatz und Ausbildungs Abteilung 500 (Replacement and Training Battalion) 500 was equipped with some of the earliest production Tiger IIs. At this period all Tiger IIs were coated in Zimmerit.

2) Tiger II 'Porsche Turm', schwere Panzer-Abteilung 503; Russia, Winter 1944–45. Tiger IIs of the 503rd fought in France against the Allied forces in the summer of 1944. Their Tigers were painted similar to that in 1.

(Peter Sarson © Osprey Publishing)

The Panzerjäger Tiger Ausf B, also known as the Jagdtiger ('Hunting Tiger'), was a truly monstrous vehicle, armed with a 12.8cm PaK 44 L/55. It was also an expensive and unnecessary distraction at a late stage of the war. (AirSeaLand/Cody)

ABOVE More German paratroopers on the rear hull of a Tiger II in the Ardennes. As an interesting side note, the para on the left has armed himself with a British Sten gun. (AirSeaLand/Cody)

ABOVE RIGHT German paratroopers hitch a ride on a Tiger II during the Ardennes offensive in 1944. The two heavy towing rings are visible on the lower glacis plate. (AirSeaLand/Cody)

The SS 501st sent to the Western Front as a key unit for the Ardennes offensive unloaded from the last of ten trains at Liblau-Euskirchen on 9 December. The SS 501st reported the loss of 13 Tiger IIs during fighting in December before a status report dated 15 January revealed a total of 31 Tiger IIs, of which 18 were operational. As ordered on 24 January 1945, the SS 501st was transferred to the Eastern Front with the I. SS-Panzer-Korps.

schwere Heeres Panzer-Abteilung 507

The 507th was ordered to return from the Eastern Front to Sennelager on 25 February 1945 to rebuild with Tiger IIs. The unit received four Tiger IIs on 9 March, 11 on 22 March and the last six on 31 March. They also acquired six Tiger IIs that had been previously issued to the 510th and 511th, making a total of 21. The front came to the 507th, deployed in defence of the local area.

3. Kompanie/schwere Heeres Panzer-Abteilung 510 and 3. Kompanie/schwere Heeres Panzer-Abteilung 511

The last 13 Tiger IIs produced by Henschel were picked up directly from the factory on 31 March, by crews of the 3./Tiger-Abteilung 510 and 3./Tiger-Abteilung 511. On 31 March, they reported that each company possessed eight Tiger IIs. Twelve of these were brand new productions from Henschel, while there were also three older Tiger IIs from the Waffenamt at Sennelager and one older Tiger II from the Waffenamt at Northeim.

A Romanian soldier talks with a Waffen-SS machine gunner in front of a Tiger II. The deep 'ribs' of the Zimmerit paste are evident here; it worked by reducing the adhesion of a flat-bottom magnetic mine, which could not sit flush against the metalwork. (AirSeaLand/Cody)

WAFFEN-SS PANZER TRAINING

As with the German Army, Waffen-SS inductees first went through several months of intensive infantry basic training; this was so rigorous that in the early part of the war one-third did not finish. Physical fitness, small-arms skill and political indoctrination were especially stressed. Upon completion of initial instruction, individuals could apply for specialized training, for example as officer candidates or engineers, or for service in the armour branch.

For the role of tanker, those with mechanical or technical skills were naturally most in demand, with training conducted at one of several armour facilities throughout the Reich. Although each crewman was to become familiar with each other's duties, the need for strong interaction among the commanders, loaders and gunners was particularly stressed, as close cooperation among this trio translated into rapid responses to battlefield threats.

Because officer candidates and enlisted personnel trained together, the sense of comradeship between the two groups was correspondingly strengthened. Where the Army instilled a distinct separation between officers and the lower ranks, the Waffen-SS promoted mutual respect and a more relaxed atmosphere in which officers were simply addressed by their rank without the traditional 'Herr' prefix. After 1943, foreign volunteers (preferably Nordic, but also non-Germanic) joined in increasing numbers, in part to fight against what was seen as a communist threat against European civilization. Although Hitler desired to incorporate these elements into the whole to instill the concept of a united 'Germania', Swedes, Norwegians, Dutch, French and others were organized according to nationality.

Tiger II crews focused on achieving surprise and executing decisions quickly. Once fields of fire were established, terrain was to be exploited for protection and concealment. Enemy armour and anti-tank guns were priority targets, and against overwhelming numbers the tankers were to scatter and regroup to a more advantageous position. Upon spotting hostile tanks, the Tiger II was to halt and get ready to engage them by surprise, estimating the enemy's reaction before launching an attack. The crew should hold fire as long as possible, and, if possible, the enemy tanks should not be engaged by a single tank so as to apply maximum firepower. As Germany's manpower pool, resources and leverage to achieve any sense of a negotiated peace dwindled, the SS Panzer battalions, like other armoured formations, were increasingly forced to train on obsolete foreign and domestic tanks.

The *Tigerfibel* (the Tiger I manual, which was also applicable to the Tiger II) defined several guidelines for the vehicle's official operation and deployment within a heavy armour battalion. In practice, however, deviations were unavoidable, and at the commander's discretion. To facilitate these, emphasis was laid on the importance of rapid communications between the battalion and its parent command, as such formations required as much time as possible in which to get organized and allocated to a threatened sector. There was also a heavy reliance on armoured engineers to strengthen bridges and clear minefields ahead of the heavy tanks.

On 1 April they engaged in combat in Kassel, with seven Tiger IIs per company, reporting that three further Tiger IIs had been lost due to bomb damage.

Ersatzheer and Waffenamt

Other units from the Ersatzheer and the Waffenamt were quickly thrown together at the last minute to defend the local areas as the front came to them. Virtually all operational Tiger IIs that had been issued for research or training were thrown into the fray at the end of the war. These units included Panzer-Kompanie Kummersdorf with a Tiger II and a Porsche Tiger with an 8.8cm KwK L/71 on 31 March 1945, and the Panzer-Abteilung 500 (Paderborn) with 17 Tigers (both Is and IIs) on 2 April.

UNITS SENT TO THE EASTERN FRONT
schwere Heeres Panzer-Abteilung 501

The first unit to be outfitted with Tiger IIs and sent to the Eastern Front was the schwere Heeres Panzer-Abteilung 501. Having been decimated by 3 July, the remnants were ordered to re-form and refit at the troop training area at Ohrdruf. Issued 45 Tiger IIs between 7 July and 7 August, the 501st was ordered to join Heeresgruppe Nordukraine on 6 August. Assigned to the XXIV Panzer Korps, the 501st was renamed to schwere Panzer-Abteilung 424 by orders dated 19 December 1944. The newly named unit was overwhelmed during the Russian winter offensive and ordered to be disbanded and used to create the schwere Panzerjäger-Abteilung 512 by orders dated 11 February 1945.

1) Tiger II, schwere Panzer-Abteilung 503; Budapest, October 1944. After returning from France on 9 September 1944, the 503rd was re-equipped with 43 new Tiger IIs with the series (Henschel) turret.

2) Tiger II, schwere Panzer-Abteilung 511; May 1945. The 3. Kompanie schwere Panzer-Abteilung 511 picked up some of the last Tiger IIs from the Henschel factory on 31 March 1945. No markings or call sign had been applied to this Tiger, destroyed in May 1945.

(Peter Sarson © Osprey Publishing)

schwere Heeres Panzer-Abteilung 503

On 9 September, the 503rd was ordered out of the West to rest and refit at Sennelager near Paderborn. Their 45 Tiger IIs were shipped from the ordnance depot between 19 and 22 September. Loaded on trains on 12 October, the 503rd was unloaded in Budapest, Hungary, on 14 October.

These Tiger IIs of schwere Panzer-Abteilung 503 are seen at the Sennelager training ground. (AirSeaLand/Cody)

schwere Heeres Panzer-Abteilung 505

The 505th was ordered out of the Eastern Front on 7 July to rest and reorganize at the troop training grounds at Ohrdruf. The 505th were sent their first six Tiger IIs from the ordnance depot on 26 July. Of these, two were traded with the 501st and two others had immediate automotive failures. The other 39 Tiger IIs were shipped from the ordnance depot between 10 and 29 August. Immediately losing three to fires due to leaks in the engme compartment, the 505th received replacements from those that had been issued to the Ersatzheer. Loaded on trains on 9 September, the 505th arrived on the Eastern Front at Nasielsk on 11 September.

schwere Heeres Panzer-Abteilung 509

The 509th had already been pulled out of the Eastern Front to rest and refit in September 1944. It was issued 11 Tiger IIs in September that were turned over to the SS 501st. After experiencing further delays in outfitting due to the severe interruptions in production at Henschel, the 509th was sent 45 Tiger IIs from the ordnance depot between 5 December 1944 and 1 January 1945. Loaded on trains on 12 January and sent to Hungary, the 509th re-entered combat on 18 January.

schwere SS-Panzer-Abteilung 501

The SS 501st, with 26 Tiger IIs, was transferred with the I. SS-Panzer-Korps to the Eastern Front. Six replacements shipped from the ordnance depot on 22 January, and a further 13 replacements on 10 February, completed their complement of 45 Tiger IIs. By 1 April, the SS 501st was back in Germany to rest and refit at Sennelager near Paderborn.

schwere SS-Panzer-Abteilung 503

The SS 103rd, formed in November 1943 and later renamed the 503rd, was unusually detained at the training grounds for over a year before being sent to a front. They had been issued a few Tiger Is that were later given to other units. Finally, on 19 October, the 503rd was sent four Tiger IIs from the ordnance depot, which they kept. This was later expanded by an additional six Tiger IIs acquired from the SS 502nd. Additional shipments of 29 new Tiger IIs were made from the ordnance depot between 11 and 25 January 1945. With a total of 39 Tiger IIs (instead of the full complement of 45), the SS 503rd loaded on to trains on 27 January and were sent to the Eastern Front in the Heeresgruppe Weichsel sector.

schwere SS-Panzer-Abteilung 502

A Tiger II turret sits rather forlornly on a rail car against bomb damage at the Henschel und Sohn factory, located in Kassel. As well as tanks, Henschel also produced many varieties of combat aircraft. (AirSeaLand/Cody)

The SS 102nd (later renamed 502nd) was ordered on 9 September 1944 to transfer to Sennelager to rest and refit. Due to shortages, the issue of Tiger IIs was slow in coming. Six Tiger IIs sent to the unit from the ordnance depot on 27 December were passed along to the sister unit SS 503rd. Finally, 31 Tiger IIs were shipped from the ordnance depot between 14 February and 6 March 1945. The SS 502nd was transported to the Eastern Front to Heeresgruppe Mitte starting in mid-March, logging their first engagement in combat at Sachsendorf on 22 March.

EVALUATION

While medium armoured fighting vehicles such as the German Panther or Soviet T-34 possessed a balanced triad of firepower, mobility and protection that permitted them to undertake a variety of combat roles, the Tiger II's greater weight relegated it to more limited defensive operations. Its size made movement through urban environments or along narrow roads difficult, while its drive train was under-strength, the double radius L801 steering gear was stressed and the seals and gaskets were prone to leaks. Limited crew training could amplify these problems as inexperienced drivers could inadvertently run the engine at high RPMs or move over terrain that overly tasked the suspension. Extended travel times under the Tiger II's own power stressed the swingarms that supported the road wheels and made them susceptible to bending. Such axial displacement would probably strain the tracks and bend the link bolts to further disrupt proper movement. Overworked engines needed to be replaced roughly every 1,000km. Although wide tracks aided movement over most terrain, should the vehicle require recovery another Tiger II was typically needed to extract it. Requirements for spare parts were understandably high, and maintenance was an ongoing task, all of which reduced vehicle availability.

The Tiger II's long main armament, the epitome of the family of 8.8cm anti-aircraft/anti-tank guns that had terrorized enemy armour since the Spanish Civil War (1936–39), fired high-velocity rounds along a relatively flat trajectory. In combination with an excellent gun sight, the weapon system was accurate at long range, which enabled rapid targeting and a high first look/first hit/first kill probability. However, the lengthy barrel's overhang stressed the turret ring, and made traverse difficult when not on level ground.

Optimally initiating combat at distances beyond which an enemy's main armament could effectively respond, the Tiger II's lethality was further enhanced by its considerable armour protection, especially across the frontal arc that provided for a high degree of combat survivability. Although the vehicle's glacis does not appear to have ever been penetrated during battle, its flanks and rear were vulnerable to enemy anti-tank weapons at normal ranges. In the hands of an experienced crew, and under environmental and terrain conditions that promoted long-range combat, the weapon system achieved a high kill ratio against its Allied and Red Army counterparts. The SS 503rd, for example, was estimated to have scored 500 kills during the unit's operational life from January–April 1945. While such a figure was certainly inflated, as accurate record keeping was hindered by the unit's dispersed application and chaotic late-war fighting where the Soviets eventually occupied a battlefield, it illustrated the success of the weapon system if properly employed and supported. As the SS 503rd never received replacement tanks like its brethren in the SS 501st and 502nd (which were given 2.38 and 1.7 times their respective 45-vehicle table of organization and equipment allotments), its Tiger II combat losses averaged less than 50 per cent.

This Tiger II, eagerly being inspected by US troops, simply ran out of fuel on the Stavelot road in Belgium towards the tail end of the Ardennes offensive. The crew set fire to the vehicle as they abandoned it. (AirSeaLand/ Cody)

Because of the chaotic combat environment throughout Pomerania, and the need to quickly allocate resources to several threatened sectors at once, the Tiger IIs were frequently employed singly, or in small groups, often at the will of a local senior commander. In much the same way as with the French in 1940, SS 503rd's armour acted more in an infantry-support capacity than as a unified armoured fist. The Tiger IIs would perhaps have been better used organizationally to fill a Panzer regiment's heavy company by strengthening existing, depleted parent formations, but instead they remained in semi-independent heavy Panzer battalions until the end of the war. Forced to rely on small-unit tactics, Tiger II crews played to their strengths by adopting ambush tactics to minimize vehicular movement and pre-combat detection, especially from enemy ground-attack aircraft.

As tankers regularly spent long hours in their mounts, the Tiger II's relatively spacious interior helped reduce fatigue, and made operating and fighting within the vehicle somewhat less taxing. A good heating and ventilation system improved operating conditions, which then reduced crew mistakes that were all too common during a chaotic firefight. Although the Tiger II had well-positioned ammunition racks that facilitated loading, projectiles that were stored in the turret bustle were susceptible to potentially catastrophic damage caused by spalling or projectile impacts. Even after Henschel incorporated spall liners to reduce such debris, concerned crews would often leave the turret rear empty, which correspondingly made room to use the rear hatch as an emergency exit.

The cost to produce the Tiger II in manpower and time (double that of a 45-tonne Panther), and its high fuel consumption, brought into question why such a design progressed beyond the drawing board considering Germany's dwindling resources and military fortunes. It was partly a response to the perpetual escalation of the requirement to achieve or maintain battlefield supremacy, and much of the blame rested with Hitler and his desire for large armoured vehicles that in his view presumably reflected Germany's might and reinforced propaganda. By not focusing resources on creating greater numbers of the latest proven designs such as the Panther G, German authorities showed a lack of unified direction and squandered an ability to fight a war of attrition until it was too late to significantly affect the outcome. Limited numbers of qualitatively superior Tiger IIs simply could not stem the flood of enemy armour.

With its monstrous 38cm rocket launcher, the Sturmmörserwagen 606/4 mit 38cm RW 61 (also known as the Sturmtiger) was a heavily urban assault vehicle. Only 14 of the massive projectiles could be stored on board. (AirSeaLand/Cody)

CHAPTER 7

PANZER CREWS

On the Eastern Front in February 1944, famous tank commander Michael Wittman poses with his crew in front of a PzKpfw VI Tiger I. Note the kill rings painted on the barrel. (AirSeaLand/Cody)

The crew of a PzKpfw III take time out from operations to relax, although this photograph – which appeared in the Nazi propaganda magazine *Signal* – looks rather contrived. (AirSeaLand/Cody)

The technical story of German tanks always masks a human story beneath. The life of a Panzer crewman was not for the fainthearted, either in war or peace. The vehicle in which they operated could, and did, play a critical role in their ultimate survivability, but it is worth giving a final thought to the practicalities of manning these powerful weapon systems.

The routine duties of a tank crew, whether Allied or German, were similar. The crew dedicated a great deal of time to their tank. Oil, fuel and air filters had to be constantly cleaned, a task which was especially important owing to the smothering dust. A clogged filter could quickly overheat and kill an engine. Track tension had to be checked and adjusted to prevent throwing a track at a critical moment. The radio operator spent many hours cleaning and tinkering with the temperamental, fragile set. Heat and dust were the crew's enemies, to say nothing of the rough ride and what this did to vacuum tubes (valves), condensers, soldered connections and the delicate tuning.

Care of the armament was crucial. The main gun and machine guns demanded frequent cleaning, even without being fired. This also applied to optical sights and ammunition. Dusty ammunition coupled with oil and carbon buildup in machine guns jammed them. Dusty main gun cartridges might fail to extract. After repeated firing or cross-country travel, the main gun's recoil system had to be checked to ensure there was sufficient fluid in the recoil buffer, and the recuperator springs, which returned the gun to battery, had to be readjusted. Live firing of all weapons prior to combat was critical to zero them, that is, to ensure the sights were adjusted to coincide with the actual point of impact at set ranges. A good tank commander ran dry fire drills at every opportunity under varied conditions, including nighttime. Pistols and sub-machine guns had to be cleaned along with other crew kit, and a spare barrel for each machine gun had to be maintained. Keeping the tank fed was an endless job.

With an operating range of 120–200 miles, during high-tempo operations a tank had to be refuelled every day or two, not so much because it actually travelled that distance, but because of the time it spent idling. Fuelling was done by hand, and it was heavy work to boost 20-litre jerry cans up onto the hot engine deck and empty each into the filler tube. A full jerry can or *Benzinkanister* (fuel container) weighed 21–22kg; a PzKpfw III required 16 of these to fill up. Fine cloth was placed over the filler hole to filter out dust and had to be cleaned between each can going in. Oil and transmission fluid had to be topped off and dozens of grease points, joints and bearings squirted. Canteens and the water cask were filled regularly.

To restock a tank with ammunition was heavy work requiring the entire crew. The crated ammunition had to be unloaded from a truck, and the metal boxes had to be opened, rounds had to be removed from sealed shipping tubes and all of the packing materials had to be reloaded on trucks. Only in action were the packing materials discarded. Each round had to be passed up through the side escape hatches and individually stowed in cramped quarters. This might have to be accomplished during lulls in combat in order to cross-level ammunition between tanks.

For their machine guns, the Germans received their ammunition loose in 1,500-round wooden boxes. The rounds had to be belted by hand in the nonexpendable belts, a tracer inserted every seventh round, the 150-round belts then correctly coiled into 25 canvas bags and finally stowed.

Worn-out and damaged tracks had to be replaced, which was a lengthy, labour-intensive job requiring all hands, as was replacing worn-out rubber-clad bogie wheels and return rollers. Spare sections of track links and bogie wheels were stowed on the hull as spares and for additional protection. Periodically, platoon and company commanders inspected the crews and machines. All work done on the tank had to be recorded in a log book (in German, *Fristenheft*). All necessary tools, crew and individual equipment, and spare parts were accounted for. Equipment included shovels, picks, axes, pry bars, jack, wire cutter, track tension tool, normal mechanic's tools, tow cable, fire extinguishers, camouflage net, first aid kit, flashlights, binoculars and compass.

The infantry may have been jealous of tankers riding into battle, but it was hot, heavy, demanding work to keep their machines going. Spare parts shortages were common on both sides. As a result, it was critical to recover broken down or damaged tanks and to place them back in action or cannibalize them for parts. More often than not a knocked-out tank, what the Germans called a *Panzerleiche* (armour corpse), could be

This German tank commander, the leader on a Sturmhaubitze 42, is using S.F.14 Scherenfernrohr Gi H/6400 periscope-type artillery ranging optics to spot potential targets. (AirSeaLand/Cody)

returned to action in short time. Tankers may have ridden, but they did not ride in comfort. Even on sand roads, much less cross-country, it was a jolting experience riding on seats with minimal padding. Gun sight rubber eye and forehead protectors produced black eyes and bruises. The desert heat, easily in excess of 43°C, was one thing, but the inside of a tank frequently reached 49°C, and that was with all hatches open and the tank moving. Dust flooded through hatches, and the crew members who could, sat in the hatches. The driver, though, was confined inside, and with his hatch open he faced a full blast of dust from leading vehicles. The PzKpfw III was even driven with the break service hatches open to ventilate the front compartment.

Going into combat, a tank had to shut all hatches, although the commander normally only closed his when absolutely necessary in order to effectively observe and be aware of the developing situation and terrain. Even in Europe, a buttoned-up tank could heat up to over 38°C with little air circulation. The engine and transmission generated more heat, as did weapons firing. Propellant fumes from the main gun when it ejected cases and from the machine guns flooded the interior, already ripe with the smell of gasoline fumes, oil, sweat and urine. Owing to the high-powered engine, the running gear and grinding treads, the ride was incredibly noisy, whether the hatches were open or not. Intercom or speaking tubes had to be used to communicate with the man at one's shoulder.

A buttoned-up tank offered only very limited observation through vision slits, ports, periscopes and gun sights, all with narrow fields of observation. There were many blind areas around tanks; obstacles and attacking infantry could not be seen if near the tank. Dust and smoke all but blinded a buttoned-up tank. In combat, crewmen relieved themselves into a can, bottle or empty main gun cartridge case to be emptied out of the escape hatch, although spilled contents were a regular and unfortunate occurrence.

A tank crew could carry a couple of days' rations along with cooking gear. A ration tin with a hole punched in the lid could be heated on an exhaust manifold. The Germans had gasoline stoves, but more often used their little Esbit cookers heated by fuel tablets. Another means of cooking was to fill a large used ration tin half full of sand and soak it with gasoline. The sand prolonged the burn while an open ration can or mess kit was heated over it. And yes, an egg, purchased from an Arab, could be fried on the engine deck with a dash of cooking oil. The Germans issued few pre-packaged rations, but rather tinned sausage, meat spread or sardines, compressed dried beans and peas, black bread from field bakeries or packaged preserved bread, tubes of cheese, ersatz coffee and Italian tinned meat and hardtack, neither of which was popular. Rations were issued on a daily basis, and crews cooked them collectively, although an effort was made to serve a hot soup or stew meal once a day from the battalion kitchen. Fresh foods were seldom issued, but some, such as onions, olive oil and marmalade, were procured from local sources. A 100-gram chocolate disc (Scho-ka-kola) in a tin or fibreboard container was issued as emergency rations and was quite tasty. Captured British and American rations were highly valued.

Waffen-SS soldiers conduct maintenance on their PzKpfw IV in Normandy in 1944. (AirSeaLand/Cody)

For sleeping arrangements, the German crews used triangular-shaped shelter-quarters also worn as rain capes. Four could be buttoned together to make a pyramid-shaped, four-man tent. Often the shelter-halves or shelter-quarters were pitched as an awning, tied along the downwind side of the tank's track guard and the lower edge staked to the ground. This was also done when sleep could be caught during the day, although the awning was pitched on the shady side. When shelter was unnecessary, tankers often bedded down at the rear of the tank to capture radiating engine heat. Troops bundled up in overcoats and wool blankets, with two often used for insulation from the cold ground.

Near the front, slit trenches were dug in which to sleep. In some instances, a shallow pit was dug to the length and inside width of the tracks and the tank parked over it, providing the crew with overhead cover. In bivouacs or laagers in forward areas, tanks and other AFVs parked facing outward in an all-around perimeter. If the ground was broken, the tanks positioned themselves in hull defilade. One crewman manned the turret, usually pulling one- or two-hour shifts.

During lulls in action crews simply slept the best they could in their stations; again, at least one man remained awake. The Germans issued Benzedrine, also known as Pervitin or Isophan, a methamphetamine and known today as 'speed', to keep them alert and awake during prolonged combat. The bottles were marked only as 'Stimulant' and with the directions '1 or 2 [5mg] only as needed to maintain sleeplessness'. In 1941, German reports were enthusiastic of its use, but by the year's end they were more cautious, and warnings were issued in early 1942. While reducing the desire for sleep, the resulting fatigue led to loss of efficiency and difficulty in accomplishing complicated tasks. It was directed that the drug's use should be confined to emergencies and not taken routinely. It was to be given only if there was a reasonable expectation that the crisis would end within 12 hours. Pervitin would not be given indiscriminately to large bodies of troops, nor to those whose duties required difficult decisions. It was to be administered under the control of a medical officer. Nonetheless, there were soldiers who became addicted to Stimulant.

Lack of water was also a constant problem. There was seldom enough for drinking, much less for washing and shaving. Fortunately, tanks used air-cooled engines. The long-term result of doing with less water was gradual dehydration, headaches, lightheadedness, muscle and joint aches, weight loss and high blood pressure. The worst effect of water deprivation is that blood volume is reduced and one's blood thickens. When wounded and succumbing to shock, blood vessels contract and the thickened blood aggravates the effects of shock.

Combat was unnerving, fast-paced, confusing and highly stressful. Sleep was infrequent and meals irregular. While comparatively immune to small-arms and mortar fire and all but a direct artillery hit, there were many lethal threats to the tankers and their tanks. More tanks were lost to anti-tank mines than any other single cause. Anti-tank guns, tank-destroyers and other tanks were deadly.

One of the hardest-working crewmen was the loader. In heavily gunned tanks, hefting the rounds was indeed strenuous work. It was not so difficult for the light 3.7cm and 5cm guns, but still he had to work in cramped quarters retrieving rounds from difficult-to-access locations about the tank. He also had to avoid the gun's recoil and watch out for ejected cases. Loaders also restowed spent cartridges or tossed them from an escape hatch and shifted rounds from less accessible stowage to more rapidly accessed racks.

The driver was another hard worker. He steered using two hand-operated braking/steering levers and also had to manually shift gears with a hand lever and clutch pedal. Additionally, there was the usual strain of driving, observing and paying attention to the commander's 'backseat driving'. Good drivers steered their own course, seeking cover and clear routes. During motor marches to the front and even during combat, other crewmen might relieve the driver. Often drivers were spared watch duty to ensure their rest. The radio operator, because of his relatively easy job, often accepted other duties such as preparing meals and looking after the quarters. The Germans called him a *Stullenmax* (untranslatable, but equating to 'gofer').

Tank crews developed close bonds owing to the shared experiences of intense training and combat. They learned one another's strengths and weaknesses, who would cheer them up in bad times and who pulled through no matter what the circumstances. The Germans called it *Kameradschaft* (comradeship), having a deeply serious meaning when strong bonds developed between men who fought together.

The tanks described in this book were little worlds unto themselves, spaces of humour, boredom, excitement and occasionally terror, and every other emotion around them. From the humblest light Panzer to the mighty Tiger II, the crewmen would become as wedded to their vehicle as each other.

This photograph of a loader in a Tiger I tank of the Das Reich Division on the Eastern Front in summer 1943 evokes the physically limited space inside a German tank, even one as large as the Tiger. (AirSeaLand/Cody)

FURTHER READING

OSPREY TITLES USED IN THE PRODUCTION OF THIS BOOK

New Vanguard Series:
NVG 01 – Tom Jentz & Hilary Doyle, *Kingtiger Heavy Tank 1942–45* (1993)
NVG 05 – Tom Jentz & Hilary Doyle, *Tiger I Heavy Tank 1942–45* (1993)
NVG 22 – Tom Jentz & Hilary Doyle, *Panther Variants 1942–45* (1987)
NVG 26 – Bryan Perrett, *German Light Panzers 1932–42* (1998)
NVG 27 – Bryan Perrett, *Panzerkampfwagen III Medium Tank 1936–1944* (1999)
NVG 28 – Bryan Perrett, *Panzerkampfwagen IV Medium Tank 1936–1945* (1999)
NVG 39 – Tom Jentz & Hilary Doyle, *Panzerkampfwagen IV Ausf.G, H and J 1942–45* (2001)
NVG 67 – Stephen A. Hart, *Panther Medium Tank 1942–45* (2003)
NVG 215 – Steven J. Zaloga, *Panzer 38(t)* (2014)

Duel Series:
DUE 2 – Stephen A. Hart, *Sherman Firefly vs Tiger: Normandy 1944* (2007)
DUE 4 – Robert Forczyk, *Panther vs T-34: Ukraine 1943* (2007)
DUE 10 – Gordon L. Rottman, *M3 Medium Tank vs Panzer III: Kasserine Pass 1943* (2008)
DUE 13 – Steven J. Zaloga, *Panther vs Sherman: Battle of the Bulge 1944* (2008)
DUE 33 – Steven J. Zaloga, *Panzer IV vs Char B1 bis: France 1940* (2011)
DUE 37 – David R. Higgins, *King Tiger vs IS-2: Operation Solstice 1945* (2011)
DUE 63 – Steven J. Zaloga, *Panzer III vs Somua S 35: Belgium 1940* (2014)
DUE 66 – David R. Higgins, *Panzer III vs 7TP: Poland 1939* (2015)
DUE 70 – Steven J. Zaloga, *Panzer IV vs Sherman: France 1944* (2015)
DUE 78 – Steven J. Zaloga, *Panzer 38(t) vs BT-7: Barbarossa 1941* (2017)
DUE 80 – Steven J. Zaloga, *Pershing vs Tiger: Germany 1944* (2017)

SECONDARY SOURCES:

Bender, James & Odegard, Warren W., *Uniforms, Organization and History of the Panzertruppe*, R. James Bender Publishing, San Jose, CA (1980)

Bernage, Georges, *The Panzers and the Battle of Normandy June 5th–July 20th 1944*, Heimdal, Bayeux (2000)

Blumenson, Martin, *Kasserine Pass: Rommel's Bloody, Climactic Battle for Tunisia*, Houghton Mifflin, New York (1966)

Ellis, Chris & Doyle, Hilary, *Panzerkampfwagen: German Combat Tanks 1933–1945*, Argus Books, Auburn, CA (1976)

Freiser, Karl-Heinz, *The Blitzkrieg Myth: The 1940 Campaign in the West*, Naval Institute Press, Annapolis, MD (2005)

Glantz, David & House, Jonathan, *The Battle of Kursk*, University of Kansas Press, Lawrence, KS (1999)

Gudgin, Peter, *Armoured Firepower: The Development of Tank Armament 1939–45*, Sutton Publishing, Gloucestershire (1997)

Hartmann, Bernd, *Panzers in the Sand: The History of Panzer-Regiment 5*, Stackpole, Mechanicsburg, PA (2010)

Hastings, Max, *Das Reich: The March of the 2nd SS Panzer Division through France*, Holt, Rinehart, & Winston, New York, NY (1981)

Jentz, Thomas, *Panzer Truppen, Volume 1: 1933–42*, Schiffer, Atglen, PA (1996)

Jentz, Thomas & Doyle, Hilary, *Germany's Tiger Tanks: DW to Tiger I*, Schiffer, Atglen, PA (2000)

Jentz, Thomas & Doyle, Hilary, *Germany's Tiger Tanks: VK45.02 to Tiger II*, Schiffer, Atglen, PA (1997)

Jentz, Thomas & Doyle, Hilary, *Panzerbefehlswagen Ausf D–K: Panzer Tracts No. 3-4*, Panzer Tracts, Boyds, MD (2007)

Jentz, Thomas & Doyle, Hilary, *Panzerkampfwagen III Ausf A–D: Panzer Tracts No. 3-1*, Panzer Tracts, Boyds, MD (2007)

Jentz, Thomas & Doyle, Hilary, *Panzerkampfwagen III Ausf E–H: Panzer Tracts No. 3-2*, Panzer Tracts, Boyds, MD (2007)

Jentz, Thomas L., *Germany's Panther Tank: The Quest for Combat Supremacy*, Schiffer Military History, Atglen, PA (1995)

Jentz, Thomas L., *Panzertruppen 1: The Complete Guide to the Creation & Combat Employment of Germany's Tank Force, 1933–1942*, Schiffer, Atglen, PA (1996)

Jentz, Thomas L., *Panzertruppen: 1943–1945*, Schiffer Military History, Atglen, PA (1996)

Jentz, Thomas L. & Doyle, Hilary, *Panzerkampfwagen II: Ausf.a/1, a/2, a/3, b, c, A, B, and C – development and production from 1934 to 1940: Panzer Tracts No. 2-1*, Panzer Tracts, Boyds, MD (2008).

Kolomyjec, Maksym & Ledwoch, Janusz, *Panthers and Tigers in the Kursk Bulge 1943*, Wydawnictwo Militaria, Warsaw (2004)

Kurowski, Franz, *Elite Panzer Strike Force: Germany's Panzer Lehr Division in World War II*, Stackpole, Mechanicsburg, PA (2011)

Lefevre, Eric, *Panzers in Normandy Then and Now*, After the Battle, London (1983)

Luck, Hans von, *Panzer Commander*, Praeger Publishers, Westport, CT (1989)

Nevenkin, Kamen, *Fire Brigades: The Panzer Divisions 1943–1945*, Fedorowicz, Winnipeg (2006)

Ritgen, Helmut, *The Western Front 1944: Memoirs of a Panzer Lehr Officer*, Fedorowicz, Winnipeg (1995)

Schneider, Wolfgang, *Panzer Tactics: German Small-Unit Armor Tactics in World War II*, Stackpole Books, Mechanicsburg, PA (2005)

Sharp, Charles C., *German Panzer Tactics in World War II*, George F. Nafziger, West Chester, OH (1998)

Spayd, P.A. (ed.), *Bayerlein: After Action Reports of the Panzer Lehr Division Commander from D-Day to the Ruhr*, Schiffer, Atglen, PA (2005)

Spielberger, Walter, *et al.*, *Panzerkampfwagen IV and its Variants 1935–1945 – Book 2*, Schiffer, Atglen, PA (2011)

Steinhardt, Frederick, *Panzer Lehr Division 1944–45*, Helion, Solihull (2007)

Tieke, Wilhelm, *SS-Panzer-Brigade Westfalen: Activation–Operations–Destruction March–April 1945*, J. J. Fedorowicz, Winnipeg (2003)

Vuksic, Velimir, *SS Armor on the Eastern Front 1943–1945*, Fedorowicz, Winnipeg, Canada (2005)

Walden, Gregory, *Tigers in the Ardennes: The 501st Heavy SS Tank Battalion in the Battle of the Bulge*, Schiffer, Atglen, PA (2014)

Watson, Bruce, *Exit Rommel: The Tunisian Campaign 1942–43*, Praeger Publishers, Westport, CT (1999)

Weidinger, Otto, *2 SS Panzer Division Das Reich*, Vol V, Fedorowicz, Winnipeg (2012)

Weiss, Willi, 'Pershing versus Tiger at Elsdorf', *After The Battle*, No. 153 (2011), pp.32–43

Wilbeck, Christopher, *Sledgehammers: Strengths and Flaws of Tiger Tank Battalions in World War II*, Aberjona, Bedford, PA (2004)

Winninger, Michael, *OKH Toy Factory – The Nibelungenwerk: Tank Production in St. Valentin*, History Facts, Andelfingen (2013)

Wood, M. & Dugdale, J., *Waffen SS Panzer Units in Normandy 1944*, Books International, Farnborough (2000)

Zetterling, Niklas, *Normandy 1944: German Military Organization, Combat Power and Organizational Effectiveness*, Fedorowicz, Winnipeg (2000)

INDEX

Page numbers in **bold** refer to illustration captions